The Peacebuilding Puzzle

Political Order in Post-Conflict States

Transformative peace operations fall short of achieving the modern political order sought in post-conflict countries because the interventions themselves empower post-conflict elites intent on forging a neopatrimonial political order. *The Peacebuilding Puzzle* explains the disconnect between the formal institutional engineering undertaken by international interventions and the governance outcomes that emerge in their aftermath. Barma's comparative analysis of interventions in Cambodia, East Timor, and Afghanistan focuses on the incentives motivating domestic elites over a sequence of three peacebuilding phases: the elite peace settlement, the transitional governance period, and the aftermath of intervention. The international community advances certain forms of institutional design at each phase in the pursuit of effective and legitimate governance. Yet, over the course of the peacebuilding pathway, powerful post-conflict elites co-opt the very processes and institutions intended to guarantee modern political order and dominate the practice of governance within those institutions to their own ends.

NAAZNEEN H. BARMA is Assistant Professor of National Security Affairs at the Naval Postgraduate School, Monterey. Her research focuses on international interventions in post-conflict states and the political economy of development and has appeared in scholarly and policy publications. She has worked with the World Bank as a governance and institutional reform specialist in the East Asia Pacific Region and is a founding member and co-director of Bridging the Gap, an initiative devoted to enhancing the policy impact of contemporary international affairs scholarship.

The Peacebuilding Puzzle

Political Order in Post-Conflict States

NAAZNEEN H. BARMA
Naval Postgraduate School, Monterey

CAMBRIDGE
UNIVERSITY PRESS

CAMBRIDGE
UNIVERSITY PRESS

University Printing House, Cambridge CB2 8BS, United Kingdom

One Liberty Plaza, 20th Floor, New York, NY 10006, USA

477 Williamstown Road, Port Melbourne, VIC 3207, Australia

4843/24, 2nd Floor, Ansari Road, Daryaganj, Delhi - 110002, India

79 Anson Road, #06-04/06, Singapore 079906

Cambridge University Press is part of the University of Cambridge.

It furthers the University's mission by disseminating knowledge in the pursuit of education, learning and research at the highest international levels of excellence.

www.cambridge.org
Information on this title: www.cambridge.org/9781107169319

When citing this work, please include a reference to the DOI 10.1017/9781316718513

First published 2017

A catalogue record for this publication is available from the British Library

ISBN 978-1-107-16931-9 Hardback

To my parents, Tarifa and Haider
and my madricha, Barbara

Contents

Figure and Tables

Figure

Tables

Acknowledgments

This book emphasizes the importance of viewing international peacebuilding with an expanded horizon, thereby better situating it in the context of what came before and after. In acknowledging the numerous intellectual and personal debts upon which the researching and writing of this book rests, it occurs to me that they, too, must be viewed with a long temporal lens. I started this project in 2004 as a doctoral candidate at the University of California, Berkeley, but the initial inspiration came when I was working at the World Bank before graduate school, circa 2000. It was then that I took my first trips to war-torn countries (Cambodia and East Timor), as one small cog in the vast, bright-eyed machinery of the post-conflict reconstruction bureaucratic machine. I was instantly enthralled – even after spending two dank weeks living in a fevered haze in a container in Dili, East Timor, and suffering a waist-deep fall into an uncovered drain in the pitch-black night that left me limping for weeks. I knew that this major contemporary policy challenge was what I wanted to study at graduate school, which I began in 2001. Having done so – and, quite simply, figured out what on earth was going on and how to fix it all – I was resolved to then return to the policy world to continue working operationally in fragile countries.

I did exactly that, finishing my PhD at Berkeley in 2007 and going back to the World Bank. And then I realized, as I gained more exposure to the realities of governance and institutional reform in post-conflict and developing Asia and the Pacific, that my intellectual journey was very much incomplete. In many ways my own trajectory mirrored that of the international peacebuilding endeavor: the hubris that came with the end of the Cold War peaking at the turn of the century, followed by the often grim reality and soul-searching that soon followed. My task became how to find my own stance between Pollyanna's unrealistic expectation and Cassandra's cynicism. I wanted to understand better what I had seen on the ground, instead of wringing my hands in despair.

The intellectual side of it called to me – and I was extremely fortunate to be offered in 2010 a tenure-track position at the Naval Postgraduate School with the promise of being able to focus my scholarly research on contemporary policy challenges.

This book is the combined result of my dissertation, my time in the policy world, and my return to academia. At Berkeley, I was supported by a dissertation committee composed of four brilliant scholars who had the grace to let me do what I wanted without letting me take any shortcuts. Steve Weber, my advisor, has been an exemplary mentor, always pushing me, often by example, to ask big questions and to find creative and elegant answers to them. Margaret Weir, Peter Evans, and Pradeep Chhibber together inspired me to think systematically about the state and how elites govern society and equipped me with the intellectual appetite and tools to do so. Only now do I fully recognize my great fortune in having these extraordinary scholars as guides in the early stages of my own scholarly journey. I sincerely hope that they will be proud of the way this book turned out. While at Berkeley, I also had the formative opportunity to learn from Steve Vogel, Nick Ziegler, John Zysman, and the late Don Rothchild of UC Davis, among others. I was very fortunate to receive major funding from Berkeley's Political Science Department and Institute of International Studies; as well as the University of California's Institute on Global Conflict and Cooperation and the United States Institute of Peace.

The Berkeley Political Science Department also gave me the great and lasting gift of camaraderie with a group of people who are both exceptional peers and my dearest friends, to whom I shout out my deepest affection and gratitude: Jennifer Bussell, Rebecca Chen, Thad Dunning, Brent Durbin, Jill Greenlee, Rebecca Hamlin, Amy Lerman, Abe Newman, Ely Ratner, Jessica Rich, Sarah Snip Stroup, and Regine Spector. Thanks for all the discoveries and capers, intellectual and otherwise – I simply cannot imagine a better group of people with whom to have shared it all.

I interviewed and talked with over one hundred individuals over the course of this project and I am extremely grateful for their time and patience in sharing their knowledge with me; I also thank them for their commitment to the best version of peacebuilding. Since joining the faculty at the Naval Postgraduate School I have learned from and been inspired by our students, many of them returning from tours in

Afghanistan and Iraq and all of them diligent and dedicated public servants. Pieces of the analysis in this book were first published in the *International Journal on Multicultural Societies* (now *Diversities*) and *Conflict, Security & Development*, and I thank UNESCO and Taylor & Francis, respectively, for their permission to repurpose that analysis and empirical material here. Parts of the argument here were presented at different stages at the Australian National University, the London School of Economics, the University of California, Santa Cruz, and the World Bank, as well as at the annual conferences of the International Studies Association and the American Political Science Association, and I am grateful for those opportunities to discuss the work and for the feedback I received from those in attendance.

As I reconsidered the puzzle that motivated this study and turned my dissertation into this, quite different, book, I have incurred numerous additional debts of gratitude that it is a pleasure to acknowledge. When Barbara Nunberg hired me to work with her at the World Bank in 1998 she quite literally set my life on a new pathway. She has shaped my intellectual outlook and my political and global sensibilities and she has been for almost two decades a dear friend and mentor. I am also indebted to her and another amazing boss and friend, Nick Manning, for my introduction to the three countries on which this study is built. My respect and thanks, too, to the other colleagues and friends I picked up through the World Bank: especially, Jana Orac, Amanda Green, Elisabeth Huybens, Mark Abdollahian, Mick Moore, Shabih Mohib, Saysanith Vongviengkham, Habib Rab, Catherine Anderson, Doug Porter, and Lorena Viñuela; and my YPeeps, Peter Lafere, Jamus Lim, Elizabeth Ninan, and Peter Dulvy. I am also grateful to my other DC pals, especially James Kvaal, Oliver Fritz, Sara Porsia, and Ely Ratner, for all the rollicking conversations and warm friendship. Each of these folks has influenced the way I see the world and the practice of development, politics, and public policy – and I admire them greatly for their commitment to making the world a better place and the integrity with which each of them pursues that goal.

Two major intellectual realizations shaped the rewriting of my dissertation into this book: both a product of what I was reading and teaching and what I had learned on the ground. First, I came to see that peacebuilding operations can only be truly understood if they are viewed as temporal sequences that link conflict, intervention, and aftermath. In this regard, this book is singularly inspired by Paul Pierson's

Politics in Time, which led me to more consciously apply a historical institutionalist lens to this study. Second, I also grasped that post-conflict countries could fruitfully be viewed as a special subset of the developing world, which brought me back to the foundational concept of political order and a political economy lens.

As I grappled with the implications of these new viewpoints, I received a great deal of help along the way. I am grateful to John Haslam, my editor at Cambridge University Press, for two extremely thoughtful and constructive anonymous peer reviews, and to the production team who helped shape this into a book. I am deeply indebted to those who read large portions of this book or helped me think through different parts of its argument, providing insightful comments as well as generous encouragement: Kent Eaton, Maiah Jaskoski, and Ben Read for that wonderful impromptu book workshop; and, also, Ed Aspinall, Susanna Campbell, Bjoern Dressel, Paul Hutchcroft, Naomi Levy, Clay Moltz, Jessica Piombo, and Sarah Stroup. Their feedback has improved this book immeasurably. I am grateful to others for timely advice on the mysteries of academic careers and publishing and, more importantly, their warm collegiality and support: Séverine Autesserre, Joshua Busby, Anne Clunan, Jeff Colgan, Erik Dahl, Mike Glosny, Jim Goldgeier, Bruce Jentleson, Matt Kroenig, Mohammed Hafez, Aila Matanock, Abe Newman, Jordan Tama, Chris Twomey, and Rachel Whitlark. I owe more than I can say to my book buddy extraordinaire, Brent Durbin.

And I owe my deepest gratitude to my family. Antonia Jindrich, Elkova Sallaberry, Karen Manville, and Shelly Grabe: thank you for your unconditional friendship and encouragement. Karen, Tom, Heather, and Wyatt Rowley, and Jessi Hempel: you embraced me into your family and into your hearts and you are always and everywhere in mine. Tyzoon Tyebjee, I miss you; and, Joyce Hemmer, thanks for keeping the delicious dinners and elder statesmanship going. My Barma cousins: you boost me up and make me laugh, a winning combination. Papa Taher: you were proud of my future even when it was yet unknown and I hope that I've begun to live up to your dreams for me. Sakina: thanks for always having my back and embodying the best of stolid support. Inseeyah: thank you for all the laughing, crying, and soul-good living we've been blessed to enjoy together; and for bringing the amazing Sven and Iva Stieldorf and the resultant adventure into our lives. Tarifa and Haider, Mum and Dad: thank you for setting the example of the life rooted in community to which I aspire and for your unfaltering support and encouragement in everything I undertake, no matter how far afield it takes me. Scout: thanks for the beach time that honed my California state of mind. Zalia: thank you for the gift of presence and for all the joyful days on which you distracted me from this book and also invigorated me to finish it. Erin: thank you for your love and the gift of stillness, for your unshakeable faith that I would finish this book, and for moving heaven and earth to help ensure that I could. (We'll always have Cambodge.) To have shared these fortunate and joyful years with all these remarkable people makes this book theirs as much as it is mine.

Introduction

International peacebuilding interventions in post-conflict countries have become widespread since the end of the Cold War – yet they have often confounded expectations, ending in reversals and disappointment. The international community's approach to building sustainable peace in war-torn states rests upon the notion that an engineered process of simultaneous statebuilding and democratization can bring modern political order to post-conflict states. Indeed, the United Nations (UN) has, at great cost, made implementing that theory one of its signature undertakings in its transformative peacebuilding endeavor. But in all too few of the post-conflict countries in which this transformation has been attempted have real improvements in the quest for effective and legitimate governance been achieved. In turn, human security and global stability remain compromised by persistent political instability, weak and corrupt governance, and chronic underdevelopment in ostensibly post-conflict countries.

This book explains why international post-conflict interventions have fallen short of the weighty aspirations they embody. It reframes the peacebuilding puzzle by presenting a new theory of how domestic elites construct political order during and after peacebuilding interventions. A comparative analysis of the UN's transformative peacebuilding attempts in Cambodia, East Timor, and Afghanistan shows that while international peacebuilders want to build effective and legitimate government, domestic elites essentially do not. As is the case in much of the developing world, post-conflict elites use strategies to prioritize their own political survival and power that result in a neopatrimonial political order that better delivers on their goals. Peacebuilding interventions thus generate a set of unintended yet predictable effects. In all three cases, the UN's efforts at peacebuilding through elite settlement followed by a process of simultaneous statebuilding and democratization were co-opted by a small subset of domestic power-holders who successfully closed down the political space and stunted state capacity.

To be sure, each of these countries is better off than before the peace operations. Yet the goals of intervention have not truly been met. Instead, there are striking similarities in the patterns of neopatrimonial order that emerge in the aftermath of intervention. This book makes the case that the peacebuilding approach is, at least in part, itself responsible for the eventually disappointing governance outcomes that emerge in post-conflict countries.

This introduction briefly presents the core argument of the book, highlighting the theoretical advances it makes in the context of the existing literature on peacebuilding and discussing its significance in light of the contemporary practice of peacebuilding. It sketches the empirical dynamics associated with the interaction between international interventions and domestic elite incentives in Cambodia, East Timor, and Afghanistan. It then outlines the structure of the book.

The Politics of Peacebuilding

The study of the processes and implications of peacebuilding has developed significantly over the past twenty-five years, alongside the evolution of actual policy efforts on the ground over that timeframe. A large body of work emerging from both the scholarly and practitioner realms has yielded valuable contributions in terms of exploring the multiple dimensions of conflict cessation and peacekeeping through negotiated settlements, defining peacebuilding and its many different dimensions, distinguishing the effects of different types of international peace operation, identifying some of the contextual factors necessary for success or explaining particular failures, and generating policy implications.[1] Yet there remain surprising gaps in the study of peacebuilding and related shortcomings in its practice. In particular, scholars and practitioners have tended to focus on the processes of peacebuilding, emphasizing the institutional contours of peace settlements and the mandate

[1] On peacekeeping and conflict cessation, see Fortna 2008; and Stedman, Rothchild, and Cousens 2002. On the multiple dimensions of peacebuilding, see Jarstad and Sisk 2008; Paris 2004; and Paris and Sisk 2009. On different types of peace operation, especially the machinery of international transitional administration, see Caplan 2005, 2012; Chesterman 2004; and Tansey 2009. On contextual factors conditioning peacebuilding success, see Autesserre 2010; Doyle and Sambanis 2006; Girod 2015; and Howard 2008. For policy implications, see Call 2012; Fukuyama 2004; and Ghani and Lockhart 2008.

and mode of implementation of peace operations. The most rigorous analyses have centered around what contextual factors condition the probability of peacebuilding success and failure, but they have largely neglected the conjunctural nature of the causal interaction between peacebuilding interventions and domestic political dynamics that truly determines whether a stable and lasting peace is achieved. Peacebuilding research has also been relatively myopic, focusing on the immediate question of whether international efforts help to establish peace and prevent a return to conflict, with much less attention to the aftermath of these interventions and the political dynamics and outcomes they set in motion.

This book, by contrast, approaches the study of peacebuilding through a historical institutionalist lens, viewing it as a hyperpolitical undertaking that interacts over time with the reconstruction of political order in post-conflict states. I illustrate that post-conflict elites react to, shape, and co-opt international interventions across countries in a sequence of recognizable patterns that undermine the quest for sustainable peace. The peacebuilding literature's analytical focus to date on the peace operations themselves – their mandates, mechanisms, and immediate outcomes – is partly a result of the recent nature of the surge in international attempts at peacebuilding. Now that enough time has elapsed from the wave of peacebuilding efforts initiated following the end of the Cold War, it is also time to focus more squarely on post-intervention outcomes in fragile and conflict-affected countries. This book takes on the least-studied aspect of post-conflict interventions by tying the implementation of peacebuilding interventions to what happens after the international community leaves. In doing so, it demonstrates that peacebuilding outcomes are best understood as the result of a dynamic contest between two alternative visions of post-conflict political order – that of the international community and that of domestic elites.

The Argument and its Significance

Since the end of the Cold War, the international community has invested a great deal in what I term the UN's "transitional governance" strategy of transformative peacebuilding – a period of simultaneous statebuilding and democratization over which international peacebuilders govern in tandem with domestic elites. In each country in which this approach is applied, it has resulted in new institutions intended to form the basis for effective and legitimate governance. But, in case after case, initial euphoria at the successful holding of elections and design of the formal institutions of the modern state has eventually turned into dismay at the poor governance outcomes that result. This book seeks to explain why – and, in so doing, to shed some light on how peacebuilding strategies might be improved. It does so by pursuing a comparative analysis of the UN transitional governance interventions in Cambodia (1991–1993), East Timor (1999–2002), and Afghanistan (2002–2005), conducted on the basis of fieldwork in each country and extensive complementary secondary research.[2] In each case, as in other post-conflict countries, the UN made reconstructing state capacity and building a democratic political system the explicit goals of a peacebuilding intervention.

The core contribution of this book is a new historical institutionalist theory about how post-conflict political order is constructed. It explains the unintended governance outcomes that emerge as a result of competing international and domestic visions of post-conflict political order at three critical phases along the temporal sequence of the peacebuilding pathway: the peace settlement that ends violent conflict; the implementation of a transformative peace operation; and the aftermath of the intervention. Elite peace settlements are intended to mark an agreement on a country's post-conflict future – but, in reality, they serve more as the terms upon which conflict continues by political means. A sharper understanding of elite political contest leading into and coming out of the conflict is crucial to understand how domestic elites embarked, in tandem with the international community, on reshaping post-conflict political order. In turn, the implementation of transitional governance, a process of institutional engineering intended to strengthen the state and initiate a process of democratization, becomes co-opted in practice by specific elites intent on entrenching their emerging grips on power. By choosing elites with whom to govern, peacebuilding interventions confer power upon them – and those elites use that power to enact subtle strategies of institutional conversion to their own ends. In the aftermath of intervention, finally,

[2] Throughout this book, I refer to and discuss the country case studies in the sequence in which the peacebuilding interventions occurred. In addition, following scholarly convention, I refer to East Timor by its anglicized name, rather than by its official name, Timor-Leste.

elites consolidate a neopatrimonial political order in which traditional, patronage-based governance co-exists with the formal institutions of modern governance.

Post-conflict states thus come to rest in a suboptimal political economy equilibrium that falls well short of the type of political order the international community aims to transplant through peacebuilding interventions. This outcome, as illustrated by the post-intervention political landscape of the three cases examined in this book, is characterized by discretionary instead of rule-bound law and policymaking, weak state capacity and poor service delivery, and attenuated democratic political practices. The cases illustrate, in subtly different ways, how the neopatrimonial political order that emerges in post-conflict states is perversely enabled by the transitional governance model's simultaneous pursuit of state- and democracy-building and its unique need for a domestic counterpart to aid in governance. In undertaking peacebuilding through transitional governance, the UN acts on an implicit theory about how best to change the domestic political game in order to create the foundations for sustainable peace. Yet, in practice, at each phase of the peacebuilding pathway domestic political realities trump international objectives.

In Cambodia, for example, the UN emphasized a quick route to elections to excise the Khmer Rouge, which was hostile to the peace process, from the legitimate body politic; but this tactic strengthened the hand of Hun Sen and his Cambodian People's Party (CPP). The UN's reliance on the CPP as its de facto counterpart in administering the country during the transitional period served to further entrench the CPP in the state apparatus, to the extent that even losing the country's first election was not enough to sever that grip. Since then, the struggle among Cambodian elites for an unassailable locus of power in the country has bloated the weak bureaucracy and oriented it toward patronage politics. Over time, Hun Sen and CPP elites have cemented in place a hegemonic regime, propped up by extensive and pervasive patronage networks, for which elections and the power-sharing formula stipulated by the constitution serve as window-dressing.

East Timor's major peacebuilding hurdle after the independence referendum was the hollowed-out state infrastructure left behind when the Indonesian government pulled out of the tiny nation. The UN peace operation there allowed only a limited degree of Timorese participation in executive governance of the country during the transitional period.

Moreover, its assumption that Timorese elites were united and its desire to maintain its neutrality in Timorese politics meant that the necessary elite political settlement was neglected. As a result, it mishandled the growing demands for increased "Timorization" by appointing as its preferred counterparts a small, yet powerful clique of revolutionary-era leaders who returned from a long exile to govern their country. These elites failed to translate their electoral mandate into inclusive policies for the Timorese population and the country's reconstruction. Intra-elite schisms, in the absence of countervailing state authority, spiraled into renewed violent conflict. The country's current leadership perpetuates a hierarchical governance structure as well as the reliance on patronage distribution for political support, a dynamic that has intensified on the basis of East Timor's petroleum wealth.

In Afghanistan, the tension between state- and democracy-building was at the core of the international community's dilemma in developing a peacebuilding strategy. It was framed as the struggle between the imperative to stabilize the country and the goal of giving the country, torn apart by many years of war, a new lease on democratic nationhood. The UN and the United States assumed that for the state to function at all, the loci of power held by the *mujahideen* leaders would have to be incorporated into the new government. Indeed, the country's first contemporary president, Hamid Karzai, invited such warlords to serve in his cabinet and as his provincial governors. Once bestowed with this legitimacy, these well-resourced veterans of Afghan political society were adept in consolidating their own patron–client networks; and elites around Karzai mimicked their behavior in the struggle for political support. The result is a weak and fragmentary state that struggles to resource even the limited activities it undertakes and to protect its society against the predatory rent-seeking and violence perpetuated by entrenched political elites at both the central and subnational levels.

Post-conflict developing countries, such as the three discussed in this book, hardly offer the fertile soil necessary for strong and effective states to take root and flourish. Indeed, a reasonable null expectation is that international peacebuilding interventions will have no real impact whatsoever. Yet the evidence from post-conflict Cambodia, East Timor, and Afghanistan, as I demonstrate in this book, tells a more nuanced story. Remarkably similar transitional governance processes in each case were surprisingly successful in (re)constructing the minimal basis for effective state administration and enabling local elites to come to some form of agreement on post-conflict institutional foundations. Elites in each of the three countries, guided by the UN, reached some consensus on a suitable administrative and democratic architecture for the local context and then held democratic elections to mark the endpoint of the transitional phase. Despite those successes in initiating the processes of statebuilding and democratization, however, each country has since faced significant challenges in consolidating effective and legitimate governance. This book argues that these hurdles are a result of the interaction between the international interventions and the domestic elites with whom they work.

These conclusions are by no means intended to damn peacebuilding efforts in their entirety. On the contrary, in each country, the political settlement has successfully prevented the return to full-scale violent conflict, a major achievement considering that post-conflict countries face a very high risk of renewed civil war in the absence of intervention.[3] This study is not a challenge to the comprehensive body of empirical evidence and relative consensus in the literature that international peacekeeping interventions help to maintain ceasefires and prevent a return to civil conflict.[4] In the three cases studied, as with the majority of the broader universe of countries in which the international community has mounted peace operations, political violence has been quelled, at least to some degree, by the international presence.[5] In addition, each country has recovered some measure of state capacity and political stability – each has increased revenue collection and the provision of public services and has held a series of elections. The point, rather, is to elucidate the difficulties in the complex endeavor of implanting state capacity and democracy in developing post-conflict countries within a short timeframe – and to make the case that a big part of the challenge is the logic underpinning the UN's transitional governance approach.

The theory and argument advanced here help to shed light on a number of crucial and practicable policy implications for reforming

[3] Collier, Hoeffler, and Söderbom 2008. [4] Fortna 2004, 2008.

[5] Although low-level political violence persists in Cambodia and East Timor, their civil wars were terminated through international involvement. Afghanistan, however, remains a country in civil conflict: there, the number of battle deaths per year fell below 1,000, the typical threshold above which a conflict is identified as a war, only in 2003 and 2004; otherwise it has remained above 1,000. UCDP/PRIO Armed Conflict Dataset, as presented in Gleditsch et al. 2002; and Themnér and Wallensteen 2014.

the practice of peacebuilding, detailed in the book's conclusion. A better understanding of how international peacebuilding objectives meet reality on the ground in post-conflict countries can help design better interventions in two major ways. From a theoretical perspective, it becomes apparent that some objectives may be simply too unrealistic to be retained in their entirety. It is a significant policy oversight to not squarely acknowledge that the different components of modern political order – stability, government effectiveness, and democratic legitimacy – emerge in different ways and are by no means always mutually reinforcing. In practical terms, nonetheless, it may yet be possible to adjust the manner in which peacebuilding is undertaken in order to prevent the undermining of core objectives. Second, viewing the peacebuilding pathway in temporal continuity and with an emphasis on elite incentives highlights, for example, that major policy setbacks have emerged from an overemphasis on specific institutional form, when instead the focus should be on the governance functions served at critical junctures on the pathway to peace.

Structure of the Book

The first two chapters lay the foundation for the book's analytical approach and contributions. Chapter 1 discusses the utility of the study in light of the contemporary practice of international peacebuilding. It defines the main focus of inquiry, which is the UN's transitional governance approach to transformative peacebuilding, and situates the book's argument within the existing peacebuilding literature, highlighting its unique contributions. It then introduces the historical institutionalist lens the book adopts to better understand peacebuilding and describes the research design of the study. Chapter 2 develops the book's core theory that international interventions enable and are co-opted by post-conflict elites intent on forging a neopatrimonial political order. Linking scholarship on conflict and peace to that on political, institutional, and economic development, it builds a theoretical framework that outlines what we should expect to see of elites attempting to build post-conflict political order. It lays out the logic underpinning the book's narrative, which spans a sequence of critical peacebuilding phases that form the course of international interventions: the peace settlement phase, the transitional governance period, and the aftermath of intervention. This causal argument is woven from a number of thematic threads concerning the manner in which elites negotiate and respond to moments of transition and shape institutions and political order coming out of those formative junctures.

The three chapters that form the main empirical body of the book then focus on each of these peacebuilding phases in turn, analyzing case material from Cambodia, East Timor, and Afghanistan at each juncture. This phase-by-phase narrative structure, in contrast to the more typical case-by-case approach, enables scholars and practitioners to better understand how critical junctures and path dependence contribute to the overall outcome of neopatrimonial political order in post-conflict states. Chapter 3 demonstrates how internationally mediated peace settlements in Cambodia, East Timor, and Afghanistan attempted to not merely bring an end to conflict but also to resolve the problems that created conflict at the outset. Through a comparative assessment of the politics leading into and out of the conflict, it demonstrates that these settlements are best understood as conditional elite pacts that initiate a new phase of elite conflict over the construction of political order. Chapter 4 focuses squarely on the peacebuilding interventions implemented by the United Nations in tandem with domestic counterparts. Based on the notion that statebuilding and democratization are mutually reinforcing, the UN attempts to implement both simultaneously to reorient domestic politics away from conflict. The chapter shows that there are, in fact, deep contradictions between these two processes and that they undermine each other when pursued together. In the three cases, conferring legitimate power and resources upon specific domestic elites enabled them to restrict political competition and dominate the process of post-conflict institutional design. Chapter 5 addresses the neopatrimonial political order that persists in Cambodia, East Timor, and Afghanistan in the aftermath of their international interventions, examining the consequences of the institutional decisions made during the transitional governance process. Through the historical institutionalist lens, it examines how power shifts and settles through the institutional system, paying particular attention to the manner in which domestic elites operate within and convert the institutional infrastructure to their own political–economic advantage. In all three countries, the neopatrimonial equilibrium has proven unfortunately resilient in undermining the quest for rule-bound, effective, and legitimate post-conflict governance.

The conclusion reviews the key findings of the book and discusses its implications for the future practice and study of peacebuilding. It probes the validity of the argument through a brief examination of other peacebuilding interventions. The bulk of the conclusion is devoted to a discussion of how peacebuilding might be improved on the basis of the book's findings. First, it disentangles the statebuilding and democratization imperatives that have been linked together in the pursuit of transformative peacebuilding. It then offers six targeted policy implications, along with a caveat, for improving peacebuilding practice. Finally, it reflects on the implications of this book for future research on peacebuilding and other challenges facing post-conflict developing countries.

1 *Rethinking the Peacebuilding Puzzle*

State formation and democratization have proven to be inherently organic, long-term, and complex processes that are extremely difficult to impose from the outside. Post-conflict countries are the least favorable environments in which strong and effective governance can take root and democracy can flourish. They are typically quite poor, having lost years of potential economic growth and development; they have low levels of institutional and human capacity that have been further attenuated by extended conflict; and they are home to populations with sociopolitical cleavages that have led to, and become hardened by, violent civil conflict. Nevertheless, the international community, led by the United Nations, acts on the belief that a strong state and a democratic political system are best suited to managing political conflict and presumes to be able to build the necessary administrative and democratic institutions to underpin modern political order and peace in these fragile countries.

The crux of the puzzle addressed in this book is why the international community has been relatively unsuccessful in building the peace it thinks it is building in post-conflict states. This chapter lays the foundation for the book's approach to this puzzle and describes the manner in which it builds its conceptual, empirical, and practical contributions. It begins with an overview of the practice of international peacebuilding interventions, defining, in particular, the aspirational underpinnings of the transitional governance approach to transformative peacebuilding that is the focus of this inquiry. Next, through a brief review of the existing literature I make the case that we need to better understand the limitations of transformative peacebuilding, and I outline the unique argument this book builds in doing so. The chapter then outlines the empirical approach underlying this research, describing the outcomes of interest and the logic behind the case selection and research design.

What is Peacebuilding?

Peacebuilding is the most extensive and transformative type of peacekeeping intervention undertaken by the international community. Where traditional peacekeeping entails international assistance to maintain a ceasefire among former combatants, peacebuilding constitutes a project to transform a post-conflict country's sociopolitical landscape so as to prevent the possible recurrence of conflict. In the aftermath of the Cold War, the UN's peacekeeping and peacebuilding portfolio became one of its fastest-growing and most distinctive endeavors for two main reasons. First, violent civil conflict around the globe peaked in the early 1990s as the stability wrought by the Cold War ended, although the proportion of countries embroiled in civil conflict then started to decline steadily.[1] Second, the end of the bipolar global rivalry between the United States and the Soviet Union meant that the UN Security Council could finally begin to agree to peacekeeping mandates under Chapters VI and VII of the UN Charter.[2] The Security Council tripled the peacekeeping operations it mandated between 1987 and 1994 and the UN's annual peacekeeping budget climbed from $230 million to $3.6 billion in the same period.[3] The figure is double today: the approved UN peacekeeping operations budget in the fiscal year from July 2014 to June 2015 was just over $7 billion. Over the past two decades, the UN's peacekeeping budget has been about triple its regular operating budget.[4] Moreover, peacebuilding is essentially a UN affair: its interventions are by far the predominant form of multilateral peace operation since 1945.[5]

[1] Blattman and Miguel 2010; Fearon 2010; and Fearon and Laitin 2003.

[2] The two sections of the UN Charter deal with dispute resolution: Chapter VI authorizes the UN to issue recommendations, while Chapter VII authorizes the Security Council to take forceful measures where necessary. Charter of the United Nations, San Francisco, 1945.

[3] Doyle and Sambanis 2006: 6, citing Boutros-Ghali 1995.

[4] The UN's current two-year operating budget is set at $5.4 billion.

[5] Different elements of peacebuilding have been pursued over the same period by multilateral regional groupings under the rubric of the United Nations (for example, the peacekeeping missions deployed by the Economic Community of West Africa States, or ECOWAS, in Liberia and Sierra Leone in the 1990s and in Guinea-Bissau in 2012). The United States' invasion and occupation of Iraq, beginning in 2003, was undertaken unilaterally, but in many respects the nation-building project pursued there via the Coalition Provisional Authority paralleled the logic of the transitional governance experiences described here.

The broad mandate of the UN Department of Peacekeeping Operations covers a large range of activities – including ceasefire monitoring, humanitarian assistance, military demobilization, power-sharing arrangements, support for elections, transitional administration, and operations to strengthen the rule of law and promote economic and social development.[6] Former UN Secretary-General Boutros Boutros-Ghali laid out the conceptual foundations of the newly ambitious and growing UN role in peace and security that he presided over as the Cold War ended in his seminal report, *An Agenda for Peace*.[7] He detailed the interdependent roles – preventive diplomacy, peacemaking, peacekeeping, and post-conflict peacebuilding – that he foresaw the UN carrying out in the rapidly evolving international system. Over the course of the past quarter-century, the practice of peace operations has indeed grown in complexity and ambition, as Boutros-Ghali anticipated. Although this evolution has not been strictly chronological, a number of analysts have fruitfully classified UN peacekeeping strategies in generational paradigms.[8] The bulk of the UN's peace operations since the end of the Cold War have focused on post-conflict peacebuilding, which Boutros-Ghali defined as "action to identify and support structures which will tend to strengthen and solidify peace in order to avoid a relapse into conflict."[9] Similarly, the influential *Brahimi Report* on UN peace operations defined peacebuilding as "activities undertaken on the far side of conflict to reassemble the foundations of peace."[10]

The Transitional Governance Approach to Transformative Peacebuilding

This book defines peacebuilding, following scholarly and practical convention, as the international community's attempts to transform a post-conflict country through intervention. What I term transitional governance, the focus of this book, is a specific type of peacebuilding endeavor for a particular environment: it is a transformative approach to forging sustainable peace in nations riven by civil war by crafting

[6] For further discussion of the UN Department of Peacekeeping Operations mandate and role in post-conflict countries, see Brahimi 2000; Doyle and Sambanis 2006; Durch 2003; Howard 2008; Jones 2004; and Ratner 1995.

[7] Boutros-Ghali 1992.

[8] For example, Goulding 1993; Ratner 1995; and Thakur and Schnabel 2001.

[9] Boutros-Ghali 1992, para. 20.

[10] Brahimi 2000, para. 13.

the administrative and political governance institutions to underpin lasting peace. Often other important peacebuilding dimensions – such as improving internal security, resettling refugees and internally displaced persons, and reconstructing a market-based approach to economic development – go hand in hand. The presence of an international coercive force, represented iconically by UN blue helmet troops and police but sometimes handled by NATO and other alliances, is often a crucial element of multidimensional peace operations.[11] Here, nevertheless, I restrict the analytical lens to focus on the engineered attempt at simultaneous statebuilding and democratization in post-conflict countries. Via this form of peacebuilding through transitional governance, the UN pursues state effectiveness and democratic legitimacy as the two essential ingredients of modern political order and the necessary underpinnings of lasting peace.

To date, the UN has not laid out an explicit model of transitional governance. Hence, I offer here an inductive definition, built through an examination of the mandates of the peace operations that attempt this manner of transformative peacebuilding.[12] A negotiated peace settlement among warring elites, typically brokered by the United Nations, marks the end to violent civil conflict. Transformative peacebuilding through transitional governance begins, subsequently, when a UN transitional authority or assistance mission is mandated by the UN Security Council to assist with the implementation of the peace agreement over a specified transitional period, typically two to three years. The hallmark of transitional governance – distinguishing it from other, less transformational versions of multidimensional peacekeeping – is that the appointed mission is responsible, to some degree, for performing the executive functions of the state.[13] Over the course of

[11] This is especially the case in the early stages of major interventions, where peacekeeping is a primary international concern, and ceasefire maintenance can continue to be crucial right up to a post-conflict election. See Fortna 2008. Yet the evidence below shows that the role of domestic coercive forces is more central than that of international troops to the longer-term endeavor of establishing political order in post-conflict states.

[12] This definition is condensed from that elaborated in Barma 2006, 2007. See also the definitive assessment provided in Caplan 2005.

[13] Caplan 2005: 21, concurs as follows, "... what distinguishes [these missions] from peacekeeping is the scope of their interest in, if not actual responsibility for, the functioning of a territory or state."

the transitional period the UN relies on a small group of domestic counterparts – sometimes a body that explicitly shares power among competing local groups – to assist with governance and to provide some form of domestic political participation in the process. Simultaneous processes of statebuilding and democratization are thus embedded in the transitional governance approach. Finally, the transitional period culminates in a UN-organized national election for a constituent assembly.[14] Once that representative body deliberates and ratifies a new constitution, making core choices about institutional architecture along the way, it is transformed into a new, post-conflict national legislature. At this point, while the UN and many international aid organizations remain involved in various forms of post-conflict assistance, a legitimate domestic government takes hold of the reins of administrative power. Figure 1.1 depicts the staged process that comprises the transitional governance approach between dotted lines showing its relationship to what comes immediately before and after this period.

The UN's strategy of peacebuilding through transitional governance represents the conviction that transformative peacebuilding is possible. It also represents an implicit theory: the notion that an engineered process of simultaneous state- and democracy-building is the strategy through which international interventions can help conflict-affected countries to transform the sociopolitical dynamics that activated and perpetuated conflict. In turn, the formal institutions pursued in post-conflict countries are the trappings of Weberian, rationalized bureaucracy and procedural liberal democracy because these forms of governance fit the international community's model of statehood. In other words, international norms concerning what is effective and legitimate domestic governance play a major role in shaping the UN's choice of the transitional governance strategy and the formal institutional outcomes it seeks in mounting post-conflict interventions to build sustainable peace.[15] The international organizations that undertake different elements of peace operations – including the United Nations,

[14] Zaum 2012 notes that only in Cambodia and Bosnia did UN mandates specify that elections would mark the end of the peace operation. Nevertheless, elections have served broadly as the main practical mechanism of transition from international to domestic governance.

[15] Autesserre 2014; Meyer et al. 1997; and Paris 2003.

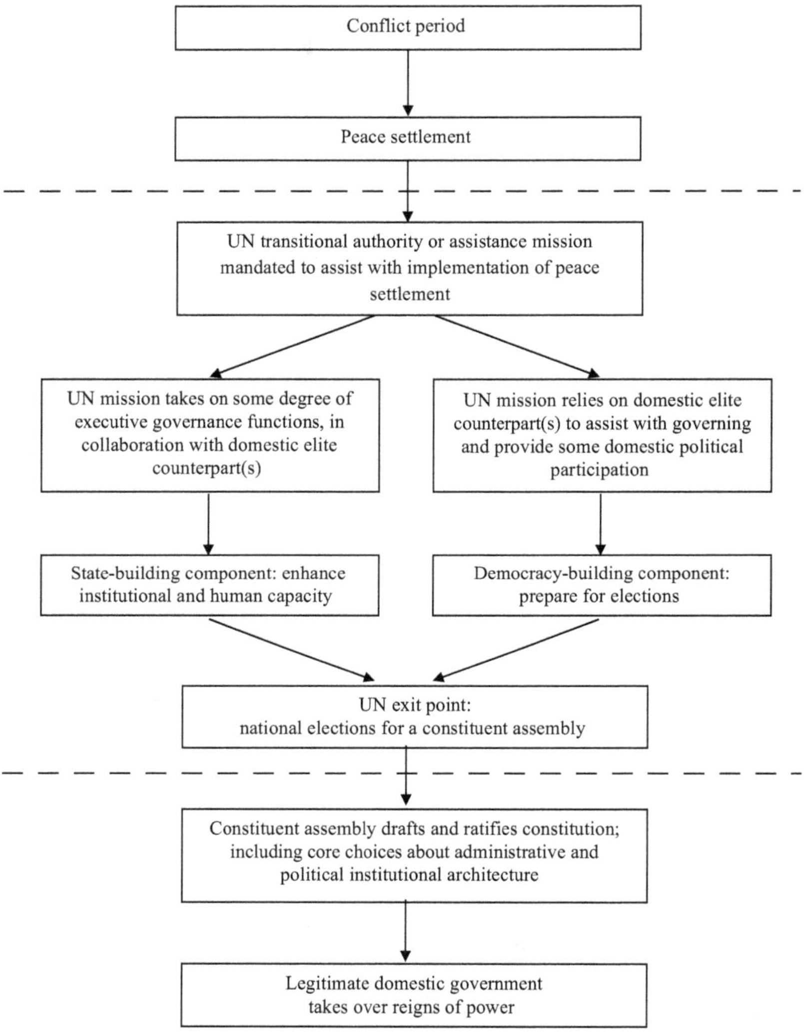

Figure 1.1 The transitional governance approach to transformative peacebuilding

the World Bank, and multilateral security groupings such as the North Atlantic Treaty Organization (NATO) – are, in turn, the repositories and promulgators of such international norms.[16] These norms persist even in the face of evidence from developing countries that the formal

[16] Barnett and Finnemore 1999, 2004; and Meyer and Rowan 1977.

structures of bureaucracy and democracy are often fairly ineffective at performing their intended governance functions.[17]

This book tells a particular story about how these international norms and objectives about modern political order meet reality on the ground in recipient post-conflict countries. The theoretical framework advanced in the following chapter, along with the empirical investigation of peacebuilding through transitional governance in Cambodia, East Timor, and Afghanistan, explain and illustrate why and how domestic political elites adapt and use the symbols, resources, and institutions associated with peacebuilding in constructing, instead, their own version of political order, one rooted in neopatrimonialism. Each chapter deals with one particular phase of the peacebuilding pathway, describing the international objectives animating that part of the sequence and then illustrating systematically how pursuit of those objectives was co-opted and upended by domestic elites. I turn now to a brief review of the existing literature in order to explain how this book's argument builds upon and adds to our understanding of peacebuilding.

What Do We Know About Peacebuilding?

Scholars have delved deeply into what began in the early 1990s as a relatively new theoretical space at the intersection of international relations, comparative politics, and public administration in order to examine the increasingly regular and significant phenomenon of post-conflict peacebuilding. Resting on various subdisciplinary perspectives, research on peacebuilding has evolved from the initial set of largely descriptive and policy-prescriptive assessments of peace operations to work that develops a deeper emphasis on the interaction of international and local actors and a more nuanced approach to the politics of peacebuilding. Nevertheless, thinking on peacebuilding tends to inadequately capture the agency of domestic elites on long-term governance outcomes because it underemphasizes the importance of taking a historical perspective on the central challenge of building political order. The bulk of the peacebuilding scholarship, as I illustrate in this section, comes from perspectives that place the peace operations themselves at the center of the inquiry. They thereby explain outcomes on the basis of

[17] Herbst 2000; Jackson 1990; Jackson and Rosberg 1982; and Scott 1998.

an intervention's scope, its size, the way it is organized, and so on, contextualized within the constellation of factors that condition its success or failure. My argument differs from these rival explanations in that the analysis privileges the role played by post-conflict elites – their interests, their actions, their agreements – in dealing with international interventions along the temporal sequence represented by the peacebuilding pathway.

The study of peacekeeping has its genealogical roots in international relations, originating with a body of work concerned with explaining when and why interventions successfully achieve and maintain peace. The first wave of research in this field was focused squarely on the peace operations themselves, with a view to understanding why some failed where others succeeded, and primarily based on a case-by-case analysis of post-conflict countries.[18] Single-country case studies of peace operations abound, many written by experienced practitioners. These are rich in empirical description but pre-theoretical, tending to underplay the causal mechanisms leading to success in outcomes as well as the interaction of international peacebuilding strategies with the domestic political environments in which they unfold. Another line of inquiry focuses on the machinery and processes of transformative peacebuilding – comparing the various mechanisms through which the international community has attempted to aid post-conflict states.[19] These studies typically come from a liberal internationalist perspective that takes as given the appropriateness of the norms pursued and, while acknowledging the importance of political context in shaping outcomes, many are oriented as evaluations geared toward improving policy and practice. Thus they tend to attribute the relative success of peacebuilding exercises less to causal political dynamics and more to technocratic details subject to policy manipulation such as the scope and implementation of the operational mandates themselves.

The second wave of research on peacebuilding approached similar questions through the adoption of a more deliberate focus on methodological and theoretical rigor, with the aim of developing systematic

[18] Fortna and Howard 2008 outline the development of the first two waves of research discussed here. They also point to an earlier wave of work that was focused on peacekeeping in interstate wars.

[19] Bellamy, Williams, and Griffin 2004; Caplan 2005; Chesterman 2004; Chesterman, Ignatieff, and Thakur 2005; Chopra 1999; Diehl and Druckman 2010; and Fukuyama 2004.

causal arguments that can be generalized across cases.[20] Much of this work was concerned with the extent to which peace lasts in post-conflict countries, with the inquiry focused on the factors that either impede or enhance the prospects for peace. The analytical logic driving this work is thus typically probabilistic or what Paul Diehl has termed "behavioral."[21] One line of scholarship has essentially confirmed the simple and important finding that peacekeeping operations lengthen the duration of peace after civil wars – peace lasts longer when there are international forces deployed than when former parties to conflict are left to themselves.[22] Other path-breaking research has identified a number of key determinants limiting the success of peace operations in terms of the incidence of violence and the success of democratization and reconstruction efforts.[23] These approaches tend to be rationalist, focusing on the degree to which optimal interaction was achieved between the characteristics of an intervention and the context in which it is undertaken. In general, however, this strand of peacebuilding scholarship is restricted to binary outcome measures of the presence or absence of peace and democracy at some relatively short remove from the end of an intervention.[24] The probabilistic, rationalist, and variable-centered nature of this body of work has yielded important knowledge about the likelihood of specific governance outcomes obtaining in a given timeframe after a peace operation. Yet, overall, this analytical approach has fallen short of developing a causal understanding of longer-term governance outcomes. We still lack a comprehensive explanation of the conditions under which a genuine transformation takes place in post-conflict societies, or a causally reasoned account of why that so often fails to transpire – a gap that the conjunctural and contingent logic of this book's approach seeks to fill.

In its early incarnations, a large body of the peacebuilding scholarship was fused to the desire of peacebuilding practitioners to be more successful. Practice and theory on this topic emerged contemporaneously and many of the first crop of peacebuilding analysts were

20 Fortna and Howard 2008. 21 Diehl 2014.

22 Fortna 2004, 2008; Hartzell, Hoddie, and Rothchild 2001; and Walter 2002.

23 Call 2012; Doyle and Sambanis 2000, 2006; Girod 2015; Jarstad and Sisk 2008; Paris and Sisk 2009; Stedman 1997; and Stedman, Rothchild, and Cousens 2002.

24 Call 2008 identifies the four standards for measuring success that have been common in the peacebuilding literature.

themselves also practitioners concerned with policy results. Roland Paris argued that this quirk of the peacebuilding scholarship led to a "cult of relevance" that limited theoretical and empirical advances in the field.[25] A third wave of peacebuilding research connects itself more deliberately, by contrast, to broader debates in international relations theory. Some scholars have, for example, framed the pursuit of peacebuilding goals and norms in relation to broader thinking about the construction and transmission of international norms. Deploying a constructivist or sociological institutionalist lens, these studies have focused on issues such as the replication of externally legitimate norms of statehood, the mechanisms of organizational learning at the United Nations, and the operative frames employed by expatriate peacebuilders working in post-conflict contexts.[26] Others have considered from a more rationalist ontological perspective the implications of theories of international governance and state sovereignty for peacebuilding practice and policy.[27]

The peacekeeping literature rooted in international relations generally stops short of analyzing the dynamics of transitional governance processes in terms of how international objectives interact with domestic forces. Turning to comparative politics for insight on these domestic dynamics of peacebuilding, other theoretical shortcomings become clear. Scholars have much to impart about the effects of elections and constitutional design on post-conflict peace as well as the connection between peacebuilding and democratization.[28] Externally imposed and managed interim governments in post-conflict countries have been analyzed in comparison to other types of provisional governance arrangements during major regime transitions.[29] There has been much lively debate on whether power-sharing, in its various forms, is a valuable

[25] Paris 2001. One particular problem that resulted from this closeness to policy concerns was an overreliance on the UN's narrative and data concerning specific peace operations. Della Porta 2013 argues, similarly, that dominant approaches to understanding terrorism are biased by their closeness to the United States government's interests and data. I thank Maiah Jaskoski for making this connection.

[26] Autesserre 2010, 2014; Barnett et al. 2007; Howard 2008; Ottaway 2002; Paris 2004; Westendorf 2015.

[27] Fearon and Laitin 2004; Keohane 2003; Krasner 2004; Krasner and Risse 2014; Lake 2016; and Matanock 2014.

[28] Jarstad and Sisk 2008; Reilly 2002; Reynolds 2002; and Roeder and Rothchild 2005.

[29] Shain and Linz 1995; also Gutierri and Piombo 2007.

post-conflict peacebuilding tool – an intellectual legacy of the predominance of ethnicized civil conflict in the post-Cold War period.[30] Yet while this focus on institutional form is certainly warranted, it is also essential to explicitly consider the interaction of institutions with the political environment in which they exist and the agency of domestic elites who both control and are constrained by them.

This latter point is made in a different manner by a final group of scholars, who have turned a critical theoretical eye on the very concept and practice of peacebuilding. Some have focused their critique on the implementation of peacebuilding through "neotrusteeship," or the imposition of governance by an external power, and on the mechanics of international involvement and donor-driven assistance.[31] Others have reappraised the "liberal peacebuilding" model itself, questioning the international community's motivation in applying it and the appropriateness of its content – Weberian bureaucracy, liberal democracy, and neoliberal economics – in the post-conflict countries in which it is attempted.[32] One strand of this critique focuses on expatriate peacebuilders' myopia about local, indigenous practices of peace and governance, arguing that peacebuilding should better resonate with the actual needs of the society emerging from conflict.[33] Overall, this most critical strand of the literature focuses on how international norms and objectives are externally imposed on a recipient country.

In sum, in theorizing about peacebuilding and studying its outcomes, analysts have tended to focus on the processes and institutional forms comprising the practice of peacebuilding. There are notable exceptions advancing the perspective that peacebuilding attempts can be improved only by better apprehending the political incentives of domestic elites – and emphasizing, contrary to the conventional assumption, that the strategic interests of international and domestic actors rarely coincide.[34] Yet the various strands of the peacebuilding literature tend overall to suffer from a short-term focus, a probabilistic or variable-centered logic, and an overemphasis on the institutional forms

30 Hoddie and Hartzell 2005; Horowitz 2002; Jarstad 2008; Lijphart 2002; and Sisk 1996, 2013.
31 Barnett 2006; Butler 2012; Call 2008; and Paris 2010.
32 Chandler 2006; Hughes 2003; Pugh 2005; Richmond 2006; and Richmond and Franks 2009.
33 Mac Ginty and Richmond 2013; and Richmond 2014.
34 Barma 2012a; Barnett and Zürcher 2009; Call 2012; Curtis 2013; Lake and Fariss 2014; Manning 2007; Tansey 2014; and Zürcher et al. 2013.

associated with peacebuilding. In order to truly understand whether peacebuilding approaches can and do achieve their objectives of building sustainable and lasting peace, it is necessary to explain longer-term governance outcomes by focusing on the causal and conjunctural mechanisms through which domestic elites interact with interventions and continue to build political order in their aftermath.

This book thus emphasizes how domestic post-conflict elites have been extremely adept at co-opting international peacebuilding interventions for their own political concerns and objectives. The approach of peacebuilding through transitional governance is not undertaken in a political vacuum even when formal institutional structures have collapsed. On the contrary, peacebuilding is a hyperpolitical undertaking; and the political–economic incentives facing domestic elites in the course of peacebuilding are crucial in explaining outcomes. Recognizing this issue in practice, the policy community on peacebuilding and development has recently converged on the broad consensus that the ability of an institution to deliver good governance – in the sense of producing public services and achieving legitimacy – is not simply a technocratic matter; instead, successful institution building is embedded in political processes, power structures, and societal sources of legitimacy.[35] The narrative presented in this book pays careful empirical attention to the elite incentives that define and condition their pursuit of political order. In particular, it examines how post-conflict elites garner political support and legitimacy, focusing on how they use political and administrative institutions to deliver the various benefits that underpin their compact with society.

Rethinking the Peacebuilding Puzzle

What explains the relative disappointment in the pursuit of effective and legitimate governance through peacebuilding interventions despite the tremendous financial, human, and intellectual resources devoted to this endeavor? The answer presented here rests upon two theoretical innovations that help to reframe the peacebuilding puzzle. Uniquely, I approach the study of peacebuilding through a temporal perspective, adopting a historical institutionalist lens. The book's causal

[35] Barma, Huybens, and Viñuela 2014; Jones and Chandran 2008; OECD 2011; Whalan 2013; Westendorf 2015; and World Bank 2011.

narrative – as outlined briefly below – is structured around the pathway of three critical peacebuilding phases that form the course of international interventions: (1) the settlement phase, which marks an end to outright violent conflict; (2) the transitional governance period, over which a transformative peacebuilding intervention is implemented, in tandem with domestic elites, with the intent of creating a sustainable peace through statebuilding and democratization; and (3) the aftermath of the intervention and the pivot of a "post-conflict" country to a "normal development" phase. Emphasizing the temporal dimensions of political phenomena in this manner – viewing political processes "in time" as Paul Pierson coins it – can be essential to uncovering elements of the causal mechanisms at hand.[36] One crucial insight that emerges from the temporal causal picture presented here is that international peacebuilding efforts do not, contrary to their implicit logic and expressed goals, bring about a fundamental break with the political patterns of the past. Instead, we can only achieve a true understanding of the outcomes of peacebuilding when we see these efforts in temporal continuity. Over the course of the peacebuilding pathway that forms the narrative arc of this study, the manner in which domestic elites interact with an international peacebuilding intervention in shaping political order – unintended consequences and all – comes into sharp relief.

Intertwined with the historical institutionalist approach, this book imports a new political economy perspective to the study of peacebuilding. The study of intra-state conflict was revolutionized by an attention to the economic incentives that influenced the behavior of warring parties.[37] The study of how societies end and recover from conflict requires a similar emphasis on the political–economic motivations orienting the parties to peace. The vast majority of post-conflict countries are developing countries in which the central governance challenge is the construction of a viable modern political order conducive to economic productivity. Yet those who study post-conflict peacebuilding, typically rooted in the study of violent conflict and its resolution through peacekeeping and institutional engineering, have

[36] Pierson 2004. See also Thelen 1999 on the importance of temporality in historical institutionalist approaches to politics, as well as the significance of examining politics as a dynamic process that often results in unintended consequences.

[37] Ballentine and Sherman 2003; also Collier and Hoeffler 1998.

paid scant attention to the study of the political economy of development – which is focused on how institutions and resources shape elite incentives, the state–society compact, political order, and economic development. We cannot fully explain post-conflict governance outcomes unless we understand the incentives motivating elites as they attempt to construct political order and see how the choices of these actors are conditioned by context – features that come into sharp relief over the course of the peacebuilding pathway.

The empirical chapters in this book advance the following causal argument through a comparative analysis of UN peacebuilding experiences and post-intervention outcomes in three countries: Cambodia, East Timor, and Afghanistan. First, I examine how warring elites come to a peace settlement in the context of the grievances and competing claims to governing legitimacy that contributed to conflict in the first place. Mediating a peace settlement is the first step taken by the international community in an attempt at transformative peacebuilding – and, in turn, serves as the basic agreement upon which the rest of the peacebuilding intervention is then predicated and implemented. Previous scholarship has emphasized that the settlement phase of peacebuilding is best understood as a conditional elite pact, yet the literature typically views and assesses these peace settlements in the limited context of marking an end to violence. A post-conflict settlement deal should, more importantly, be interpreted as a critical juncture marked by exceptionally fluid politics that, in turn, initiates a new pathway featuring heightened elite conflict in the political arena. The way elite settlements are typically pursued has the perverse effect of freezing in place an unstable equilibrium of power; this makes it more likely for elites to perceive the immediate post-conflict period as a "winner takes all" game with short time horizons. A sharper understanding of elite political contest leading into and coming out of the conflict becomes central to understanding how domestic elites embarked, in tandem with the international community, on reshaping post-conflict political order.

Second, I demonstrate how the simultaneous state- and democracy-building approach pursued by the archetypal transformative peacebuilding intervention empowers particular domestic elites to capture the legitimate political space and concentrate state resources in their own hands. In order to quickly establish basic state functions, the international community chooses specific elites with whom to govern, undermining the creation of a level political playing field to promote democratization. The new political pathway initiated by the peace settlement thus locks in advantages to a small group of elites. In turn, a self-reinforcing dynamic is established whereby these early winners continue to gain benefits in a manner that leads to a permanent reshaping of the power balance. Peacebuilding interventions themselves deliver sources of patronage to these specific political actors in the form of financial and other resources and the conferral of legitimate power. Perhaps most crucially, these elites are also centrally involved in the process of institutional engineering that takes place over the transitional governance period itself. Thus, over the course of an intervention and in the election that marks its endpoint, a small group of elites benefits from gradually increasing returns to power, while actively nurturing a political coalition and shaping institutions to their continued advantage.

Third, I explain how and why post-conflict countries tend to consolidate neopatrimonial political orders in the post-intervention phase. The UN's peacebuilding model rests on the liberal ideal that well-functioning, democratic states will deliver the public goods and services and shared prosperity that are pillars of sustainable peace. In reality, however, the political–economic incentives motivating post-conflict elites make it easier and more profitable for them to distribute public rents and patronage goods to their clients in exchange for political support. When time horizons are short and citizens cannot hold elites accountable for their commitments to provide public goods, elite incentives privilege narrow benefit provision to specific clients instead of public goods that benefit all citizens. Under these conditions, elites can channel their appeal to citizens through hierarchical patron–client networks. The formal structures of authority – such as government agencies and institutionalized political parties – are undermined, in turn, because elites do not need to build credibility with the broader populace. The patterns of political contestation evidence an inter-elite battle to gain political authority, as well as the struggle to use political power to continue to reinforce advantage.[38] This neopatrimonial political–economic order is an obviously suboptimal one that privileges the short-term interests of elites and their networks over the long-term

[38] Pierson 2015 identifies this as a major feature of how power distribution is path-dependent.

welfare of society at large. Even as a return to violent conflict is forestalled, genuine improvements in state capacity and democratization prove to be illusory.

Rethinking the peacebuilding experiences in Cambodia, East Timor, and Afghanistan through the lens of this narrative demonstrates the contest between two competing visions – international and domestic – of political order. Quite simply, during the course of transitional governance powerful domestic elites co-opt the UN-led process of institutional design, which is intended to serve as the basis for lasting peace, and subsequently consolidate their holds on power through various discernible strategies, damaging the prospects for democratic governance. Peacebuilding operations bring with them significant resources and, in turn, the allocation and control of those resources become a new site of power for elites.[39] In Cambodia today, the hegemonic ruling party quashes dissent and controls all the levers of administrative, economic, and political power in a situation of grand state capture. In East Timor, a nascent peace was upended by continuing elite factional battles that turned violent and the subsequent political–economic settlement remains contentious. In Afghanistan, competing elites maintain a pitched battle for control of the state and the country's resources – a struggle framed by the political dominance of ethnoregional patron–client networks. In subtly different ways, each country's trajectory reveals how elites faced a political–economic calculus that oriented their incentives toward the construction of a neopatrimonial political order characterized by discretionary rule-making, weak state capacity, and compromised democratic accountability.

Viewed in time and with the role and incentives of post-conflict elites firmly in mind, it becomes evident that the international peacebuilding endeavor paradoxically fails at achieving its goal of sustainable peace through state- and democracy-building because these elites instead succeed at using the peacebuilding intervention for their own ends. I wish to be clear at the outset that those ends are not unquestionably negative. In each of the three cases in this book – as well as in other countries – the post-intervention political order is undoubtedly better than the conflict that preceded it, with elements of more political stability, government efficacy, and democratic accountability. But these outcomes fall short of what the international community believed itself

[39] Barma 2012a; Hughes 2009a; and Richmond 2006.

capable of achieving. The contention here is that viewing post-conflict peacebuilding interventions as sequenced contests between two competing visions of political order explains why the desired results of the transformative peacebuilding enterprise are not fully met as well as the outcomes we see in place. Next, I discuss how I construct this argument.

A Unique Approach to Understanding Peacebuilding

This study hews to the three defining features of comparative-historical analysis identified by James Mahoney and Kathleen Thelen and their collaborators in their recent, thorough, and eloquent case for the approach[40] – which has often, until relatively recently, also been referred to as historical institutionalism. First, this book adopts a firmly *macroscopic orientation* to the study of peacebuilding, focusing on large-scale political outcomes and causal patterns, along with a *configurational logic*, whereby the mode of explanation emphasizes variables combining in patterns defined by context. Second, the study was inspired by a desire to focus on *problem-driven, case-based research*, geared toward the explication of causal mechanisms through deep understanding and retelling of case empirics as opposed to a stylized rendering of cases coded on isolated variables of interest. Third, the analysis in this book presents a *temporal emphasis*, whereby the timing and sequencing of when specific things occur matter a great deal to the way that outcomes play out, as much as any other element of context.

I have chosen to define this book's analytical logic as resting on a foundation of historical institutionalism even though "comparative-historical analysis" has perhaps become the dominant label for this approach in the political science scholarship. This choice reflects the wish to emphasize the metatheoretical reframing that the historical institutionalist approach affords the study of peacebuilding, especially through its temporal and configurational causal logic, over other, more granular methodological concerns being addressed by those in the

[40] Mahoney and Thelen 2015. In their introduction to the volume, Thelen and Mahoney 2015 discuss each of these characteristics at length, establishing the case for their analytical importance.

vanguard of comparative-historical analysis.[41] This section thus makes a particular case for a temporal understanding of peacebuilding, characterizing the international community's model of peacebuilding through transitional governance as a critical juncture and emphasizing the value of a path-dependent approach to the study of this transformational experience. It then specifies the macropolitical and institutional variables that are of interest in the study and discusses the configurational mode of explanation. Finally, it explains the selection of the Cambodia, East Timor, and Afghanistan cases and outlines the case-intensive empirical research design underpinning the study.

Viewing Peacebuilding in Time

One of the central aims of this book is to make an original contribution to the study of peacebuilding by grounding it "in time."[42] To deepen our understanding of peacebuilding and political order in post-conflict states, this book emphasizes the importance of temporal causal sequences and mechanisms and views institutions – formal rules, policy structures, and norms – as both the legacies of the concrete political struggles of the past and the contours of the political arena of the present.[43] In this light, the temporal location of peacebuilding interventions is crucial, in relation both to the conflict and political landscape that precedes them and also to their aftermath and the political dynamics and outcomes they set in motion. The analysis here is thus differentiated from the more common approach to the study of peacebuilding, which favors a probabilistic logic and typically treats interventions as *exogenous* treatments to be assessed in terms of the extent to which they met their objectives. Adopting an in time approach helps to expand our conjunctural and contingent understanding of where institutional change comes from, opening it up to *endogenous* change shaped by the interaction of specific actors, and avoids the risk of an improperly truncated analysis.[44]

This book embeds the abrupt transformational experience represented by a peacebuilding intervention in a longer view of the gradual building of political order. In so doing, it recognizes that as

[41] I am extremely grateful to Paul Pierson for a clarifying exchange about use of these various labels. I alone am responsible for the choices made here.

[42] Pierson 2004.

[43] Mahoney and Thelen 2010: 7; and Pierson and Skocpol 2002.

[44] Pierson 2004.

consequential for political outcomes as the critical junctures at which wholesale change occurs is the slow and piecemeal adaptation in and around institutions that follows.[45] The rich literature on state formation and the building of political and institutional order has taught us that the sequencing of political and institutional choices and processes is central to explaining outcomes.[46] In particular, causal conjunctures – the interaction effects between causal sequences – are especially important for understanding the effects of competition over political space.[47] Institutions, in the narrative I build in this book, are both an outcome of interest and important intervening variables in generating other outcomes – they emerge from temporal processes of political struggle and are deeply embedded in social context, shaping both going forward. In short, institutions – including those that are at the heart of peacebuilding interventions – are the path-dependent products of both continuity and change.[48] When we view peacebuilding efforts in temporal perspective it becomes clear that the formal institutions they transplant into post-conflict states interact with the patterns of the past instead of serving as a break with them.

A peacebuilding intervention is a transformative moment from its inception (via peace settlement and UN mandate) through to its close (exit via elections), encompassing its implementation on the ground through transitional governance. A peacebuilding operation of this nature is thus fruitfully treated as a watershed event that, like a classic critical juncture, "establish[es] certain directions of change and foreclose[s] others in a way that shapes politics for years to come."[49] Such an intervention, like a critical juncture, can be seen as both a structural phenomenon that reshapes the polities in which it is undertaken, as well as a moment of contingent choice for the agents involved in the transformation.[50] Indeed, Giovanni Capoccia notes that the *defining* feature of a critical juncture is contingency – because of the uncertainty

45 Mahoney and Thelen 2010: 1.

46 For example, Ertman 1997; Skocpol 1979; Slater 2010; Tilly 1990; and Waldner 1999.

47 Pierson 2004; and Waldner 1999.

48 Katznelson 1997; Pierson 2004; and Thelen 1999.

49 Collier and Collier 1991: 27.

50 In this regard, I hew to the insight that the relative balance of structure and agency during this transformative event is an empirical rather than a definitional issue, as argued in Brady and Collier 2004; and Slater and Simmons 2010. Assessing this relationship is precisely one of the contributions of the empirical approach in this book.

as to what institutional arrangements will come to look like, "political agency and choice . . . play a decisive causal role in setting an institution on a certain path of development, a path that then persists over a long period of time."[51] What makes a peacebuilding intervention a particularly interesting type of critical juncture is that it represents a series of wide-ranging institutional choices superimposed by an external actor upon the fluid political landscape of a post-conflict country.

Peacebuilding Outcomes: Institutions and Governance

The transformative aspirations of the broader peacebuilding project are represented in the belief that the international community can, in a relatively short period of time, establish the institutional underpinnings for rule-bound, effective, and legitimate government. Animated by the objective of building the foundations for lasting peace, international interventions focus operationally on the construction of the formal institutional structures of the administrative and political arenas. Yet those institutional structures are transposed onto dynamic political contexts, hence eventual governance outcomes are a product of the domestic political game. The results of peacebuilding interventions are decidedly mixed, therefore, with a notable gap between the formal institutions transplanted through transitional governance and the eventual governance outcomes in the aftermath of intervention. Open contestation around formal institutional choice is only the tip of the iceberg in terms of the real power battles that are going on under the surface – such that the politics of initial institutional adoption are often very different from the politics of later implementation and adaptation.[52] Thus, I examine two sets of outcomes: the formal institutional choices surrounding statebuilding and democratization; and the extent to which effective and legitimate governance are consolidated in the post-intervention phase.

Formal Institutional Choices

In undertaking peacebuilding that aims to resolve the roots of conflict, the international community has come to believe that a political solution to stalemated civil conflict cannot be "all or nothing," and that

[51] Capoccia 2015: 148. [52] Hacker, Pierson, and Thelen 2015.

institutional design is the major policy instrument available for reconciling previously warring segments of a population. With the eventual aim of building a stable and lasting peace by establishing the foundations for democratic governance, two sets of institutional structures are emphasized in peacebuilding through transitional governance: *administrative structures* – the set of institutions through which a government exerts control or broadcasts authority over its population; and *constitutional arrangements* – the set of institutions through which a governing authority administers a polity with legitimacy. Agreement on the institutional architecture of the modern state – including an administrative structure, a constitution, and the design of an electoral system – represents the outcome of crucial political negotiations among domestic elites, as well as a critical step in the longer process of building rule-bound, legitimate, and effective government.

Post-Intervention Governance Outcomes

Transformative peacebuilding focuses, in the peace settlement and transitional governance implementation phases, on the construction of the administrative and political institutions discussed above. Its objectives, however, are to resolve the roots of conflict and thereby build a stable peace. The degree to which those institutions are the channel through which effective and legitimate governance is built and thereby serve as a stepping stone to sustainable peace can only be assessed by looking at consolidated governance outcomes in terms of state capacity and democratization. We know a strong state and its hallmarks when we see them in action. The Weberian ideal state is one that is effective, resting in turn on the autonomy and internal organization or rationalization of the bureaucracy.[53] The state is also in constant interaction with society, both shaping and being shaped by it.[54] Theda Skocpol thus argues that analysis of the state should also include the "Tocquevillian" dimension of state strength that emphasizes the state's connections with society.[55] Peter Evans captures this two-sided conception of strong state capacity with the notion of *embedded autonomy*, a term that echoes Michael Mann's distinction between "extensive" and "intensive" power.[56] The widely used working definition of

[53] Evans and Rauch 1999.
[54] Evans, Rueschemeyer, and Skocpol 1985; Kohli 2002; and Migdal 1997.
[55] Skocpol 1985. [56] Evans 1995; and Mann 1986.

a consolidated democracy developed by Juan Linz and Alfred Stepan captures the notion of democratization in a similarly inductive manner. Briefly, a democratic regime is consolidated behaviorally, when no significant actors attempt to create a nondemocratic regime or turn to violence; attitudinally, when a strong majority of the public believes that democratic procedures and institutions are the best way to govern their collective life; and constitutionally, when governmental and non-governmental forces alike are habituated to conflict resolution within the laws, procedures, and institutions laid out by the new democratic process. In short, consolidated democracy is a political situation in which democracy has become "the only game in town."[57]

It is worth noting here that the criteria outlined above – especially the latter set, concerning the consolidation of effective and legitimate governance – constitute a higher bar than most analysts of peacebuilding have adopted in assessing its outcomes. Most scholars and practitioners, while acknowledging that the situation often deteriorates as time elapses, have judged the success of UN peace operations mainly by assessing the degree to which peace obtained at the point the UN exited the country or a few short years later. There are good reasons for the adoption of this conventional approach. Some have pleaded that not enough time has elapsed to realistically analyze consolidation. Others claim that state- and democracy-building are, by their very nature, extremely difficult and time-consuming processes, and thus assessments of consolidation are based on unreasonably high standards of peacebuilding success that cannot properly be attributed to the implementation of the peace operation itself.[58] These are certainly complex and lengthy processes and evaluating proximate cause is indeed methodologically difficult.[59] Yet assessing the outcomes of peacebuilding operations in achieving their own objectives means examining critically what happens after peacebuilders leave the country in addition to understanding what they did while they were there. Fortunately, an assessment of longer-term peacebuilding records has now become possible as more time has elapsed since the close of the

[57] Linz and Stepan 1996: 5–6; they attribute the phrase to Di Palma 1990.

[58] Downs and Stedman 2002.

[59] Tansey 2014 makes a case for strengthening causal inference in the study of peacebuilding and suggests that this can be achieved through methods of process-tracing, counterfactual analysis, and control cases.

UN transitional governance missions considered here. Lengthening our perspective in this manner – alongside a macroscopic and conjunctural perspective, in contrast to a more probabilistic and evaluative logic – enables a critical assessment of the international community's assumption that a transformative process of elite peace settlement followed by simultaneous state- and democracy-building will achieve sustainable peace.

Case Selection

Transitional governance interventions are rare events. To recap, these are the transformative operations in which the UN pursues lasting peace through a strategy of simultaneous statebuilding and democratization, enacted via the implementation mechanism of shared international and domestic governance over a transitional period that begins with a peace settlement and ends with a first post-conflict election. In common with most scholars in this area, I focus on the UN as the major actor undertaking and coordinating international peacebuilding interventions. Moreover, UN transitional governance serves implicitly, due to its multidimensional and transformative nature, as an umbrella rubric for the post-conflict activities of other global actors – including international financial organizations, bilateral development agencies, and international nongovernmental organizations. Since 1948 the UN has mounted a total of 70 peace operations, 55 of which have taken place since the end of the Cold War in 32 different countries, with a number of countries having hosted multiple operations.[60] Christoph Zürcher et al. classify 19 of these as major peacebuilding operations – they meet this definition if they lasted over 6 months, comprised more than 500 personnel, and were intended to maintain peace at least in part by facilitating socio-political change.[61] Of these 19, only 6 meet the criteria established here for transitional governance: these are, in

[60] These figures are constructed from the list of peacekeeping operations maintained by the United Nations Department of Peacekeeping Operations, available at: http://www.un.org/en/peacekeeping/documents/operationslist.pdf.

[61] Zürcher et al. 2013. By this definition, missions focused solely on ceasefire or election monitoring or security sector capacity-building would not qualify as major peacebuilding operations. See also Paris and Sisk 2009, who identify an almost identical list of 21 major post-conflict peacebuilding operations during the period 1989–2007 on the basis of slightly different criteria.

chronological order, Cambodia, Bosnia, Croatia, Kosovo, East Timor, and Afghanistan.[62]

This book focuses on the transitional governance interventions that were deployed by the UN in Cambodia (1991–1993), East Timor (1999–2002), and Afghanistan (2002–2005). Cambodia, East Timor, and Afghanistan are the only three developing countries with weak institutional capacity in which the transitional governance approach has been implemented. The analysis in this book does not includes the three remaining instances of transitional governance peacebuilding – Bosnia, Croatia (Eastern Slavonia), and Kosovo.[63] All of these countries are more wealthy and institutionally advanced than the three developing nations I consider here – nevertheless, the transitional governance strategy itself remains similar in these cases, which should thus provide an opportunity for the further testing of the findings of this book. I also do not systematically examine major peacebuilding operations that do not meet the definition of transitional governance because they were not governed in tandem with the UN through a civil administration component to the peace operation, even if they encompassed UN-run elections and some elements of statebuilding. These cases would include, chronologically, Namibia, Mozambique, Haiti, Rwanda, Tajikistan, Angola, Macedonia, the Central African Republic, Sierra Leone, the Democratic Republic of the Congo, Liberia, Côte d'Ivoire, Burundi, South Sudan, and Mali.[64]

The lack of an African transitional governance case is analytically unfortunate for this book, since Africa is the region where by far the

[62] Zürcher et al.'s 2013: 59–63 systematic coding of the scale and scope of the universe of peacebuilding missions clearly delimits Afghanistan, Bosnia, Cambodia, Croatia, East Timor, and Kosovo as the only countries in which interventions took on major executive, legislative, policymaking, and even judicial responsibilities.

[63] Although the United Nations Mission in Bosnia and Herzegovina (UNMIBH) itself did not bear the executive governance roles that are the hallmark of transitional governance, these executive functions were performed by the Office of the High Representative, the ad hoc international agency established to implement the 1995 Dayton Peace Agreement and later mandated to provide guidance to UNMIBH. As such, the Bosnian case falls within the transitional governance universe in practice.

[64] The excellent volume by Zürcher et al. 2013 offers a comparative analysis of this broader universe of transformative peacebuilding cases.

most peacebuilding occurs.[65] Namibia was the first country in which a major peacebuilding operation was undertaken and some would consider it the first case of transitional governance. Per my reading of the intervention's mandate, however, the United Nations Transition Assistance Group (UNTAG, 1989–1990) in Namibia does not meet the definition of a transitional governance mission advanced here because it did not comprise a civil administration component responsible for a broad scope of governance functions. UNTAG did, in practice, take on some executive governance roles, but the range of those functions was relatively circumscribed, at best qualifying the intervention as a proto version of the more full-blown transitional governance interventions that were mandated soon after.[66] The two most recent major peace operations, in South Sudan (2011–present) and Mali (2013–present), are similarly multidimensional in scope and transformative in ambition, but with circumscribed governance functions for the UN in terms of implementation. Nevertheless, the empirical chapters below incorporate, where possible, conclusions from published research on major African peacebuilding operations that shed some light on the theoretical generalizability and empirical validity of the arguments advanced here.

Peacebuilding through transitional governance is uncommon. It does not occur very often in part because of what it entails – big, expensive, ambitious operations in countries where civil war has contributed to the disintegration of governance. To date, the East Timor intervention represents the high-water mark of the approach – and it is entirely possible that the peacebuilding ground has shifted enough over the decade since it concluded that we will no longer see such transitional governance attempts. Yet it is precisely the ambitious nature of these instances of transformative peacebuilding – and the contemporary international aspirations they represent – that makes them an important object of study.[67] This book's argument and implications

[65] See Curtis and Dzinesa 2012 for an overview and compilation of work on peacebuilding in Africa.

[66] See Howard 2008: 52–87 for an excellent focused discussion of the UN's role in Namibia and the relative success of the UNTAG peace operation.

[67] Steinmo 2008 notes that scholars working with a historical institutionalist approach are often interested in important and rare events.

will remain relevant even as the precise manner in which the international community's transformative peacebuilding endeavor is pursued continues to evolve.

Research Design

The research design underpinning this book is a comparative case study approach that traces the process of how transformative peacebuilding interventions in Cambodia, East Timor, and Afghanistan led to a series of unintended political–economic consequences that shaped post-intervention governance outcomes. I present the argument thematically, instead of in case-narrative format, delivering a structured, focused comparison of the three cases at three critical peacebuilding phases – peace settlement, transitional governance, and the aftermath of intervention. The analytical strategy for doing so echoes Charles Call's insight that the transition from warfare to peace, in general, goes through a series of temporal junctures or critical moments, at which typical clusters of decisions arise.[68] Peacebuilding disappointments in post-conflict states are overdetermined; the odds are stacked against success and numerous causal pathways can be identified in leading to failure. But a robust comparative methodological approach that also relies upon process-tracing can be used to identify a plausible causal chain. Employed together, a controlled comparison and process-tracing offer a "middle ground" approach between heavily ideographic descriptions of particular cases and overstylized cross-case comparisons that lose granular texture.[69]

My purpose is to assess the merits of the international community's approach to post-conflict intervention through a critical analysis of the process it applies in interaction with domestic elites in attempting to achieve its stated outcomes. This purpose forms the basis of the structured, focused methodology employed to examine the cases. The logic of the method is straightforward: the empirical research was guided by a series of questions asked of each case intended to collect evidence on the outcomes of interest and potential causal patterns. In turn, this makes possible both systematic comparison across cases and cumulative conclusions.[70] Within-case analysis through process-tracing helps

[68] Call 2012. [69] Slater 2010: 21; also Collier and Collier 1991.
[70] George and Bennett 2005, especially pp. 67–124.

to strengthen the argument that, rather than the pre-existing conditions in each case, it was the interaction between the international intervention and domestic elite incentives that led to the observed outcomes. The approach underpinning this study is particularly well suited to generating new hypotheses about understudied phenomena, carrying out contextualized comparison, and dealing with causal complexity. Like many historical institutionalist works, the approach here begins with a specific empirical puzzle in a limited number of cases sharing a unified political experience and focuses on developing mid-range theory on the topic.[71]

The case-comparative approach grounded in historical institutionalism is sometimes regarded as being difficult to falsify. Although this is not inherently true, the criticism may apply to a specific empirical investigation – hence it is worth being explicit about what could falsify my argument. In short, empirical inklings that domestic elite incentives and actions are not truly path dependent, or linked temporally, would prove the argument wrong. Evidence that would support a more rationalist and probabilistic logic, for example, would be signs that domestic elites were repeating rounds of interaction among themselves or with the international intervention with little impact from the outcomes of previous rounds; or that powerful actors were able to impose their instrumental designs on institutions such that their preferred functions were achieved quite perfectly. My analysis of the evidence from the cases, as presented in the empirical chapters, instead supports the conjunctural, path-dependent logic that allows for, among other things, explanations for the high level of institutional ambiguity and mismatch seen in the cases. Moreover, any limitations of the approach adopted here with regards to Popperian falsifiability are, I believe, outweighed by the benefits of a problem-driven, case-oriented approach that is geared toward generating a theoretically informed causal account of the peacebuilding outcomes across these three cases.[72]

Cambodia, East Timor, and Afghanistan display a substantial degree of variance in pre-intervention pathways, in terms of their trajectories into conflict and the nature of the peace settlement that ended conflict. The three countries thus serve as a set of "most different systems"

[71] Thelen 1999: 373 identifies these features as hallmarks of historical institutionalism.
[72] Mahoney and Thelen 2015.

cases in terms of many potential explanatory variables, including: the nature of the conflict; the configuration of competing groups and elites that engaged in conflict and came to a peace settlement; and the nature of sociopolitical cleavages and macrohistorical context. In Cambodia, three major coherent factions opposed to each other on ideological grounds fought a 21-year civil war against the backdrop of Cold War geopolitics and a genocidal regime. The peace settlement of 1991 was the result of a mutually hurting stalemate between still hostile groups. In East Timor, the settlement marking the end of a 24-year resistance struggle against Indonesian occupation was the independence vote in 1999. The revolutionary front served as an umbrella group that, albeit quite incoherent, dominated the political landscape in the transitional phase. Afghanistan emerged in 2001 from 22 years of conflict that saw an anti-imperialist struggle morph into civil war among many fairly coherent ethno-tribal groupings. A peace agreement was struck among a coalition that had come together, aided in the end by the US military, to defeat the Taliban – but political, financial, and armed resources in the country continued to be spread widely across still hostile groups.

Despite the many differences between the cases, each country underwent the transformative critical juncture of a peacebuilding intervention through transitional governance. My argument here thus emerges from the method of agreement:[73] the shared transformational experience that all three countries went through is the transitional governance process – hence any similarities in outcomes that result from that process should be more compelling given their differences. While the comparative case material presented here generates a causal logic, it cannot rigorously demonstrate the external validity of that logic.[74] The theory-building research objective here is a heuristic, building-block approach that seeks to inductively identify causal patterns to better understand peacebuilding.[75] As discussed above, the transitional

[73] Mill 1843; also George and Bennett 2005; and Przeworski and Teune 1970.

[74] One complementary research agenda would examine a set of cases of indigenous peacebuilding in which the international community did not implement a transitional governance process. See, for example, Barma, Levy, and Piombo 2015; and Weinstein 2005.

[75] Eckstein 1975; and George and Bennett 2005, especially pp. 74–78.

governance approach is one type of broader peacekeeping and peacebuilding intervention. The scope of the research here is necessarily limited; nevertheless, the analysis I develop in this book fills a gap in and contributes to the more general theory of peacebuilding being developed by scholars and practitioners today. In addition, this book generates a theory of the politics of international intervention and its interaction with domestic elite incentives that is generalizable beyond the issue of peacebuilding.

My analysis rests on the approximately one hundred personal interviews I conducted from 2002–2014 in Cambodia, East Timor, and Afghanistan, as well as in Canberra, London, New York, and Washington, DC.[76] Each interview lasted between one and two hours and was conducted on a semi-structured basis using an interview guide adapted for each country or for other specific purposes. Interviewees were identified using snowball sampling – i.e., a nonrepresentative chain of referrals – and included legislators, government officials, national- and provincial-level civil servants, journalists, civil society and private sector representatives, scholars, natural resource sector experts, and officials representing international organizations, bilateral development agencies, and international nongovernmental organizations. Almost all of my interviewees requested that they not be quoted directly and that they not be identified in relation to specific responses. In the text below interviewees are therefore identified only by their general role in relation to certain findings; the appendix to this book provides a full list of all interviews. The analysis also draws upon the rich case study evidence available in published work and policy reports on international peacebuilding interventions.

The research was organized as a series of questions that map to the three critical phases along the peacebuilding pathway, around which sequence this book is structured: the peace settlement phase; the transitional governance period; and the aftermath of intervention. It is during these critical moments marking the course of an intervention

[76] These interviews were conducted in Kabul, Afghanistan, in July 2002; Phnom Penh, Cambodia, in May and October 2005 and October 2014; in Dili and provincial capitals in East Timor in April 2005, November 2009, and February 2013; and in Canberra, London, New York, and Washington DC over numerous occasions from 2002 to 2014.

that the dynamics of interaction between the international community and domestic elites are thrown into sharp relief – and political and administrative institutions serve as a crucial arena in which these interactions play out. The following chapter establishes the theoretical framework that orients the study, presenting it in terms of the peacebuilding pathway.

2 *Political Order in Post-Conflict States*

A Theoretical Framework

Peacebuilding interventions typically fall short of achieving their aspirations because of a mismatch between the objectives of the international community and those of post-conflict elites. The United Nations is intent on building the basis for effective and legitimate governance through a transformative approach to peacebuilding. Domestic elites, by contrast, are intent on forging a very different type of political order, one geared toward bolstering their own political survival and power, with claims to governing authority that are rooted in the distribution of patronage spoils. These post-conflict elites are empowered by the strategy of institutional engineering pursued by international peacebuilding interventions and, in turn, manipulate it, pursuing different tactics of institutional conversion that result in a neopatrimonial political order. This chapter advances a theoretical framework for understanding why and how this transpires, arguing that peacebuilding outcomes are best understood as the result of a phased contest over the course of the peacebuilding pathway between two alternative visions of post-conflict political order.

The practice of externally supported attempts to simultaneously construct states and democracies in developing countries is relatively new and offers fertile ground for mid-range theory generation. My approach to understanding the puzzling outcomes of peacebuilding interventions begins with the premise that the pursuit of effective and legitimate governance through peacebuilding must be situated in the context of the broader quest for modern political order. The first part of this chapter thus lays out a general framework for understanding the nature of political order and what we know about how it is typically established over time – focusing on the incentives elites everywhere face and the consequent choices they make in ordering power in specific ways. In that light, I then build a sequenced causal framework suggesting the outcomes we should expect to see obtain over the course of a peacebuilding intervention – one that links scholarship on conflict and peace to that on political, institutional, and economic development. At each stage of this causal sequence, I weave together relevant thematic threads from different literatures in comparative politics, international relations, and political economy about the manner in which elites negotiate and respond to moments of transition and shape the political order emerging from those formative moments. These insights are grounded in a historical institutionalist approach, viewing institutions as the arenas in which agents interact with structural historical forces and emphasizing the temporal dimension of causal processes, especially their sequencing.[1] Through this lens, institutional arrangements can be seen as both an outcome of the power struggles of the past and a crucial factor in determining the form of political order that emerges as a result of transformative peacebuilding.

In post-conflict states, through the transitional governance approach, the United Nations attempts to create administrative and political institutions to underpin effective and legitimate governance and serve as the foundations for lasting peace. In practice, these formal institutional arrangements become the site of contest between the international community's vision of political order and the political–economic interests animating the power struggles among domestic elites. At each of the three critical phases of the peacebuilding pathway, therefore – the peace settlement phase, the transitional governance period, and the aftermath of intervention – we see a mismatch between the goals of the intervention and what transpires in the real world. The theoretical framework advanced in this chapter explains this gap, suggesting what we should expect to see at each phase as domestic elites attempt to build post-conflict political order and resist and manipulate international interventions as they do so. At the peace settlement phase, elites preoccupied with their own survival and empowerment come to an agreement to end the conflict. But that settlement, instead of serving as an end to conflict, becomes the next stage over which their internecine struggles to create a political order continue. In turn, during the transitional governance phase, the simultaneous attempt at statebuilding and democratization becomes co-opted by a small subset of domestic power-holders, paradoxically closing down the political space and stunting state capacity. In the aftermath of the intervention, domestic elites attempt to find the balance between

[1] Pierson 2004; and Thelen 1999.

distributing patronage through their clientelist networks to build political support and delivering a measure of stability and public goods in order to create an environment of some collective stability and prosperity. Thus, in post-conflict countries, we see a hybrid political order emerging that is neopatrimonial in nature – forestalling the effective and legitimate governance of the modern state to which international peacebuilding aspires.

The Pursuit of Political Order

How different societies construct political order is one of the single most important questions in the study of politics and perhaps the most elemental.[2] What are the forces that propel societies to move from the "traditional state," characterized by persistent violence and patrimonialism, to a "modern state," defined by stable, effective, and legitimate government?[3] Political philosophers grappled with this basic inquiry as they articulated social contract theory. Thomas Hobbes's *Leviathan* still gives us the label by which we understand that some concentration of sovereign authority in the hands of an individual or group of individuals is necessary to achieve the transition away from the state of nature; even as the debate between Hobbes's insistence on the necessity of authoritarian rule in that transition and John Locke's rebuttal in favor of the merits of constitutionally constrained government continues to the present day.[4] The study of political order has a distinguished contemporary intellectual history, serving as the core subject matter upon which landmark theoretical works in the political science canon have been written.[5] It has also enjoyed a resurgence in the past decade, with much of the renewed interest in the subject coming from the

[2] Margaret Levi, in her address as President of the American Political Science Association, noted that political science is "driven by a common desire to understand what makes for good governments and how to build them," defining good governments as effective and accountable. Levi 2006: 5.

[3] Here, I use the term "modern" in its Weberian sense, which is normative concerning the qualities of political order, as opposed to meaning "contemporary." This conventional usage means that "traditional" or non-modern forms of political order can and do exist today.

[4] Hobbes 1968 [1651]; and Locke 1963 [1698].

[5] Bates 2001; Ertman 1997; Huntington 1968; Levi 1989; Skocpol 1979; and Tilly 1990.

economics discipline.[6] Yet the links between the search for modern political order and the putative goals of peacebuilding – despite their great similarity – have been made surprisingly rarely in the peacebuilding literature, albeit with some notable exceptions.[7]

A political order constitutes the underlying system by which a society organizes its political actions and behavior. Institutions – formal rules, policy structures, and norms – are the cornerstone of this political order and are central to understanding how it evolves over time. These institutions are the legacies of the concrete political struggles of the past and, in turn, provide the contours of the political arena of the present – shaping the incentives facing individuals and organizations, guiding the patterns in which they interact, and constraining their political behavior.[8] The process of defining a political order is thus best understood as the process of institutional development. It concerns the building of stable institutional arrangements that govern political behavior, including, especially, the rules and norms that give elites control over resources and social functions and constrain these elites from using violence. The process of ordering power, in other words, is in large part about how elites organize themselves – including, crucially, alliances among elite factions – to govern their subjects.[9] In turn, institutions and the public policies they create reflect, magnify, and perpetuate the distribution of political power, actively empowering some groups and individuals while marginalizing others from the political sphere.[10] These institutional outcomes need not necessarily reflect any particular set of interests – they can be compromises between actors

[6] Acemoglu and Robinson 2012; Boix 2015; and North, Wallis, and Weingast 2009.

[7] These exceptions include Barnett 2006; Boege, Brown, and Clements 2009; Hamieri 2010; and Paris 2004.

[8] This definition of institutions follows the historical institutionalist perspective on institutions, for example in Pierson 1996; Pierson and Skocpol 2002; and Thelen 1999. Thelen 1999 observes that historical institutionalism emphasizes how institutions emerge from and are embedded in temporal processes, while rational choice institutionalism views institutions more as coordination mechanisms that generate equilibria; she also notes that this distinction, however, does not preclude much fruitful overlap and cross-fertilization between the two approaches. The theoretical framework in this chapter does indeed bring together both rational choice and historical institutionalist approaches to political order.

[9] Slater 2010; also Waldner 1999.

[10] Weir 1992.

with different goals or even the unintended consequence of conflict – and this, especially, makes them open to change.[11]

The concept of "political order" is often discussed with a positive valence, connoting political stability and good governance – with its opposite, "political disorder" or "political decay," seen as the undesirable outcome on the other end of the spectrum.[12] Here, I adapt this usage in part to conceptualize a political order as a set of political institutions and practices that rest in equilibrium. A political order is thus an institutional arrangement itself rather than a set of governance outcomes that are inherently desirable and the modifying adjective is crucial in telling us what kind of order we are talking about. In turn, there are three crucial elements by which a political order can be characterized: the control of violence through the rule of law; government effectiveness through state capacity; and mechanisms of legitimacy and accountability. The modern state is thus characterized by peaceful stability, state strength, and democratic accountability, or – to use the language of transformative peacebuilding – a stable and lasting peace, underpinned by effective and legitimate governance.

Conceived of in this way, political order can more usefully be seen as a characteristic of political systems that, as it varies in degree, also varies in kind. The governance challenge facing post-conflict countries is fruitfully viewed through this lens on political order. Fragile and conflict-affected countries are evidently in, or close to, the Hobbesian natural state of political instability, violence, and disorder. Indeed, state failure is commonly defined by the disintegration or absence of the main qualities of modern political order.[13] There are also, importantly, hybrid forms of political order distinct from both the natural and modern state. There are four crucial things to note about these hybrid or intermediate states of political order. First, most obviously, measures of the control of violence, of government effectiveness, and of democratic accountability are at intermediate levels. Countries with intermediate forms of political order are those with some political stability and some elements of effective and legitimate governance – but recognizably not, for example, what peacebuilding interventions are intended to achieve. Second, the three components vary independently, to a degree, such

[11] Mahoney and Thelen 2010: 8.
[12] For example, Fukuyama 2011, 2014a; and Huntington 1968.
[13] OECD 2008a; and Rotberg 2004.

that different pathways to the modern state are entirely possible. This logic runs counter to modernization theory, where all good things go together, a point I expand on below. Third, the three elements are, nevertheless, mutually reinforcing, which means that the hybrid or intermediate state is an equilibrium just like the modern state, albeit a suboptimal one. Fourth, each of these components or characteristics of political order – indeed, the process of political development itself – are potentially reversible – they can improve or they can disintegrate.

What closes the "political gap," as Samuel Huntington coined it, between underdeveloped and developed political systems?[14] What is the process by which a country succeeds in "getting to Denmark," a land of peaceful stability, rule of law, effective government, and democratic accountability?[15] Max Weber gave us the bare bones of the answer in his very definition of the modern state: creating the leviathan requires endowing it with a monopoly over the legitimate use of violence. In practical terms, achieving a monopoly of violence for the state becomes a question of how to contain, in Robert Bates's inimitable phrase, society's "specialists in violence," or rulers by might.[16] In traditional political orders, these elites retain the ability to mobilize violence in the service of their own particular interests and to their own benefit. Carles Boix notes that individuals can either exploit or cooperate to survive.[17] Getting to modern political order – rule-bound, effective, and legitimate governance – thus requires elites to agree to some binding of their power. Dan Slater frames this, in his study of developmental authoritarian regimes in Southeast Asia, as the intrinsic challenge of elite collective action, asserting that "severe threats to elites' property, privileges, and persons are a *necessary* condition" for elites to give up some of their individual power to establish the leviathan.[18] Stable, effective, and legitimate governance materializes when elites recognize that their interests are best served by deploying their coercive powers not for predation but to invest in the institutions, policies, and public goods that instead enhance the productive use of society's resources.

[14] Huntington 1968: 2. [15] Pritchett and Woolcock 2002; also Fukuyama 2011.
[16] Bates 2001, 2008a. [17] Boix 2015: 7.
[18] Slater 2010: 13, italics in original. On the importance of threat as an impetus to elite collective action in the service of statebuilding, see also Bates 2001; Ertman 1997; and Waldner 1999.

Why do elites – those with recourse to violence in the service of their own ends – form an agreement to restrict themselves? Elites bind themselves to cooperate in a coalition because their reward is access to the coalition's spoils, through processes of rent creation and distribution. The political and economic foundations for development come together when those who are specialists in violence realize that their interests are best served by creating the environment for economic prosperity.[19] Once a government has accumulated enough hegemonic power to ensure its survival, thereby lengthening its own time horizon, it serves the interest of that government to make the territory as rich as possible so that it can extract as much as possible over multiple time periods. Mancur Olson famously referred to this type of hegemonic government as a "stationary bandit," recognizing that societal stability is achieved at the cost of institutionalized extraction.[20] Restricting access to the privileges of the coalition only to its members gives them a stake in the coalition and makes their commitment to protecting it credible, leading Douglass North, John Wallis, and Barry Weingast to dub this type of regime a "limited access order."[21] These elites secure political order by creating a monopoly on economic activity and, thereby perpetuating an extractive, instead of inclusive, political–economic equilibrium.[22] The form that the elite collective bargain takes, in turn, structures the nature of the state's interactions with society.

The Neopatrimonial Equilibrium

Patrimonial political orders are the default institutional pattern through which elites have reached these governing pacts with society over most of human history, including into today.[23] In a patrimonial system, authority is personalized – individuals rule through personal prestige and power, privileging their own preferences. The ruler ensures basic political stability and his own political survival by providing some measure of security and by distributing patronage spoils

[19] Bates 2001; also Boix 2015. [20] Olson 1993.
[21] North, Wallis, and Weingast 2009. [22] Acemoglu and Robinson 2012.
[23] North, Wallis, and Weingast 2009 calculate that about 85 percent of the world's population in some 170 of the world's countries live in various forms of neopatrimonial (or limited access) orders, compared to 15 percent in 25 countries in modern (or open access) orders.

to his clients in exchange for their support.[24] In other words, the way in which most human societies have escaped the brutish state of nature is to endow some measure of sovereignty in one all-powerful individual or in a small group of elites. Patrimonialism is thus the prevailing form of political order that has to be overcome in constructing rule-bound, effective, and legitimate government. This is no easy task. Patrimonial political orders are stable equilibria, taking on the institutional forms they do because these systems benefit elites. Rulers in these orders sit atop hierarchical patron–client networks and the logic of instrumental exchange between patron and client serves as the ordering logic of the political system.[25] Weber drew a distinction between patrimonial authority, the principle of governance in traditional polities, and the rational-legal authority that is the hallmark of the modern state – a system in which the public and private spheres are distinct and the former is governed by the routine application of law and bureaucratic institutions.[26]

The reality in much of the contemporary developing world is that the patrimonial and rational-legal systems of authority coexist, creating systems of personalized politics within the bureaucratic and legal trappings of the modern-state. It is conventional to use the label *neopatrimonial* to characterize these "hybrid political systems in which the customs and patterns of patrimonialism co-exist with, and suffuse, rational–legal institutions."[27] What appears formally as a modern state apparatus is undermined by practices abusing the state in the service of systematic patronage distribution. The ruling group dominates and stands above the state apparatus. Officials lower down use their bureaucratic positions to gain access to state resources in order to enrich themselves and their networks and to demonstrate loyalty to their patrons. Typically, parallel structures of power such as party cliques and other patron–client networks hold more authority than the formal administrative structures. As a result of rivalry among elites to secure the top spot or, at least, for the top ruler's favor, politics is often secretive and opaque. Neopatrimonial systems, moreover, have self-reinforcing properties. Upward mobility in these systems occurs in

[24] Bratton and Van de Walle 1997: 61. [25] Scott 1972.

[26] Bratton and Van de Walle 1997; and Weber 1978.

[27] Bratton and Van de Walle 1997: 62; also Bratton and Van de Walle 1994; and Jackson and Rosberg 1984. This paragraph draws heavily on these seminal definitions of neopatrimonialism.

the context of the patron–client hierarchy and perpetuates rather than transforms the system. Elites enrich and empower themselves through patrimonial activities and accrue a traditional form of legitimacy on the basis of particularist patronage distribution through their networks. In turn, they use the rational-legal capacity of the state to the bare minimum degree required to deliver a modicum of public service delivery and collective welfare to the populace at large, earning some measure of output-based legitimacy; and rely upon the trappings of democracy to garner at least a stamp of the normative dimension of legitimacy sought by the international community.

Transformative peacebuilding represents the assertion that it is possible to guide countries in the move from political disorder to the effective and legitimate order of the modern state in a short period of time. Yet this assertion seems implausible at best, if not simply hubristic, when examined in the light of what the literature has established about the dynamics of building political order and, in particular, the pervasiveness and stickiness of neopatrimonialism in the contemporary developing world. International peacebuilding interventions attempted to transpose modern political order onto the post-conflict landscapes of Cambodia, East Timor, and Afghanistan, specifically by facilitating a process of administrative and political institutional engineering. Few would deny that some important successes were achieved in terms of stability, state effectiveness, and legitimate government: in all three countries, violence is below the levels scholars qualify as civil conflict, some degree of state infrastructure and a public service delivery footprint has been developed, and successive elections have been held. In no way do I wish to imply that any of the three countries considered here are worse off than they otherwise would have been as a result of peacebuilding through transitional governance. Indeed, they are all fundamentally more stable than before the interventions and maintain a basic degree of the government effectiveness and accountability that are the hallmarks of the modern state and among the essential ingredients of a modern political order.

Yet what best characterizes Cambodia, East Timor, and Afghanistan is the hybrid state of neopatrimonial political order. In these post-conflict countries, a patrimonial logic pervades the institutional trappings of the modern state and orders the political system, structuring political incentives and behavior. The evidence from the three countries demonstrates that no matter how well administrative and political institutions are designed, during the course of transitional governance powerful domestic groups co-opt the process of determining new institutional arrangements and, through strategies of institutional conversion, subsequently consolidate their holds on power. As they do so, they move the political order away from the goal of rationalized and democratic governance, coming to rest, instead, in the suboptimal political economy equilibrium of neopatrimonialism. The remainder of this chapter elaborates a theory about how this happens over the course of peacebuilding interventions. At its heart, this theory is a story about how the dynamic contest between two alternative visions of post-conflict political order plays out over the temporal course of the peacebuilding pathway.

Elites and Transformative Events

Theories of political order typically cast the process of organic institutional development as a gradual, even glacial, process of change over time. Yet historical institutionalist accounts of political development also emphasize the importance of seeing continuity and change as two sides of the same coin.[28] Establishing political order may take a long time – but it is not a uniform, linear process of change. It happens in fits, starts, and reversals, which are often the most revealing parts of the process. At these crucial moments, it is the interaction of structural patterns with exogenous shocks and the actions of individuals, especially elites, that serve in establishing patterns of political order. Transformative peacebuilding represents an attempt to make a deliberate break with the past, through a conscious process of institutional engineering and political management. Yet a peacebuilding operation cannot be understood simply as an exogenous event to be analyzed for its treatment effects on desired outcomes. The patterns through which these interventions unfold are, like all other transformative political events, the product of temporal processes that combine the effects of structure, shock, and agency. They are critical junctures of extraordinarily fluid politics that, in turn, set in motion specific pathways of post-conflict order building along which elites undertake recognizable strategies, especially vis-à-vis institutions, to continue to gain and bolster authority. Thus, the established scholarship on other key junctures

[28] Pierson 2004.

of political transformation – such as democratization, the transition from socialism, revolutions and mass movements, and so forth – offers a number of stylized lessons to apply to our understanding of peacebuilding.

The central argument of this book is that the incentives motivating post-conflict elites interact with international interventions and shape their outcomes, paradoxically undermining the possibility and quality of effective and legitimate governance in the longer term. The role of domestic elites – their incentives, their interactions, their choices – is thus crucial in creating the outcomes that obtain. Peacebuilding is a hyperpolitical process, seeking to fundamentally transform polity and society in the quest for sustainable peace. It is therefore inherently a highly contested process, in which local stakeholders are central over the course of intervention – agreeing on an elite settlement, engaging with the interactive dynamics of state- and democracy-building, and shaping both the institutions and the governance outcomes that result. It is domestic political actors who make specific institutional choices within the parameters established by international interventions. In turn, these powerful elites maneuver within those formal institutions to shape the political order that emerges.

The "spoiler" concept has served as the main lens for understanding the role of elites in implementing peace operations.[29] In his seminal article on spoilers, Stephen Stedman defined them as the "leaders and parties who believe that peace emerging from negotiations threatens their power, worldview, and interests, and use violence to undermine attempts to achieve it."[30] He cast spoilers as the greatest source of risk in a peace process, implying, in turn, that successful interventions require implementers to correctly diagnose and manage spoilers. Extensions of the spoiler concept emphasized that the preferences and strategies of spoilers must be understood in light of the structural context in which they are embedded and that their sources of power and legitimacy are historically formed. An excessive reliance on the agency of spoilers was seen to underemphasize structural factors, particularly the opportunity structure and relative power balance that define spoiler behavior.[31]

29 Greenhill and Major 2007; Hoddie and Hartzell 2010; Newman and Richmond 2006; Nilsson and Söderberg Kovacs 2011; and Stedman 1997.
30 Stedman 1997: 5.
31 Greenhill and Major 2007. On opportunity structures, see Tarrow 1998.

This book's approach to understanding the peacebuilding pathway broadens the emphasis on elites from a focus on their spoiler behavior or potential, focusing instead on the incentives motivating elites in concrete situations along the peacebuilding pathway. The causal narrative I develop here rests on the view that peace agreements themselves are elite settlements, and that the subsequent transitional process and its attendant process of institutional engineering are dominated by the elites designated by the UN as counterparts and legitimate contenders to power. The nature of these elites and their resource bases can vary dramatically, as evidenced by the cases considered here. In Cambodia, the leaders of the major political factions that fought the civil war were the key power-holders in society, supported by their factional armies and, in the case of what became the dominant Cambodian People's Party, by the institutional power vested in their control of the state. In East Timor, the organizational backbone of the guerrilla front stepped into the power and institutional void left at the nation's independence, bolstered by the powerful shared symbology of a widespread national resistance movement. In Afghanistan, the United States and United Nations played kingmaker, installing a compromise choice from the Afghan diaspora as the core leader – one who, in his subsequent attempts to consolidate the central state, was hamstrung by the diffuse loci of power throughout the country.

Yet, such differences among elites notwithstanding, a crucial part of my argument is that the political actors empowered by UN transitional governance interventions – no matter what *type* of elite they might be – act, surprisingly, in roughly parallel ways as they engage with and, eventually, undermine those interventions over the three phases of the peacebuilding pathway. The political landscape in contemporary post-conflict states is populated by elites who are attempting to solve the practical puzzle of protecting and expanding their own power bases while attempting to assure the international community that they are also acting in the service of legitimacy and political inclusion. The post-conflict context has been mistakenly inferred to resemble an institutional vacuum. The reality is that the political trajectory of the past, including the conflict itself, is enormously significant for what transpires next. Potential contenders to authority compete with each other, with different claims to authority based on their relative power and other political resources such as financing and social support. A perspective that focuses on the process of state engagement with other social forces highlights the mutual transformation of the state and social groups that must be inherent to any statebuilding process.[32] These political struggles and compacts must be viewed temporally, since they necessarily emerge from a country's historical experiences with political order. In turn, the temporal sequence through which domestic elites interact with international interventions matters a great deal. The following causal framework suggests what we should expect to see at each of the three phases of the peacebuilding pathway as domestic elites attempt to build their version of post-conflict political order and interact with and shape international interventions as they do so.

Elite Settlements: The Continuation of War by Other Means

Peace settlements have been emphasized as a crucial factor in explaining the relative successes of international peacekeeping operations in bringing an end to civil conflict. Treating peace settlements as mediated elite pacts, scholars have built a large body of knowledge along two main avenues of investigation. First, how are peace settlements negotiated? Here, the focus has been on the processes of bargaining and deal-making, with an emphasis on the mechanisms put in place to build credible commitment into peace deals.[33] Second, how can the substance of a peace deal be constructed to lead, in turn, to successful implementation and the desired outcomes? Here, the analytic focus has been placed on institutional design, with a particular emphasis on the merits and drawbacks of power-sharing in peace settlements.[34]

Peace agreements are, in practice, conditional elite pacts. Political dynamics are heavily elite-driven at the peace settlement stage of transformative peacebuilding, reflecting the high level of contingency associated with critical junctures. This is, in part, a direct result of the conflict itself: during periods of civil war political participation becomes militarized, as civil society organizations and other institutional channels for nonviolent political participation wither away. The predominance of elites at this stage is also a result of the fact that, to stand a chance of

[32] Herbst 2000; Mann 1986; and Skocpol 1985.

[33] Fearon and Laitin 2008; Licklider 1995; Martin 2013; Toft 2010; and Walter 1999, 2002, 2009.

[34] Hartzell and Hoddie 2007, 2015; Horowitz 1985; Jarstad and Nilsson 2008; Lijphart 1977; and Sisk 1996, 2013.

being successful, post-conflict peacebuilding must rest significantly on reconstructing the state's societal support.[35] Domestic elites are critical in helping to remedy both of these shortcomings since they are central in mobilizing political support and building social consensus around the legitimacy of new rules and institutional structures for the political and administrative arenas.[36]

Yet post-conflict peace settlements should not be seen as the outcomes of rational deal-making, or as compromises that satisfice among the various claims to authority and legitimacy advanced by domestic elites. Instead, peace settlements are better viewed as the legacies of preconflict political trajectories and the particular power balances emerging out of conflict. Nor should they be reified as just outcomes or as a stable resolution of the preceding civil violence. Instead, they should be understood as momentary terms of settlement within an ongoing elite power struggle. Elite bargaining is better seen not as pertaining to a single isolated event – for example, embodied in the discrete settlement deal itself – but rather as a series of decisions embedded in a longer bargaining process.[37] In this light, a peace treaty does not represent an end to political bargaining. As Michael Doyle observes: "After the parties agree to the creation of a peacekeeping operation, they continue to compete for advantage. The agreement becomes, as do so many other constitutional texts, an invitation to struggle."[38] Mediated settlements at moments of duress may represent the only possible solution at that particular point in time, but they are inherently unstable equilibria. In short, peace settlements should be interpreted as initiating a new phase of elite conflict through politics – the continuation of war by other means.[39]

A peace settlement is hence the beginning of the peacebuilding pathway, rather than the end goal of an elite negotiation process. It is a crucial transformative moment, serving as the pivot away from violent conflict. As such, it is useful to view the elite settlement phase in light of what we know about how elites act at other moments of fundamental

[35] Doornbos 2002; and Zartman 1995.
[36] Barma 2006; Migdal, Kohli, and Shue 1994; and Snyder 2000.
[37] Walter 2009 makes this point in analyzing why more civil wars do not end through negotiation. The same logic applies when considering why elite pacts might not hold in the post-conflict aftermath.
[38] Doyle 1995: 66.
[39] Carl von Clausewitz's famous dictum that war is the continuation of politics by other means seems to hold equally true inversed in post-conflict countries.

political transition that are similarly critical junctures. In understanding how such pivotal transformations occur during democratic transitions, revolutions, and social movements, scholars have built explanations that combine attention to structural conditions with the central roles that elites play as agents of change. Crucially, as elites engage in the political bargains around moments of sociopolitical transformation, they do not simply rely on and reward existing support but also find it necessary to continually mobilize and manipulate new support.

Elite negotiations and pacts are a central feature of the democratization scholarship. Dankwart Rustow's landmark essay on democratic transitions explicitly abandoned the quest for the functional requisites of democracy rooted in modernization theory and other structural perspectives and argued that democracy was the fruit of the conscious decisions of political elites.[40] In this view, elite consensus on the new rules of the game is an essential requisite for a successful transition from authoritarianism to democracy. A particular emphasis has thus been placed on the role of elites, their strategies, and the pacts among them, in crafting democratic transitions and consolidation, as well as on the importance of the links between elites and their supporters.[41]

The literature on social revolutions echoes this emphasis on the centrality of elite bargains as well as their social bases of support. Arthur Stinchcombe conceived of a revolution as a period of uncertainty about who will govern – and crystallized the challenge of rebuilding authority coming out of that Hobbesian state as lying in the "difficulties of finding a set of bargains among the interests contending in a revolution and a reliable apparatus to enforce them."[42] In revolutions, elite competition for authority spurs leaders to mobilize and manipulate the mass participation of groups that were previously politically excluded. In turn, the elite group that finally consolidates its hold on power systematically reconstructs state organizations in order to embody direct control by their supporters. Other competing political forces are, in the process, eliminated from structures of control and authority, again through mass mobilization and the manipulation of major public institutions, including the legal system, schools, civil bureaucracies, and

40 Rustow 1970. On modernization theory see Lipset 1959; Parsons 1951; and Rostow 1962.

41 On "crafting" democratic transitions, see DiPalma 1990; on elite links with supporters, see Bermeo 1997; Haggard and Kaufman 1997; and Karl 1990.

42 Stinchcombe 1999: 50.

military forces.[43] Some scholars argue that social movements fall onto the same continuum of mechanisms for political change as revolutions – the difference being the extent to which existing power structures are put at risk.[44]

One crucial insight from these other transformative moments is that elites are central not only in terms of their own individual preferences but also because they are the leaders of specific sociopolitical coalitions. In negotiating peace settlements, elites are hence playing a two-sided game. They must negotiate with other elites and survive the collective battle for authority, while simultaneously satisfying the groups that keep them in power. Elites are thus not only self-interested; they are, of course, embedded socially, drawing on groups for their support. In turn, the status of such groups influences the resources that elites bring to the bargaining table. As I explain below, post-conflict elites manage this two-sided game by constructing a neopatrimonial political order. A peace settlement marks a new opportunity to create a political order – and it necessarily echoes the basic political order and struggles of the past. Understanding the sources of elites' power, especially their conflicts with each other and their relationships with their supporters, is crucial to explaining the political dynamics around the peace settlement phase. The process of coming to a settlement is, quite simply, a fascinating political struggle that should be seen not as resolving all the issues at play but as reflecting and perpetuating them.

Transitional Governance: A Process of Inherent Contradictions

The hallmark of the transitional governance approach to peacebuilding is that the UN works with domestic elites simultaneously on two aspects of peacebuilding over a transitional period of two to three years: it governs the country in collaboration with domestic counterparts during this period, which ends with the holding of an election; and it works concurrently with domestic elites to reconstruct the institutional and human capacity of the state apparatus and to build a democratic political system. The approach is thus designed around two intertwined assertions. The first proposition is that it is possible for the international community to help post-conflict countries build the foundations for a lasting peace by imposing and assisting a process of

[43] Skocpol 1988. [44] McAdam, Tarrow, and Tilly 1997.

simultaneous state- and democracy-building in these countries. The second proposition is that the best mechanism for implementing a transformative peacebuilding intervention is a particular form of governance collaboration between domestic elites and the UN peace operation. In this section, I argue that both assertions are unfounded, illustrating that we should expect otherwise based on what we know about the dynamics of state formation and other transformative events starring powerful entrenched interests, especially post-socialist transitions.

The simultaneous state- and democracy-building process that is the centerpiece of the transitional governance approach has rarely, if ever, obtained organically. It is not accidental that the notion of "state formation" is expressed more passively than is the more muscular late twentieth century activity of "statebuilding." Western European countries became states through a time-consuming process and only later evolved into democracies – and this is the quintessential trajectory upon which much of the state formation literature is based. The experience of the United States, which is rarely considered in comparative assessments of state formation, tells the opposite story in which statebuilding was purposefully retarded and central administrative institutions were intentionally kept weak by strong party machines to protect their political interests in the context of a flourishing democracy. Successful statebuilding in the developing world has generally preceded and hampered, and sometimes foreclosed, democratization, as evidenced by the strong, developmental, and long-time authoritarian states of East and Southeast Asia.

Political science scholarship, although filled with rich accounts of statebuilding processes on the one hand and democracy-building processes on the other, has no real conceptualization of the complementarities or tensions embodied in the combined approach. Indeed, Francis Fukuyama recently noted that "one of the most understudied and undertheorized relationships is that between democracy and the state."[45] Even Samuel Huntington's seminal thesis that the level of political institutionalization in the developing world must stay one step ahead of social mobilization in order to channel popular participation focused on *political* institution building, rather than articulating a theory of how *state* institution building interacts with democratization.[46] Cutting into the Gordian knot of indeterminate causality that plagued

[45] Fukuyama 2014b: 1326. [46] Huntington 1968.

classical modernization theory, Huntington argued that all good things do *not* go together and that it matters a great deal in which sequence they occur. Political instability and disorder in the developing world results from the unequal dynamics of modernization. For Huntington, achieving political stability requires the level of political institutionalization to stay one step ahead of the forces of social mobilization brought about with economic development. Logically, and troublingly, then, the sacrifice of democratic pluralism is the price to be paid for stability in politically modernizing developing countries.

Others have extended this logic to the state realm as well, agreeing with the basic thesis that institutionalization must come first to properly handle the other fruits of modernization. Roland Paris's influential work on peacebuilding proposes the normatively easier to digest "institutionalization before liberalization" approach to democracy-building in post-conflict states.[47] He suggests postponing the electoral aspect of democratization until after complementary institutionalization has first been undertaken in both the political and state realms. Fukuyama echoes the basic sequencing thesis that a strong state must come first for modern political order to be consolidated, arguing that democracy coming first is a recipe for patronage and corruption.[48] Martin Shefter offered a causal explanation for this phenomenon in his pioneering studies of the presence or absence of clientelist politics in the United States and Europe. He critiqued the existing sociological approach to clientelism, which focused on social structure and political culture as the explanation for patronage, delivering instead a historical institutionalist explanation hinging on how the process of state formation interacted with patterns of political and social mobilization.[49] Shefter argued that when the rise of professional bureaucrats occurred before democratization, the clientelistic logic of spoils distribution did not take hold and parties were compelled to appeal to voters with programmatic appeals.

Conventional accounts of the rise of the modern, bureaucratic nation-state emphasize its functional advantages at collecting revenue, broadcasting authority over a territory, and providing security.[50] Modern – i.e., rule-bound, effective, legitimate – government was,

[47] Paris 2004. [48] Fukuyama 2011; also Linz and Stepan 1996.
[49] Shefter 1977, 1994; also Kitschelt and Wilkinson 2007: 5.
[50] Levi 1989; Skocpol 1979; and Tilly 1985, 1990.

therefore, first and most easily established in the states in which authoritarian governments had to wage war to ensure security, such as nineteenth-century Prussia.[51] State formation in this account is inherently violent: in addition to protecting the state from without, the leviathan also had to take away the ability to impose violent coercion from all other agents within. By contrast, countries that democratized before they established modern state bureaucracies, such as the United States, developed patronage-riddled public sectors.[52]

Post-socialist transitions offer a further illustration of the obstinate powers of entrenched interests in the face of reforms – along with the deliberate strategies vis-à-vis institutions through which they can powerfully resist and even prevent change. Scholars of Central and Eastern Europe have identified a common sequence of bureaucratic opposition to neoliberal economic reforms.[53] New institutional blueprints associated with reform threaten bureaucrats who in turn attempt, with their political supporters, to sabotage the implementation of those reforms. What begins as a backlash turns into strategies of institutional drift and conversion, manifesting through a process of bargaining and tinkering with institutional and policy reforms so that outcomes better suit the political balance of forces.[54] Post-socialist transitions also display the crucial significance of elite objectives and sequencing in the exceptionally fluid environment in which new institutional arrangements are forged.[55] Another important insight from political and economic transition in Eastern Europe is that social change emerges from a reconfiguration of institutional orders in different realms – political, economic, and social – that are in many ways incongruous instead of coordinated.[56] Thus, understanding how politics writ large changes over time is often squarely about the interaction of different, sometimes competing, ongoing political processes.[57] This fact is often obscure, however, to international agents supporting transformation because of their own particular normative and operational frames.

[51] Tilly 1990. Cf. Ertman 1997, who elaborates four distinct combinations of regime type and state apparatus, each marking a different path-dependent sequence in early modern European state formation.

[52] Shefter 1977, 1994; and Skowronek 1982.

[53] For example Bockman and Eyal 2002; and Hellman 1998.

[54] Hacker, Pierson, and Thelen 2015.

[55] Smith and Remington 2001.

[56] Stark and Bruszt 1998.

[57] Thelen 1999.

Historical institutionalist accounts of the relationships between statebuilding, democratization, and patronage politics illuminate more generally the shaky foundations of the assumptions underpinning the transitional governance approach to peacebuilding. Investigating the varying pathways out of socialism, Conor O'Dwyer demonstrates that many of the new democracies of Eastern Europe suffered from the excessive politicization of their state institutions, thereby undermining government effectiveness even in these administratively better endowed nations.[58] In particular, rapid democratization in an environment of unconsolidated state structures led to a rapid overexpansion of the bureaucracy as a result of patronage politics.

Two key patterns emerge in considering the prospects of a process of statebuilding and democratization. First, most obviously, simultaneity is an unpromising strategy – sequencing is crucial. The foregoing discussion has established that democratization in an under-institutionalized context contributes to instability and patronage-oriented politics. Second, more subtly, there is never truly a level playing field among contenders to power – incumbents hold a distinct set of advantages. Elites supported by formal or informal institutional power – resting, for example, in bureaucratic, party, or traditional power structures – retain and rely upon those resources and the legitimacy they generate. Paul Pierson catalogs the mechanisms through which "power may beget power," including the ability of powerful elites to control the stock and flow of resources and encourage others to fall in line. Furthermore, these elites are adept at mobilizing new sources of power and legitimacy in their favor – by altering political discourse they change other elites' and society's views of what is desirable and target institutions and policies in ways that change societal preferences to their benefit.[59] Scholars have vividly described, for example, how post-conflict domestic elites have been able to successfully re-appropriate the resources and symbols of international peacebuilding strategies in their countries in ways that reinforced their own authority.[60]

Institutional change and innovation often occur when entrenched stakeholders exercising vetoes over reform are neutralized. The transitional governance model tries to do that in principle by attempting to

[58] O'Dwyer 2006. [59] Pierson 2015: 134–141.
[60] For example, Curtis 2013 on Burundi; and Hughes 2009a on Cambodia and East Timor.

create a level playing field among legitimate domestic elites. In practice, however, it does exactly the opposite. By appointing domestic counterparts, the UN gives certain elites the power to exercise a veto against reform, without other checks and balances, like the rule of law, a strong state, or enough democratic accountability to ensure that, if necessary, some other political force can "throw the rascals out."[61] Domestic elites view the politics of the transitional governance period and its aftermath as a "winner-takes-all" game. In turn, their determination to survive in the context of that game leads them into cementing a neopatrimonial political order, undermining both the consolidation of autonomous state structures and nascent democratic accountability. State capacity-building is hampered since the rulers of the state use it for patronage distribution; and democracy-building is thwarted by the use of patronage resources to bolster a hegemonic hold on power. State- and democracy-building, when pursued together, act at cross-purposes so that the objectives of neither are met.

Neopatrimonial Political Order: A Hybrid Form of Governance

The peacebuilding literature focuses for the most part on the implementation of peace operations and the extent to which they achieve their goals. Most such studies assess the durability of a peace operation's performance by examining outcomes after the end of the mandate – but even the most sophisticated of these studies use a relatively short timeframe for assessment, for at least three reasons.[62] First, a short-term perspective is due to the recent nature of such interventions; not enough time has elapsed across a large enough sample of cases to go much further. Second, this type of study reflects the scholarly perception of an international intervention as an exogenously imposed treatment, the effect of which can be fruitfully assessed through cross-sectional analysis. Third, it also reflects the relatively broad consensus that international peacebuilding seeks uncontested objectives; thus a reasonable topic of study is the extent to which the effective and legitimate governance of the modern state has indeed been met in post-conflict states subject to interventions.

[61] Powell 1989: 119.

[62] For example, Doyle and Sambanis 2006 focus on outcomes two years after the termination of conflict while Zürcher et al. 2013 assess outcomes five years after the start of a peace mission.

This book aims to add a new perspective to the peacebuilding scholarship by emphasizing that international interventions represent and seek to establish *one* particular conception of political order. Domestic elites in post-conflict states, by contrast, seek to establish a very different form of political order. It is necessary, therefore, to examine the dynamic contest between these two visions over time – and, especially, as long into the aftermath of interventions as possible. Doing so makes it apparent that post-conflict political order is typically neopatrimonial in nature. The analytical stance here is in line with new scholarship in the political economy of development that emphasizes that neopatrimonialism should be understood as a core element in explaining how states *function*, not simply advanced as a reason for their failure.[63] Clan-based and other forms of patrimonial governance, along with the "competitive authoritarianism" they regularly exhibit, coexist with more rational-legal and democratic systems of governance, often for long periods of time.[64] It is crucial to understand these hybrid political orders as resting in an equilibrium of their own, which is not simply a deviation from the pathway to modern political order.[65]

Poor governance and economic outcomes in the developing world are not a result of inept leaders, nor of international organizations dispensing faulty advice. Political and economic institutions are the way they are because elites have an interest in structuring them that way; over time, those institutions replicate and perpetuate the power struggles of the past. Acemoglu and Robinson observe, for example, that there is a mutually reinforcing synergy between economic and political institutions.[66] Typically, inclusive economic institutions – featuring secure property rights, the unbiased rule of law, and equitable public service provision – create a more equitable basis for political power; in turn, inclusive political institutions, rooted in pluralism, ensure continued economic inclusion. Similarly, extractive political institutions that favor the political elite allow them to write the economic rules to benefit themselves at the expense of broader society; in turn, the

[63] Smith 2014 elaborates this point in the case of conflict-affected countries that have found their own pathways to peace without international interventions.

[64] On competitive authoritarianism, see Levitsky and Way 2002.

[65] Boege, Brown, and Clements 2009.

[66] Acemoglu and Robinson 2012. The discussion of inclusive and extractive institutions rests on their work.

extractive economic institutions that are structured to privilege powerful elite interests entrenches their future extractive potential and thus political dominance. Crucially, however, there is sometimes a mismatch between economic and political orders and these are typically unstable equilibria. Of particular note here is the negative spiral that can unfold. An extractive economic order can, over time, effect changes to an inclusive political system so that the political balance also becomes more extractive. In turn, the narrow interests that gain a concentrated hold on political order will gradually transform economic institutions into more extractive ones that more narrowly benefit and empower themselves.

A rich vein of contemporary scholarship takes as a starting point the insight that a better understanding of patronage and clientelism is crucial to better understanding stunted democratic consolidation across the developing world.[67] Programmatic and unbiased delivery of public goods and services to the population is a hallmark of a well-functioning democracy. By contrast, pervasive clientelism is both a cause and effect of a lack of democratic consolidation. In this book, I rely on Scott's seminal definition of patronage or clientelism as the logic of instrumental exchange – biased distribution of public goods and services from patrons to clients in exchange for votes and other forms of political support from clients to patrons.[68] Similarly, Stokes et al. have more recently defined clientelism as nonprogrammatic distribution of public resources in conditional exchange for political support.[69]

Neopatrimonial political orders in Cambodia, East Timor, and Afghanistan, as in other developing and post-conflict countries, encompass both the patron–client relationship between elites and their immediate networks, typically referred to as patronage, and the less personalized and yet still instrumental exchange of goods and favors for broad political support, commonly labeled clientelism. In describing post-conflict political orders as neopatrimonial – hybrid systems where both patrimonial and rational-legal elements of governance coexist – I use the terms patronage and clientelism interchangeably.[70] In post-conflict states, the concern is not electoral clientelism per se but, more

67 See, especially, Kitschelt and Wilkinson 2007; and Stokes et al. 2013.

68 Scott 1972.

69 Stokes et al. 2013: 18.

70 Kitschelt and Wilkinson 2007 also use the terms interchangeably. Cf. Stokes et al. 2013, who distinguish patronage as the subset of clientelist practices targeted at party members.

broadly, relational clientelism, which constitutes a broader set of distributional strategies that deliver ongoing benefits to clients.[71] This broader form of political clientelism is essential in the democratizing developing world as a means through which to achieve inter-elite accommodation and compromise, more so than to bind the population to different elite patrons. In other words, state and public resources are used to forge and cement alliances among different groups of elites, instead of serving the logic of mass party patronage.[72]

This book emphasizes the clientelism and patronage associated with the building of post-conflict political order, focusing especially on the ability of elites to make credible commitments to each other and to the populace. This commands attention, in turn, to how political and administrative institutions shape time horizons and elite incentives; and to how the elites who control the state deliver the patronage goods and benefits that underpin their neopatrimonial compact with society. The liberal ideal embedded in the UN's peacebuilding model is that democratically elected elites will interpret social preferences and will use the state apparatus to deliver the programmatic policies, collective public services, and shared prosperity that serve as pillars of sustainable peace. The post-conflict reality, however – as illustrated in the empirical chapters that follow – is that the political–economic incentives facing elites are such that it is easier and more profitable for them to focus, for the most part, on distributing narrowly targeted public rents and particularist patronage goods to their clients in exchange for political support.[73]

The relative weakness of party organization in post-conflict and other developing countries, moreover, makes clientelism even more appealing as a strategy for gaining political support.[74] In particular, while outsider parties with no access to state resources will attempt to make more programmatic appeals as their only viable strategy, incumbent parties with access to state resources will be more likely to mobilize those material resources in clientelist appeals for support.[75] At the same time, incumbents can continue to consolidate power by altering social discourse and by using targeted policies to reshape social preferences.[76] In furthering all such practices, elites find that they are

71 Gans-Morse, Mazzuca, and Nichter 2014.
72 Van de Walle 2007: 55; also Slater 2010.
73 Joshi and Mason 2011; and Keefer and Vlaicu 2008.
74 Reilly 2013.
75 O'Dwyer 2006; and Shefter 1977, 1994.
76 Pierson 2015.

able to channel their appeal to citizens through hierarchical patron–client networks, thus obviating their own need to build credibility with the populace – through, for example, institutionalized political parties – and undermining the formal structures of authority.[77] This equilibrium not only privileges elites and their networks over society at large; it also has adverse consequences for peace because underlying it is a new form of persistent insecurity.[78]

Elite factions in limited access orders curb violence by structuring the creation, extraction, and distribution of rents; they also structure violence itself, serving as the main fault lines of conflict in patrimonial societies.[79] Most of what I have said about violence to this point has been implicit. The fact of violence – including coercive threats of violence – is, of course, central to theories of political order.[80] The logic is simple: those who have access to violence will use it to extract what they can from the rest of the population, unless they are constrained in some way – through a pact with others who have access to violence or because the costs of using it outweigh the benefits of using it. A modern, rational-legal political order limits violence through institutions, including both formal measures and informal norms. Yet Kalyvas, Shapiro, and Masoud observe, "... much of what we identify as order is simply violence in disguise. Political institutions are often erected on violent foundations, and maintained through implicit and explicit threats of bloodshed should obedience be withheld."[81] It should not surprise us that post-conflict orders rest on a delicate knife-edge balancing a certain degree of order with the ever-present specter of violence.

A suboptimal political economy equilibrium of the sort I have described here may be relatively common to new democracies suffering from weak credibility. Yet transformational peacebuilding purports to build legitimate and effective governance – and this book demonstrates that it fails to do so because domestic elites succeed instead at using the resources of international interventions to aid them in establishing a neopatrimonial political order. This neopatrimonialism has proven obstinate in the face of attempts to impose the

[77] Keefer and Vlaicu 2008; Olson 1993; and Scott 1972. [78] Barma 2012a.

[79] North, Wallis, and Weingast 2009: 36.

[80] Weber defined violence as the essential feature distinguishing the political from the social, economic, and cultural. As noted in Bates 2008b.

[81] Kalyvas, Shapiro, and Masoud 2008: 1, fn. 1.

rule-bound, effective, and legitimate governance of the modern state. The post-conflict regimes under study here are neopatrimonial before the outbreak of conflict; they retain some elements of neopatrimonialism during the political disorder that characterizes conflict; and, in the end, even after experiencing a peacebuilding intervention designed explicitly to shape a different political order, they return to neopatrimonialism.

The Peacebuilding Pathway

Peacebuilding is "a matter of political crafting," with elites playing a crucial role in the unfolding of the pathway, especially through the strategies they use to gain and reinforce power through institutions.[82] This chapter has distilled a series of stylized expectations from other types of major transformative events and the political economy of the contemporary developing world to suggest what we should expect to see as elites in post-conflict states and international interventions interact with competing visions of political order. Transformative peacebuilding efforts represent the international community's attempt to transpose the rule-bound, effective, and legitimate governance of the modern state in post-conflict countries. Peacebuilding through transitional governance tries to move post-conflict elites toward this modern political order by constraining their behavior through a process of institutional choice that represents the norms of international statehood. International interventions thus guide post-conflict states through the negotiated elite settlement that marks the initiation of a peace operation; through a deliberately managed transitional governance process of shared domestic and international authority that simultaneously pursues statebuilding and democratization; and through the electoral, constitution-writing, and legislative rule-making process that marks the end of a transitional governance experience.

Yet post-conflict elites are adept at maneuvering within the parameters of this internationally engineered, sequenced competition over political space and thereby shaping interventions and the resulting institutions to their advantage. They aim to assuage the international

[82] DiPalma 1990: 8 uses the notion of political crafting to describe democratization.

community's concerns about modern forms of governance, while trying simultaneously to ensure their own political survival and enrichment. As a result, their actions over the phases of the peacebuilding pathway are geared toward establishing and bolstering a neopatrimonial political order that embeds the instrumental logic of patron–client exchange within the institutional trappings of the modern state. A peace agreement becomes, in this light, not the final resolution to civil conflict but the new impetus for continued internecine political struggle. The impact of the de facto power recalibration that takes place during this phase becomes apparent quite quickly as the initial victors act to assert their first-mover advantages. In turn, the transitional governance approach and the formal institutional engineering process it emphasizes become the new arena for political conflict between elite factions. The truncated timeframe of transitional governance forces upon the post-conflict elites in question a specific series of institutional choices and outcomes, setting in motion one particular pathway and foreclosing other potential pathways. Moreover, through the transitional governance model of shared governance, even as they attempt to impose particular constraints on domestic actors, peacebuilding interventions are simultaneously giving specific elites new and unmatchable resources in the form of funding, legitimacy, and authority. In turn, elites are adept at manipulating the outcomes of the intervention to mobilize and reward supporters, attract new support, and more firmly establish their grips on power.

In the aftermath of intervention, finally, a crucial insight of temporal analysis becomes apparent: because of the dynamics of sequencing, alternatives forgone due to the exigencies of transitional governance become increasingly difficult to reach as time passes and countries continue to move along the peacebuilding pathway. Post-intervention, when external support for compliance has waned, those domestic elites who have been given the responsibility to implement and enforce new rules of governance find it more beneficial to subvert those institutions. Thus we see outcomes making it clear that elites might honor the letter of the new governance rules but violate their spirit such that they are obviously being exploited.[83] They govern, within the formal institutional constraints, in ways that attempt to eliminate competing political forces from authority. In the neopatrimonial order that is

[83] Mahoney and Thelen 2010: 13.

established, the formal institutions of the modern state, so deliberately unveiled at the end of the transitional governance period, are undermined in the service of systematic patronage distribution that cements the grip on power of specific elite factions. Savvy elites know that they will acquire an aura of legitimacy by cooperating with the UN's rules – and that they will in time be able to reassert their power based on their underlying resources. In each of the cases examined here, powerful elites cooperated with the transitional governance process only to make a bid for hegemonic power once the UN presence had ended. Thus, the vision of political order acted upon by domestic elites outlasts and outmaneuvers that of international peacebuilders.

This causal narrative serves as the logic underpinning the analysis presented in the rest of the book, which focuses on the international community's model of peacebuilding through transitional governance as a transformative experiment. The empirical chapters that follow bear out the expectations derived in this chapter, through the post-conflict peacebuilding experiences of Cambodia, East Timor, and Afghanistan. Much has been written about these cases, so much so that there is little new to be gleaned on the details of the interventions themselves. Yet I aim to make a twofold contribution through my presentation of the case material and additional evidence collected through interviews. First, as this chapter has articulated, the historical institutionalist approach to examining these interventions and the consequent emphasis on neopatrimonial political order offers a new comparative take on the particular details of the cases that are worth emphasizing and thereby streamlines their presentation. Second, the temporal dimension of the analysis connects familiar historical details in new ways, especially by highlighting specific elements of the cases in light of the phases along the peacebuilding pathway.

For these analytical purposes, the empirical narrative in this book is structured through the sequence of critical peacebuilding phases: moving post-conflict countries from conflict to settlement; implementing transitional governance measures of statebuilding and democratization; and post-intervention governance outcomes. At each phase, I emphasize how domestic elites interpret and interact with international interventions in patterns that condition the possibility and quality of a stable and lasting peace in the longer term. The next chapter delivers a comparative assessment of the politics behind the elite peace settlements that mark the first critical juncture in the process of transformative peacebuilding. These settlements are the hinge between the country's past political trajectory, including the conflict itself, and the post-conflict future that the international community aspires to help shape. They offer a crucible through which to examine competing domestic and international conceptions of appropriate strategies to build political order.

3 From Violent Conflict to Elite Settlement

The international peacebuilding endeavor is framed as the attempt to create sustainable peace in post-conflict countries by transforming the root sources of conflict in these societies. The crucial first stage is to bring together the leaders of warring factions in constructing a peace settlement by which all sides agree to abide. A peace settlement can be reached in a number of different ways, as illustrated by the case studies in this book: as a result of a stalemated conflict as in Cambodia; attained as part of the journey toward independence as in East Timor; or forged through a decisive externally assisted military victory as in Afghanistan. No matter how it is reached, however, the contours of the peace deal are the manifestation of the terms on which parties previously locked in conflict are willing, at a particular moment in time, to attempt to coexist with each other. The peace settlement is, in effect, an externally imposed critical juncture that sets in motion the peacebuilding pathway that follows. In addition, an elite peace pact offers a snapshot of the domestic power balance emerging out of conflict and a strong indication of the goals and motivations of the parties to it, providing essential clues into the political realities of the peacebuilding challenge. Like other critical junctures, the peace settlement phase represents a moment of highly contingent politics, where the choices made by political actors have lasting repercussions.

Internationally mediated peace settlements in Cambodia, East Timor, and Afghanistan attempted to resolve the problems that created conflict at the outset – and served, in turn, as the basic agreements upon which the subsequent peacebuilding interventions were predicated and implemented. Each country narrative presented in this chapter analytically explores the causes and nature of the conflict period and illustrates how the peace settlement was achieved. The historical overviews emphasize those structural elements of each country's political trajectory that had lasting effects on the domestic elite power balance and political culture. In particular, they focus on the ways in which elites use the infrastructure and resources of the state in their power struggles and in building neopatrimonial networks of political support – in attempting, in short, to establish political order. In the previous chapter, I made the case that a peace agreement is, in practice, a conditional elite pact that is best understood not as a rational deal that strikes a stable compromise between elite factions but rather as the concrete representation of the legacies of the pre-conflict political trajectory and the particular power balance that emerges from the conflict. The empirical evidence presented in this chapter illustrates how the extraordinarily fluid politics of the settlement phase, against the structural backdrop of the preceding political trajectory, initiate a new phase of regularized elite conflict over the construction of political order.

For each country, I begin with a brief historical background, paying particular attention to the basic challenges of governance and political order – focusing especially on the political–economic objectives of different elite factions and the rivalries among them as well as the overall institutional infrastructure and capacity of the state. I then turn to a discussion of the conflict, emphasizing the composition of the warring factions, the contours of their grievances and the nature of their claims to state authority. In outlining the nature of political group competition in each of the cases I build on Michael Doyle's insightful notion of "ecologies of transitional politics" to characterize the nature, coherence, and orientation of the different factions to conflict and settlement.[1] The political–economic characteristics of the factions must be understood in a dynamic sense, since they change over time, and they are crucial for explaining the subsequent interaction between international peacebuilders and domestic elites during the transitional governance phase. The coherent Cambodian factions may have originally been resigned to the peace process but, over time, they became increasingly hostile to it and to each other. The umbrella national resistance movement in East Timor, seen as the natural broad-based counterpart to the United Nations, fractured quite quickly after independence. In Afghanistan there were a handful of relatively coherent factions that have, since the country's liberation from the Taliban, proliferated into many smaller groups with particularist claims. The narratives in this chapter attempt to capture the dynamics of fluid elite factional interests that are,

[1] Doyle 2001: 547–550; and Doyle and Sambanis 2006: 321–333.

in turn, central to understanding how post-conflict political order is constructed.

The Cambodian Civil War

Modern Cambodian political history combines the legacy of an ancient indigenous empire, the effects of colonization, independence, and Cold War external influences, and the agonies of civil conflict and the genocide perpetrated by the Khmer Rouge. The combination of these factors contributed to the length and severity of the civil war, as well as to the difficulty of the political settlement to the conflict. In turn, the legacy of weak state capacity and compromised political legitimacy have deepened the challenge of constructing post-conflict political order.

The ancient Khmer empire, immortalized in the temples of its capital city Angkor, controlled a large part of what now constitutes modern Thailand, Laos, and Vietnam from the ninth to the thirteenth centuries CE. With the decline of the Angkor empire, Cambodia became vulnerable to periodic invasion and occupation by these neighbors. The wars fought between Thailand and Vietnam on Cambodian soil in the 1830s and 1840s severely weakened the small kingdom's fragile institutions and carved up its territory. Cambodia's place on the map was saved when France imposed a protectorate upon the country and its obsolescent monarchy in 1863. As in their other colonies, the French prevented the development of a cohesive political or bureaucratic elite in Cambodia. Instead, they brought into the country a super-class of Vietnamese civil servants, merchants, and farmers who, along with a small overseas Chinese population, came to dominate the administrative and commercial realms in Cambodia.[2] The French constructed some degree of infrastructure in the country, but the Cambodian economy remained largely based on subsistence agriculture and traditional extractive practices in commodities such as rubber and other agricultural products.

The colonial French authorities designated the 19-year-old Prince Norodom Sihanouk king in 1941, marking a landmark event in contemporary Cambodian political history. Originally installed on the throne as a colonial puppet, Sihanouk proved over the following seven decades to be a shrewd political operator and remained one of the

[2] Gottesman 2003; Shawcross 1994; and Strangio 2014.

dominant figures of Cambodian political life until his death in 2012.[3] He played a central role in winning Cambodian independence in 1954, having decided at an early stage that his political survival hinged on his ability to emerge as a champion of Khmer nationalism against French rule. In 1955, Sihanouk abdicated the throne in favor of his father to become eligible to participate in national politics. In the election that followed his party won every seat in the national assembly. His party remained dominant for the next 15 years and he governed with no intermediaries between himself and his people, claiming legitimacy on the basis of his semi-divine connection with the peasantry. Like the French, he prevented the development of an independent political class in Phnom Penh, and continued the tradition of personalized political authority practiced by Cambodian rulers before him.

From 1970 onward, Cambodia underwent two decades of extreme political instability and a brutal civil war that included a tragic genocide. That year Sihanouk was overthrown and his regime was replaced by a right-wing civilian–military alliance supported by the United States and led by General Lon Nol. Sihanouk, who had been exiled in Beijing, decided to throw in his lot with the North Vietnamese and the small group of Cambodian communists he dubbed "les Khmers Rouges." By making common cause with the latter and assuring the rest of the world of their benign intentions, he endowed them with a measure of legitimacy and political prominence that had earlier eluded them.[4] Between 1970 and 1975, the "carpet-bombing" of Cambodian territory by the United States and the radical insurgent tactics of the Khmer Rouge made it increasingly difficult for peasants to live on the land, destroying the agricultural economy as well as the fabric of Cambodian peasant society. On April 17, 1975, following a series of victories in provincial cities throughout the country, the black pajama-clad peasant soldiers of the Khmer Rouge seized the capital city of Phnom Penh and ousted Lon Nol's government. The very same day they embarked on a radical Maoist agrarian program to return the

[3] The discussion of Sihanouk's political career draws heavily on Shawcross 1994: 6–7.

[4] By contrast, American foreign service officers stationed in the region alerted Washington – where they were met with relative disinterest – in mid-1973 to the already disturbing violence and forced migration being pursued by the Khmer Rouge in the southern Cambodian zones they then controlled, and again in 1975 soon after the Khmer Rouge took Phnom Penh. Strangio 2014: 13 and 17.

Cambodian economy and society to "Year Zero," emptying the city and forcing people to migrate to provincial labor camps. In September of the same year, the Khmer Rouge brought Sihanouk back to a ghost city and declared him the titular head of state. He resigned in April 1976 and was held captive on the grounds of the royal palace for three years until he returned to exile in Beijing. The infamous Pol Pot became prime minister at the head of the Democratic Kampuchea regime and Cambodia was governed by the reign of terror imposed by the Khmer Rouge's ruling party organization known as the *Angkar*.

The horrors of the Khmer Rouge regime and the genocide it perpetrated have been well documented.[5] Over one million Cambodians, out of a 1975 population of about 7.5 million, are estimated to have been killed through outright execution, starvation and disease, and the physical burdens of forced labor.[6] In addition to carrying out indiscriminate murderous rampages, the Khmer Rouge systematically destroyed the very fabric of Cambodian society by targeting for execution and displacement the most educated and trained sectors of society – including teachers, lawyers, doctors, and Buddhist monks, as well as the Vietnamese and Chinese leaders of the commercial class. The Khmer Rouge operated a network of prisons and execution centers, the most infamous of which were Tuol Sleng, or S-21, in Phnom Penh, and the Choeung Ek "killing fields" on the outskirts of the city. The chilling phrase widely repeated by Khmer Rouge cadres as they carried out their purges of "enemies of the revolution" was "To keep you is no gain; to kill you is no loss."[7] Over time, as the small inner faction around Pol Pot became increasingly paranoid, the organization also purged its own ranks. The Khmer Rouge decimated Cambodia's small elite and crushed any forms of dissent, destroying in its wake the country's civic institutions and all forms of community and religious association.

In parallel to these assaults on their own people, the Khmer Rouge carried out numerous attacks against Vietnam. The Vietnamese finally retaliated with an invasion, driving the Khmer Rouge out of Phnom

[5] See, among others, Chandler 1991; and Kiernan 1996.

[6] Gottesman 2003. Chandler 1998 puts the figure at over 1.5 million. Kiernan 2003, in a scrutiny of population and death estimates, calculates that the 1975–79 genocidal toll was 1.7–1.9 million people, or 21–24 percent of Cambodia's 1975 population.

[7] Strangio 2014: 2.

Penh in January 1979 and installing a Hanoi-backed client regime, the self-styled People's Republic of Kampuchea (PRK), headed by defectors from the Khmer Rouge. Vietnam, with the full support of its Soviet patrons, thus liberated Cambodia from the Khmer Rouge's grip at the same time as it installed an occupying regime there. Almost no country outside the Soviet bloc recognized the new regime in Phnom Penh. The Khmer Rouge retained the country's UN seat, passing it in 1982 to the newly formed Coalition Government of Democratic Kampuchea (CGDK). That coalition was headed by Sihanouk and included three armed Cambodian resistance groups: the Khmer Rouge; Sihanouk's royalist political party FUNCINPEC (National United Front for an Independent, Neutral, Peaceful, and Cooperative Cambodia);[8] and the non-communist Khmer People's National Liberation Front (KPNLF). External involvement became further entrenched, with the Chinese arming the Khmer Rouge, and the United States, Britain, and France supporting the other coalition partners. Schisms in the domestic elite became hardened by the logic of these Cold War alliances. In turn, Cambodia's societal and political divisions deepened and persisted after the civil conflict was brought to an end.

Its lack of UN recognition notwithstanding, the PRK regime controlled the country from 1979 onward. When Vietnam withdrew in 1989 it became known as the State of Cambodia before subsequently restyling itself as the Cambodian People's Party in order to contest the UN-administered elections in 1993. It was led by Heng Samrin and then Hun Sen, both Cambodian-born Khmer Rouge defectors with strong ties to Vietnam. This regime "developed out of the devastation inherited from the Khmer Rouge an effective (albeit dictatorial) authority over more than 80 percent of the territory"[9] and rebuilt and controlled the organs of the state. Yet it lacked legitimacy on both international and domestic fronts.[10] The PRK was nowhere near as brutal as the Khmer Rouge, but it remained a hardline, one-party state controlled by Vietnam. It brooked no dissent, cracked down on opponents, sometimes through the use of torture and murder, controlled the judiciary and press, and stifled civil society. The PRK also had to contend with the Cambodian population's widespread mistrust of, and

[8] The acronym comes from the party's French name, Front Uni National pour un Cambodge Indépendant Neutre Pacifique Et Coopératif.

[9] Doyle 1995: 18. [10] Shawcross 1994: 10.

distaste for, the Vietnamese. Few in the country supported the regime and few Cambodians returned from the diaspora to assist it with governing the country.

In this context, the PRK faced a major challenge in constructing a viable political order. In essence, it was an illegitimate occupying regime that needed to extract resources and some form of legitimacy from the provinces in order to govern the country from the center. It did so by constructing an extensive patronage network throughout Cambodia, primarily through a strategy of delegation that enabled personal gain for co-opted provincial officials while ensuring some measure of governance and public goods provision throughout the country. Caroline Hughes observes that the PRK's statebuilding project "comprised the establishment and cementing of clientelist networks running through the ministry, military, and provincial structures" that drew upon the cultural repertoires of clientelism that had long characterized Cambodian governance.[11] Political order rested upon, and power came to be deployed by, instrumental and highly personalized clientelist ties between top elites and the agents upon whom they relied to carry out their orders. In a classic manifestation of a neopatrimonial hybrid order, this led to the evolution of flexible, informal, even evasive, administrative and political cultures, in combination with a hierarchical and cohesive party patronage structure that penetrated Cambodia down to the village level, where kinship and patronage ties remained the basis of customary Khmer peasant relationships.[12]

The PRK mirrored earlier governing strategies deployed by Sihanouk and even Lon Nol, who, while personalizing political control, similarly tried to extend the reach of the state out to the rural areas of the country. This twin tactic served to extend the scope of patrimonial and patronage-based politics.[13] Yet the reach of the state under the PRK extended even further down to the village level. The regime consolidated the dominance of its party apparatus, concentrated political control, and lengthened the hierarchy of patron–client relationships by introducing, for example, a three-member village committee that comprised appointed representatives, as well as rice cooperatives, which collectivized rural agricultural production.[14] The extensive reach of the

[11] Hughes 2009a: 28.
[12] Hughes 2003, 2009a; and Pak et al. 2007, especially pp. 51–53.
[13] Pak et al. 2007; and Turner 2013.
[14] Gottesman 2003: 34–56; and Pak et al. 2007: 52.

PRK state apparatus into the Cambodian countryside had major consequences during and after the international peacebuilding intervention.

The competition for political control over the country developed out of the collapse of the legitimacy of the Cambodian state, which had begun in earnest under the Khmer Rouge's violent regime and continued under the Vietnam-installed regime. The PRK regime and its Vietnamese and Soviet backers considered the civil conflict against the Khmer Rouge to be a necessary counterinsurgency waged against a genocidal opponent. The CGDK coalition and its UN and US supporters saw the roots of the conflict in the armed intervention and occupation of the country by Vietnam.[15] The difficulty of finding a bargain that was palatable to all these competing sets of interests prolonged the conflict.[16] As Doyle and Sambanis succinctly observe, the challenge of building a peace in Cambodia was the challenge of joining effective government – the PRK – with legitimate sources of authority – the exile coalition, led by Sihanouk.[17] That disconnect between effectiveness and legitimacy has continued to thwart the Cambodian peacebuilding process to the present day and it remains the defining obstacle to constructing a modern political order in the country.

The Paris Peace Agreement on Cambodia

The Cambodian civil war was finally ended by the Paris Peace Agreement – the centerpiece of which was the *Agreement on a Comprehensive Political Settlement of the Cambodia Conflict*. This peace deal was arrived at by Cambodian elites as their various external backers withdrew support in the waning years of the Cold War. The settlement was intended to be a firm coda to the long battle for control of the country. Instead, it served as the preface to the next phase of the elite conflict that had long divided Cambodia. The negotiations in the run-up to the Paris Peace Agreement highlight the deeply entrenched animosities between the Cambodian factions – and reveal that the final agreement resulted from changes in the geostrategic context rather than from any real domestic political rebalancing. Vietnam began to consider the possibility of compromise between its client regime and the other Cambodian contenders to power as Soviet support for the PRK began to diminish in the mid-1980s and Vietnam sought closer ties

[15] Doyle 1995: 18. [16] Walter 2009: 253. [17] Doyle and Sambanis 2006: 217.

with its Southeast Asian neighbors.[18] In November 1987, Sihanouk had his first meeting with the PRK's leader, Hun Sen, to begin negotiations for a political settlement. In addition to the rapidly changing geopolitical context, Doyle observes that other factors, such as Sihanouk's age, Hun Sen's aspiration for international recognition, and military exhaustion on all sides, helped prompt these talks, as did the increasing desire of the Association of Southeast Asian Nations (ASEAN) to see a resolution to the conflict.[19] Informal meetings – facilitated by an ASEAN eager to assume a regional leadership role – identified the need for some degree of interim international involvement over the full transition to peace without any agreement on what that mechanism would look like.

In the search for a comprehensive settlement, the first Paris Conference on Cambodia was convened in July 1989. Yet these talks stalled initially, deadlocking over the nature of the interim control mechanism as well as the issue of power-sharing among the Khmer factions. The notion of a UN trustee-like interim administrative supervision of Cambodia was first mooted at this time.[20] A power-sharing system was proposed, whereby the control of several crucial ministries – defense, public security, finance, information, and foreign affairs – would be shared across the four major competing factions, along with additional mechanisms for scrutiny and oversight. The PRK, however, balked at allowing Khmer Rouge participation in the proposed interim quadripartite government; and the CGDK coalition of the other Khmer factions was leery of legitimizing the Vietnam-installed government in Phnom Penh and granting it an advantage in any future elections. Vietnam removed its troops from Cambodian soil in 1989, intent on normalizing relations with the United States, China, and ASEAN. Hun Sen's government, known formally from 1989 onward as the State of Cambodia (SOC), was left behind, still in control of the country. Yet the civil war continued, with the Khmer Rouge continuing to make territorial advances at the end of the 1980s. Finally, in 1990, the Permanent Five (P5) members of the UN Security Council drafted a peace plan that called for the establishment of an interim administration made up of the four factions to run the country

[18] Solarz 1990 observes, "Cambodia became Vietnam's Vietnam, an obstacle to Vietnam's economic development and a drain on Soviet-supplied resources."
[19] Doyle 1995: 21–22. [20] Solarz 1990.

under UN supervision. By this time the context had changed sufficiently to put in place the institutional arrangement that had earlier been rejected. The parties to the conflict agreed to this framework, although coming to a workable peace settlement took another year.

The Agreement on a Comprehensive Political Settlement of the Cambodia Conflict was signed in Paris on October 23, 1991. In this peace settlement, the four warring parties agreed to a ceasefire and disarmament, as well as refugee repatriation, the re-establishment and maintenance of law and order, the promotion of human rights, and principles for a new constitution committed to democratic pluralism. This negotiated peace was to be pursued in the context of UN administrative supervision and a UN-managed election. The Paris Peace Agreement was thus the genesis of the United Nations Transitional Authority in Cambodia (UNTAC). The agreement also mandated that the Supreme National Council (SNC), a quadripartite body created in the run-up to the final peace deal and endowed with Cambodian sovereignty and authority, would become the ongoing institutional manifestation of the temporary consensus achieved at the Paris Accords. The SNC would hence serve as UNTAC's parallel domestic counterpart during the transitional governance phase.

Yet the Cambodian factions did not sign the Paris Peace Agreement (sometimes also referred to as the Paris Peace Accords) out of their own desire for peace, but did so unwillingly due to the pressure applied to them by their external backers as a result of the changing geopolitical context.[21] Each of the parties continued to view itself the rightful regime to govern the country. The SOC believed itself to be in control of 90 percent of the country, while the Khmer Rouge believed it could continue to mount a guerrilla war and later did so. These "competing conceptions of how the accords would affect them . . . undermined the consent critical to peacekeeping."[22] It appears that each group agreed to the institutional terms of the settlement while planning to manipulate and even subvert them as best they could moving forward. In practice, this meant that if the parties saw the UN as acting against their interests they would react with entrenched resistance – an approach that often led to impasse. The SOC and the Khmer Rouge actively resisted UNTAC whenever it sought to implement its mandate in a manner that they perceived to be against their interests.

[21] Doyle 1995: 68. [22] Ratner 1995: 158.

Perhaps most significantly, the Khmer Rouge refused to comply with the second phase of the ceasefire in June 1992, which included the cantonment, disarmament, and partial demobilization of each of the factional armies. The SOC used this refusal to disarm as its own justification for resisting UNTAC control and soon the two factions were once again engaged in violent conflict – with each other, against opposition party officials, and even targeting civilians and UNTAC staff – as the election neared.

The resolution of the Cambodian conflict through the Paris Peace Agreement, albeit facilitated by external powers, serves as an example of how a "mutually hurting stalemate" can, as described by William Zartman, result in a convergence of preferences in the form of a peace treaty.[23] Yet although the Paris accords represented an inflection point in the Cambodian civil conflict, the peace settlement did not mark a final resolution to the civil war. In many ways, and increasingly so over time, subsequent Cambodian reconstruction occurred within the context of deep political animosity that sometimes simmered over into violence and instability and compromised the goals of the peacebuilding process from being achieved.

The East Timorese Resistance to Occupation

East Timor's national independence referendum in August 1999 marked the final victory of the country's 24-year-long fight for freedom. The challenges of constructing political order in East Timor emanate from both its long Portuguese colonial history and the shorter, yet traumatic Indonesian occupation.

The eastern half of the island of Timor was colonized by Portugal in the sixteenth century. Initially, the Portuguese ruled indirectly, through the traditional Timorese kings, or *liurai*. Binding together the country in the face of its ethnolinguistic diversity was a ritualized web of exchange relationships and political alliances, travel for trade and social purposes, and the spread of Tetum as the common indigenous language.[24] In the nineteenth century, Portuguese rule shifted toward greater territorial administration and became increasingly intrusive. The country's administrative division into villages, or *sucos*, disrupted the traditional political order associated with the *liurai*, who rebelled

[23] Zartman 1985. [24] Hughes 2009a; and Taylor 1999.

against their colonizers in 1912. The crushing of this rebellion ushered in a stable period until 1975. With the *liurai* acquiescing to the Portuguese administration, the traditional political order was overlaid by a new colonial order that empowered the *mestiço* Timorese – those with blood ties to Portugal. This colonial order created, in turn, a deep, lasting – and, later, politically salient – social cleavage between the urban, mostly Portuguese-speaking and Portuguese-oriented elite and the "Maubere" mountain people, who retained their traditional names, languages, and beliefs. The lives of the latter, who constituted the vast majority of the Timorese population, were relatively untouched by the centuries of Portuguese colonization, which had done little to build national institutions or infrastructure.[25] Overall, the colony's political and institutional development, particularly at the subnational level, had been severely attenuated. The legacies of this under-institutionalization, weak local capacity, and marginalization of the majority of Timorese from their country's governance have remained major challenges in the construction of political order in the country.

In 1974, Portugal's "Carnation Revolution" brought to power a new government in Lisbon that set in motion the dissolution of the Portuguese empire by accepting the right to self-determination of its colonies, even if they chose independence. Nascent political actors in East Timor quickly mobilized into three major competing political parties that espoused different positions with regard to the issue of self-determination. The Timorese Democratic Union (UDT) was the most conservative group, comprising the more prosperous Timorese and administration officials, many of whom were mixed race Portuguese–Timorese. UDT leaned toward the status quo, favoring a long transitional period of 15–20 years of autonomy with continued association with Portugal prior to full independence.[26] The Timorese Social Democratic Association (ASDT) advocated a quicker move to independence. In a sign of how close the parties' original political stances were, however, ASDT still began with a desire for an 8 to 10-year transition period of progressive autonomy, giving the country time to build its political and economic infrastructure. When its political program adopted a

[25] Dunn 2003; and Hughes 2009a.

[26] By convention, the acronyms for the parties' names come from the Portuguese formulation.

more radical tack a few months later, with more strident demands for Timorese inclusion in the administration and a clear demand for independence, ASDT became the Revolutionary Front for an Independent East Timor (FRETILIN).[27] The Timorese Popular Democratic Association (Apodeti), finally, was a smaller party that desired the integration of East Timor as an autonomous province within Indonesia. As James Dunn observes: "The polarization of the three main parties around three distinct goals tended to exaggerate the differences between their young leaders in that early stage of the territory's political development."[28] Yet the lines had been drawn early and would harden quickly.

In January 1975, UDT and FRETILIN, the two pro-independence parties, formed a short-lived coalition.[29] Initially, there was little difference between the viewpoints and aspirations of the leaders of these two groups. Yet FRETILIN became increasingly radical and it hardened its attitude toward other parties; while UDT moved to expel FRETILIN radicals in order to build a more conservative coalition. In a relatively short period of time, the alliance collapsed and there was subsequently a rapid escalation of the hostility between the parties. By the second half of 1975, East Timor was engulfed in a brief yet violent civil war that resulted in both urban fighting and intense battles among rural villages with competing party allegiances. In August of that year, the Portuguese governor and administration left Dili, withdrawing to the nearby island of Atauro and washing their hands of the East Timorese political situation.

FRETILIN had emphasized building its political organization across the country, outside the main towns where UDT operated, and its political strategy paid off. It was able to quite quickly gain control of much of the territory and forced UDT out of Dili within weeks. Its relatively loose political organization proved surprisingly adept at the formidable tasks of setting up a provisional administration and restoring law and order and basic services. As a result, by mid-October 1975 Dili was

[27] FRETILIN was modeled in large part on FRELIMO, the Front for the Liberation of Mozambique. Dunn 2003 points out that rather than being truly radical, FRETILIN remained an essentially populist and nationalist party that was influenced by the socialist aims of similar movements in other developing countries rather than by the objective of becoming a communist state.

[28] Dunn 2003: 62. Also Babo Soares 2003.

[29] UDT was originally the largest party in East Timor, but soon lost ground to FRETILIN. Some observers, for example, Nicol 1978, have argued that FRETILIN used the coalition with UDT tactically to win over supporters.

functioning normally. This was despite the fact that waves of Timorese refugees to both Australia and Indonesia, along with the withdrawal of the Portuguese administration, led to the loss of approximately 80 percent of East Timor's officials – leaving a particular lack of administrative personnel at the district level.[30] FRETILIN leaders recognized their administration could only be temporary and called on the Portuguese to return and implement a phased decolonization process. FRETILIN's successful, albeit brief, interregnum – whereby it established its populist and nationalist roots down at the village level and entire *sucos* shifted allegiance to it based on village chief preferences – forged a strong emotional bond between the party and the Timorese people, and had a lasting impact on the national psyche. By sending its young cadres out into rural areas to work on agriculture and literacy programs, FRETILIN "captured peoples' hearts."[31] Dunn estimates that FRETILIN's support had, by September 1975, risen to 80 percent of the population from its initial 60 percent in elections a couple of months earlier.[32]

Meanwhile, Indonesia had embarked upon a program of subversive activities intended to destabilize the country and undermine FRETILIN's claim to authority over all of East Timor, with the goal of providing the pretext for Indonesian occupation through ties with the integrationist party, Apodeti. In October 1975 Indonesia began a series of covert attacks, codenamed Operasi Komodo, to perpetuate the notion that the civil war between FRETILIN and UDT was ongoing. The FRETILIN leadership's main preoccupation became blocking Indonesia's designs over the country, preventing instead a deeper attention to reconstructing the administration and economy. FRETILIN appealed in vain to Indonesian President Suharto and the rest of the world for a negotiated solution. Its sense of isolation grew, along with the recognition that its energies would have to shift from building a new administration to defending the country. The leadership began to make preparations for a guerrilla struggle against Indonesia, sending food, supplies, and arms into the mountains.

The denouement came when Portugal agreed in November 1975 to talk with Indonesia over the status of the territory with no UN

30 Dunn 2003. The discussion of this era of Timorese politics draws heavily on this excellent source.
31 Author interviews with East Timorese and donor officials; Dili, East Timor, April 2005. See also Babo Soares 2003.
32 Dunn 2003: 221.

or Timorese representation. Although FRETILIN leaders realized they were in no position to govern an independent country, they unilaterally declared the independence of East Timor on November 28, 1975. Two days later, a coalition of pro-Indonesia parties, comprising mainly UDT and Apodeti, also proclaimed the independence of the territory from Portugal and its integration with Indonesia. East Timor had never been part of the Dutch East Indies, and Indonesia had never laid any formal territorial claim to the country. Yet, on December 7, 1975, Indonesia launched a naval, land, and air invasion of East Timor, under the pretext of preventing instability in its neighbor and eradicating what it identified, to promote Western acceptance of its invasion, as the radical leftist independence parties there.

The initial Indonesian assault was brutal. The many incidents of violence included the summary mass executions of hundreds of Timorese and Chinese residents and the abduction, torture, and rape of women and girls affiliated with FRETILIN. The remnants of the Portuguese colonial administration on the island of Atauro bore witness to the first day's assault and set sail the next. Dili was ransacked first; but similar mass executions took place in the towns of Liquiça, Maubara, and Aileu as the Indonesians extended their grip on the country. In response to the savage onset of the invasion, many Timorese fled their homes: tens of thousands fled to West Timor and, in the eastern half of the country, tens of thousands moved their households behind rebel lines in the mountains. In the area around the FRETILIN stronghold of Baucau, for example, the local population fell from about 85,000 people prior to the invasion to about 32,000 three months later and less than 10,000 a year after that.[33] All told, two-thirds of the remaining Timorese population were behind rebel lines during the course of the occupation.[34] Those who chose to surrender once famine conditions took hold in the mountains were placed in resettlement camps in which the conditions were equally dire.

Indonesia gradually increased its territorial control at FRETILIN's expense, continued its alliance with the pro-Indonesian parties, and perpetuated the fiction that the Timorese people supported the Indonesian presence. A "Regional Popular Assembly" was established to

[33] Figures reported to the governor of Baucau province, as cited in Dunn 2003: 253.

[34] Dunn 2003: 258.

determine the status of East Timor and this carefully Indonesian-assembled group petitioned Indonesia on May 31, 1976, to formally integrate East Timor. Six weeks later, Indonesia's President Suharto promulgated a law integrating East Timor into his country as its twenty-seventh province. From that point onward, Indonesia maintained that the East Timorese people had exercised their right to self-determination and had chosen integration with Indonesia, albeit under autonomous status.[35] Portugal, however, never ceded its governing authority over East Timor and the United Nations declined to recognize the authority of the Regional Popular Assembly concerning the status of East Timor. The country was all but under an Indonesian military occupation, a fact made possible by American and Australian silence on the issue.[36]

FRETILIN continued to resist East Timor's integration into Indonesia, retreating into the interior mountains of the island and fashioning itself into a guerrilla movement with an armed wing, FALINTIL (Armed Forces for the National Liberation of East Timor). Few Timorese were in favor of integration to begin with, and Dunn notes that "the rapacious and brutal behavior of the occupying forces greatly stiffened the resolve of the resistance and provided FRETILIN with a degree of popular support greater than it might otherwise have enjoyed."[37] From mid-1976 onward, the pattern of Timorese resistance shifted firmly from political action toward guerrilla warfare, and FRETILIN devoted considerable attention to ensuring adequate food supplies for the swollen mountain population.[38]

The Indonesians made some attempts to revive East Timor's economy, but they concentrated their attention on those sectors from which they could derive the most rents. The majority of Timorese who refused

[35] Martin 2001: 16–17.

[36] Australia was the only country to formally recognize the annexation of the territory, granting de jure recognition to Indonesia's claimed sovereignty in talks on settling the seabed border between Australia and East Timor. The United States never publicly objected to the annexation and continued its military support to Indonesia, which had portrayed FRETILIN as a communist movement.

[37] Dunn 2003: 253.

[38] In a fictionalized account of the island of Danu and the forging of its guerrilla resistance, Mo 2002 mirrors very closely the lived experiences of FALINTIL fighters, their relationship with Timorese civilians, and the early years of East Timor's occupation and struggle for independence.

to accept the Indonesian citizenship necessary for a government job found very few formal employment opportunities available to them. Although some Timorese officials and politicians accepted positions of authority under the new administration, the undisputed leaders of the territory were Indonesian officers from the armed forces, Tentara Nasional Indonesia (TNI), and the Kopassus special forces units. East Timor became an important financial resource and symbol to the Indonesian military elite – a fact that later fed into the TNI-inspired post-referendum violence in 1999. The political and economic marginalization of East Timorese under Indonesian occupation was more extreme than under Portuguese colonization.

FRETILIN's political and military structure coalesced during the initial years of the occupation. Nicolau Lobato became the main leader of the resistance, overseeing both political and military strategy, as other leaders who favored a negotiated settlement with Indonesia were gradually purged from the organization. Lobato was killed in 1978 and the death of this folk hero was to prove a major symbolic setback for the Timorese.[39] Caroline Hughes notes that this period marked a shift in resistance tactics: with major Indonesian assaults being stepped up against the ground it held, FRETILIN yielded its territorial control and FALINTIL units moved to secret mountain hideouts from where they initiated a new strategy of insurgent attacks on the Indonesian army.[40] Communication was essentially cut off between the guerrilla leaders in East Timor, their FRETILIN colleagues in exile in Mozambique, and the Timorese diaspora in Australia and Indonesia. The group of FRETILIN leaders in Mozambique, who came to be known as the "Maputo clique," held on to the original radical beliefs and motivations established during the movement's formation. The guerrilla leaders on the island, meanwhile, adapted their beliefs and objectives to the exigencies of continuing the insurgency and caring for the population still behind their lines.

José Alexandre "Xanana" Gusmão – later East Timor's first president, and then two-term prime minister for seven and a half years – assumed command of FALINTIL and the domestic mantle of FRETILIN leadership over the course of a two-year period from 1979

[39] Lobato was found and killed by an Indonesian special forces unit led by Prabowo Subianto, later President Suharto's son-in-law and the narrowly defeated presidential candidate in 2014.

[40] Hughes 2009a: 35.

to 1981. He took deliberate steps to move the group's political tactics away from radicalism and toward non-ideological policies intended to appeal to all Timorese. He formed the National Council of Maubere Resistance (CNRM) – later renamed the National Council for Timorese Resistance (CNRT) – which was intended to serve as an umbrella national resistance movement with a broader political appeal than FRETILIN. In so doing, he and other key guerrilla leaders embraced the ideology of Mauberism, identifying the Timorese nation with the Maubere mountain peasants and their traditions and idealizing the relationship between the FALINTIL guerrillas and the mountain people in a bond that remains politically symbolic to the present day.[41] In this manner the urban elite core of FRETILIN and the rural poor Maubere majority were joined together in a newly fashioned contemporary Timorese nationalist identity – a central plank upon which today's political order rests.

From 1982 onward, Gusmão was able to establish communications with FRETILIN leaders abroad, particularly those who had been orchestrating the party's political organization and objectives from exile in Mozambique and, in the 1990s, the Timorese diaspora in Australia. FALINTIL's strength in terms of the number of fighters and its overall military capability declined from the mid-1980s onward but the CNRM built and maintained an extensive network of popular support in the towns and villages of East Timor. Its survival and success as a resistance front depended on this grassroots network. Gusmão undertook what became a legendary walk from village to village across the interior of the country, asking the people whether FALINTIL should continue the resistance and generating an enormous groundswell of support.[42] During this time he was given the title "brother of the roots," or *Maun Bo't*, by the people and, together with the FALINTIL troops he led, attained a heroic status among the Timorese population, serving as a symbol of their resilience as a nation and a reminder that Indonesian occupation was neither complete nor final. Gusmão was arrested in 1992, but continued to command FALINTIL from prison in

[41] Niner 2009. Hughes 2009a: 36–37, notes that FALINTIL leaders began participating in indigenous animist rituals and taking on Timorese names, with Gusmão adopting the name Kay Rala and Francisco Guterres, another key FALINTIL commander, taking on the name Lú-Olo.

[42] Author interview with a donor official; Dili, East Timor, April 2005. Also Niner 2009.

Jakarta. Over the course of the next decade, he became a key interlocutor between UN and other negotiators and the FRETILIN leadership, cementing his role as the key veto player in Timorese politics.

Over the course of the latter half of the occupation, other elements of the Timorese political landscape began to take shape as various groups of political actors gained in importance. The Catholic Church assumed a growing political role in East Timor, with later Nobel Peace laureate Bishop Carlos Belo arriving on the scene in 1983. In addition, political activism blossomed among the Timorese youth. They were products of an Indonesian education system that was intended to make them more sympathetic to integration. Yet, speaking the Bahasa language in which they were educated, they formed a new front against integration with Indonesia, having equally experienced – or at least witnessed among their families – the brutality, oppression, and human rights abuses that resulted from the occupation. As the guerrilla movement neared exhaustion in the late 1980s, the student movement became crucial in the final years of the fight for freedom, as well as in the political settlement that was to come with independence. From 1995 onward, the UN convened an annual meeting of East Timorese leadership, known as the All-Inclusive Intra-East Timorese Dialogue, which drew delegates from both inside and outside the country. This event was significant in bringing together the disparate strands of the Timorese leadership, although the representatives from inside East Timor tended to lean toward Indonesia and Gusmão himself was not present.[43]

The conflict lasted through 1999, with particularly heavy loss of life in its vicious early years. Estimates of the number of Timorese who died as a result of the independence struggle, including from the famine and disease that came with massive population displacement, range as high as 200,000; the Indonesian authorities themselves acknowledge up to tens of thousands of deaths.[44] The human rights violations committed by the Indonesian army against FRETILIN cadres and their supporters were extreme. Indonesian missions behind guerrilla lines deliberately destroyed food crops to create conditions of destitution. In the

[43] Gunn 1997.

[44] Martin 2001: 17. Kiernan 2003, in a scrutiny of population and death estimates, calculates that the early 1975–1980 death toll alone in East Timor was approximately 170,000, or 24 to 26 percent of East Timor's 1975 population. He notes that, at one-fifth of the population, this is proportionately comparable to the Cambodian genocide toll of the same time period.

infamous "fence of legs" campaign, the Indonesian army forced thousands of East Timorese villagers to march in human chains ahead of Indonesian troops to comb the interior of the island for FRETILIN and FALINTIL members. Dunn reports that in a second "fence of legs" campaign in 1985, thousands of Timorese chose to go to the hills to avoid conscription, resulting in famine conditions, torture, and executions.[45] The brutality of the Indonesian troops against the guerrillas intensified the local population's hostility toward the occupiers, even turning Timorese youths into faithful FALINTIL recruits.

These human rights violations received little attention abroad until November 1991, when Indonesian armed forces opened fire on a pro-independence assembly of mourners at Santa Cruz Cemetery in Dili, killing at least 50 and possibly up to 200 people. The television images and journalist reports from the scene had a dramatic impact on the international community, raising East Timor's profile in the global consciousness. In 1992, Xanana Gusmão's own profile, and that of the movement he led, was elevated when he was captured and subsequently continued his activism from prison. Then, in 1996, the Nobel Peace Prize was awarded to Dili's Bishop Belo, who, among other things, had played a crucial role in exposing the Santa Cruz massacre, and José Ramos-Horta, FRETILIN's exiled foreign minister and leading international spokesman, "for their work towards a just and peaceful solution to the conflict in East Timor."[46]

The United Nations had remained essentially a bystander during the course of the occupation.[47] The Security Council adopted resolutions in December 1975 and April 1976 that affirmed the right of the East Timorese to self-determination and called on Indonesia to withdraw. Through 1981, the General Assembly passed annual resolutions expressing concern over the suffering of the East Timorese population and reaffirming their right to self-determination. Direct discussions between Portugal and Indonesia were initiated under the auspices of the Secretary-General in 1983, yet they failed to achieve any progress. Indonesia maintained that the Timorese had decided on their fate in 1976; Portugal, however, insisted on a legitimate act of self-determination in East Timor, thereby keeping the issue alive. Tripartite

[45] Dunn 2003: 296.

[46] The Norwegian Nobel Committee, press release on the Nobel Peace Prize 1996, as quoted in Martin 2001: 17.

[47] Martin 2001: 17–18.

talks were revitalized and the UN role became more proactive when Secretary-General Kofi Annan appointed a Personal Representative for East Timor in February 1997.

The East Timor Independence Referendum

The Indonesian occupation of East Timor was finally brought to an end by internal changes in Indonesia, beginning with the fall of Suharto in May 1998. The following month President B. J. Habibie, Suharto's successor, floated an offer of autonomy to East Timor, which was still under integrated status. The Indonesian military was staunchly opposed to any concessions that could lead East Timor down the road to independence. Special forces officers based there began setting up an extensive paramilitary organization made up of pro-integration Timorese, intended to frustrate a possible referendum. The Indonesian military paid, trained, and armed militia members and organized their operations against pro-independence groups. Militia violence – including seizures of independence activists, torture, killings, and the destruction of homes – began in October 1998 and escalated in early 1999. By that point, FALINTIL troops had moved into cantonment in the mountaintop town of Aileu and followed the still imprisoned Gusmão's order not to engage either Indonesian or paramilitary units, so as not to allow any further civil war pretext for continued Indonesian occupation. The decision was followed with agonized restraint at the time as FALINTIL troops watched their countrymen being murdered; it has since been credited as a crucial strategic move that facilitated a faster and more inclusive national healing process.[48]

Gusmão and other Timorese leaders remained firm on their demand for an eventual referendum on independence but were amenable in early 1999 to an extended period of transitional autonomy, in which Indonesia would play an active role, before a vote.[49] Yet Indonesian officials in Jakarta objected to the transitional autonomy approach, believing that a majority of Timorese would choose to remain in

[48] Author interviews with donor officials and civil society leaders; Dili, East Timor, April 2005. Also Cristalis 2002.

[49] Gusmão spoke a number of times in early 1999 about creating an environment in which the Indonesian military would not feel defeated and of the need to create the basis for friendly relations between East Timor and its large neighbor. Martin 2001: 23.

Indonesia and advancing the sentiment that they would rather withdraw entirely if the Timorese chose independence. Indonesia, Portugal, and the UN finally reached agreement, on May 5, 1999, to hold a referendum on whether the people of East Timor accepted Indonesia's integration-with-autonomy proposal. Although the independence option was not specifically on the ballot, it was clearly the alternative in the Yes–No vote; Habibie declared that if the Timorese voted against autonomy, he would call on the Indonesian parliament to grant them independence.

The UN moved quickly to organize the plebiscite, with the Security Council establishing the United Nations Mission in East Timor (UNAMET) on June 11, 1999, to manage the voting process. The UN had a little over two months to organize a free and fair vote – including the registration of eligible voters, the organization of the vote itself, and the establishment of a secure environment. This latter security concern was paramount – yet Indonesia refused to accept international peacekeepers, insisting that it alone must remain responsible for ensuring security during and after what it called the "popular consultation." Pro-integration militias directed by the Indonesian military ratcheted up their violent campaign, focusing on districts adjacent to the border with West Timor and forcing thousands of East Timorese to flee their homes and cross the border.

On August 30, 1999, in the midst of that intimidation, East Timorese voted in a national referendum – known as the *Popular Consultation in East Timor* – overwhelmingly against a special autonomy relationship with Indonesia and hence in favor of independence.[50] The country had finally been allowed the act of self-determination it had been promised in 1974 by a withdrawing Portuguese colonial administration. Just hours after the results of the referendum were announced, pro-special autonomy militias – still organized, armed, and assisted by the retreating Indonesian military forces – conducted a pre-planned, systematic "scorched earth" campaign intended to leave the small country both depopulated and in ruins.[51] Some three-quarters of buildings in the country were gutted by fire and demolished in the retreat. An estimated

[50] The vote was 21.5 percent in favor of and 78.5 percent against the proposed special autonomy relationship, with 98 percent of 451,792 registered voters (out of a population of about 800,000) participating.

[51] UN Security Council Document No. S/1999/976, Annex, Para. 1, 14 September 1999. See also Martin 2001: 24–26 and Dunn 2003, especially pp. 348–359.

80 percent of the nation's 800,000 people fled their homes to escape the violence, with about a quarter of a million displaced persons fleeing and being forcibly deported into neighboring West Timor, where it is estimated that around half of them remain today. Estimates of how many were killed are unreliable, varying from hundreds into the thousands; some mass graves remain unexamined, reports abound of bodies being dumped at sea, and many who fled to West Timor are subsequently unaccounted for. Gusmão's orders to FALINTIL to remain disengaged were tested to the limit as the fleeing East Timorese flocked to the FALINTIL cantonments with accounts of violence, yet they remained firm and were obeyed. The head of UNAMET, Ian Martin, later observed that the UN's planning around the aftermath of the referendum had been "on the basis of a best-case scenario that the UN hoped could be realized with a high degree of international attention and pressure but that was never realistic."[52]

Following two weeks of concerted international pressure, on September 12, 1999, Indonesia finally and reluctantly agreed to the presence of UN troops to help restore security. A multinational blue helmet force (INTERFET), headed by Australia, arrived in Dili on September 20, 1999, in one of the swiftest responses in the history of UN peacekeeping. Within two weeks the Indonesian troops had withdrawn totally and on October 20, 1999, the Indonesian parliament annulled its 1976 annexation of East Timor, bringing the occupation to a formal end.[53] Just five days later, on October 25, the UN Security Council authorized a mandate for the United Nations Transitional Administration in East Timor (UNTAET),[54] which became the governing authority of the territory for a transitional period that would culminate in national elections and the writing of a constitution. As UNAMET and then UNTAET were constituted, responsibility for East Timor within the United Nations shifted from the Department of Political Affairs, which had handled the ongoing dialogue since the 1980s, to the Department of Peacekeeping Operations. Critics later pointed to this switch in assessing the UN's role and actions in East Timor, arguing that the basic peacekeeping-oriented structure of the mission hindered it from achieving its mandate, which required the mission to

52 Martin 2001: 126.

53 Gusmão came home to East Timor and to a hero's welcome on October 22, 1999.

54 UNTAET was established by UN Security Council Resolution 1272 on October 25, 1999.

govern the country as well as put in place the foundations for political, institutional, and economic development.[55]

East Timor was thought by many at the UN and in wider international intervention circles to be a *tabula rasa* upon which to prove the effectiveness of internationally assisted peacebuilding and reconstruction initiatives. In many respects, the country appeared the perfect environment for success: violence was effectively over after the Indonesian withdrawal and there was remarkable political accord and goodwill within the country, with no real dissent over appropriate leadership. Yet UNTAET has subsequently been heavily criticized for the manner in which the political timetable and process was implemented.[56] The peacebuilding challenge in East Timor was viewed as very different from that in either Cambodia or Afghanistan. Unlike in most other UN peacekeeping missions, the main political challenge in this case was not to mediate between factions that had been at war. Anthony Goldstone captures the thinking at the time with the observation that the political adjudication process had already occurred with the national referendum in August 1999; so that "Instead, the political task was the relatively straightforward one of working through a political timetable that had the uncontested goal of independence as the final end point."[57] A set of interrelated challenges arose over the course of this process, however, that proved problematic for subsequent state capacity-building and democratic consolidation: UNTAET's slow incorporation of East Timorese participation into both the administrative and political arenas; the clear dominance of one party as political participation was increased; and the overall timing and sequencing of the political process in relation to the statebuilding dimension of transitional governance. Furthermore, it has become apparent with the advantage of hindsight that the international community misinterpreted the domestic political situation, in particular overestimating the degree of elite political accord and the extent to which the returned FRETILIN leadership spoke for their fellow political leaders.

The Afghan Civil War

By the time the Afghan Northern Alliance and the US military drove the Taliban out of Kabul in November 2001, Afghanistan had suffered

55 Chesterman 2002; and Suhrke 2001.

56 Chopra 2002; Goldstone 2004; and Suhrke 2001.

57 Goldstone 2004: 85.

over two decades of war. Often labeled the last proxy battleground of the Cold War, the country saw its anti-imperialist war against the Soviet Union morph into a civil war among *mujahideen* (or freedom fighter) factions, many supported by external patrons, that combined in rapidly shifting alliances. The conflict continued into 2001 even as the Taliban, one of those factions, had consolidated power over most of the country. Afghanistan in 2001 was considered the quintessential failed state, an institutional vacuum in which societal anarchy persisted and in which state-sponsored terrorism could flourish. The country was characterized by severely fragmented social and political structures and a nonexistent central state infrastructure. It was trapped in a regional conflict complex – centered around the drug, gem, and transit trades – with entrenched subnational and transnational social linkages that perpetuated the country's internal fragmentation and chaotic conflict patterns.[58]

Afghanistan has for centuries been victim to conflict emanating from both within and without – its territory being fought over in fierce tribal power battles as well as serving as a buffer between empires and contested ground for their expansionist ambitions. Modern Afghanistan was founded in the mid-eighteenth century when Ahmad Shah Durrani united the Pashtun tribes and established a political order strong enough to be the basis for territorial expansion. Yet this stability, and Afghanistan's subsequent independence, proved fragile in the face of the century-long battle between Britain and Russia for conquest of Central Asia and Afghanistan, dubbed the "Great Game." The nation was finally consolidated in the late nineteenth century, when Abdul Rahman Khan, also of the Durrani chiefly clan, reigned over a period in which external interests over the country were balanced, the Afghan tribes were consolidated, and the country's bureaucracy was reorganized into what can be regarded as the modern Afghan state. He achieved this consolidation at a great cost in terms of violence, albeit couched in a nationalist narrative, advancing a process of what Louis Dupree called "internal imperialism" to crush different claims to authority across the country and reward followers with government posts and the spoils attached to them.[59]

Establishing central government over the diverse, tribal, and independent-minded Afghan people has remained an ongoing

[58] Rubin 2000. [59] Barfield 2010; Dupree 1973; and Gregorian 1969.

challenge for successive rulers. One particular defining cleavage in Afghan politics has been the tension between a reformist, modernizing urban elite and a more conservative, traditional rural majority. The Pashtun monarchy was long at the fault line of this tension, claiming its legitimacy from its tribal chiefly roots but also embarking upon cautious modernization programs. It was finally abolished in 1973 when the last king, Zahir Shah, who had reigned for four decades, was ousted by his cousin and former prime minister Mohammed Daoud Khan. Daoud established rule as president of the Republic of Afghanistan and with his coup the pendulum of power in the republic swung in favor of Kabul-centric elite politics to the extent that the regime was faulted for not incorporating leaders from outside the immediate circle surrounding Daoud. Barnett Rubin labels this era of Afghan politics a "rentier regime," in the sense that these Kabul elites were resourced by and beholden to external patrons.[60] As a result, they were motivated more by external forces than by internal ones and the capacity of the Afghan state to govern the country withered away under the control of these elites. Daoud, in turn, was killed by the People's Democratic Party of Afghanistan (PDPA) when it seized power in April 1978. The PDPA, the principal communist organization in the country, was aligned with and aided by the Soviet Union and represented the first group of Afghan intelligentsia to come to power in the country. The radical reforms that they introduced in the countryside undermined traditional authority and social structures.[61] At the same time, the Afghan state rapidly developed a unilateral independence on the Soviets, while aid from other sources began to flow to the various Afghan resistance groups.

In December 1979, Moscow, dissatisfied with its indirect leverage over the destabilizing government in Kabul, sent troops into Afghanistan to install a more pliable government that would allow it to assert more direct control. In response, a rural resistance movement comprising various Afghan militias, or *mujahideen* factions, and backed by foreign support, united in order to drive out the invaders. After ten costly years of a war of attrition it found itself unable to win, the Soviet Union withdrew its troops from Afghanistan between May 1988 and February 1989. Without the unifying *jihadi* and nationalist impulse of driving out the invaders, the *mujahideen* alliance soon

[60] Rubin 2002: 81–105. [61] Giustozzi 2009.

fractured back into its separate political and military structures with their own objectives and strategies, competing for power in a country where the national institutional infrastructure had been shattered. Local divisions re-emerged and the preferences of international supporters diverged, preventing the *mujahideen* groups from consolidating into a plausible political alternative to the Soviet-installed Najibullah puppet regime in Kabul. Local militia commanders began to make the necessary practical deals with their opponents and foreign funders to assert their own autonomy and power. They were once again able to levy tribute payments on road transport across their territories and, often forming Potemkin *shuras* or village councils, received increasing amounts of foreign aid directly rather than through their umbrella parties.[62] While some attempted to forge independent political strategies, most emerged as local strongmen, reabsorbed into traditional social and political structures but increasingly emphasizing Islamism and establishing ties with religious parties. Various sources of foreign aid empowered warlords and strengthened their patronage networks, in turn further undermining traditional patterns of life and disrupting tribal social codes in the countryside.[63] The overall result was fertile ground for warlordism to flourish.[64]

As conflict widened over territory and control of the Afghan state itself, broader regional coalitions formed where social control was relatively more cohesive, often along tribal or loosely ethnic lines. The fierce political competition enabled elites to make ethnicity salient as a political resource; this was a context in which conflict *became* partially ethnicized, rather than being provoked by ethnic tensions. Armed forces and ethnic groups were pulled back into the country's ethnoregional power networks, and a strong degree of regional autonomy developed in the face of national turmoil.[65] Rubin observes that the extent to which regional commanders could marshal autonomous political and bureaucratic organizations marked the differences among regions in the country.[66] The Pashtun areas in the South and East remained fragmented, although in the East the army of the Pashtun Gulbuddin Hekmatyar, supported by Pakistan, remained powerful. In other parts of the country regional strongmen consolidated their power

[62] Rubin 2002: 256–257. [63] Marten 2012. [64] Giustozzi 2009.
[65] Thier and Chopra 2002: 895.
[66] Rubin 2002: 258–264. This section draws heavily on this authoritative work.

in patterns that have lasted into contemporary Afghan politics. In the Northeast, Ahmad Shah Massoud, bolstered by the legitimacy of being a national resistance hero, commanded a regional capital and substantial contiguous territory along with the social network that formed the basis of Tajik power. In the North, the Uzbek Rashid Dostum still commanded over 40,000 militiamen, more than triple those led by Massoud, with whom he was still loosely allied.[67] Ismail Khan's Persian-dominated organization in the West, centered in the city of Herat, allowed him over the next decade to function essentially as an independent *emir* earning revenue from tolls and providing some public services to the population.

In the meantime, the Pashtun-dominated central state, still nominally under the control of Najibullah, disintegrated as the external aid that had held it together dried up. Rubin observes that the more clientelist and locally rooted tribal Pashtun culture was not well equipped to compete in the struggle for power, with the exception of Hekmatyar's organization, to which other Pashtuns turned for leadership.[68] A series of battles for control of Kabul followed – for control of the central state, indeed control over the very definition of Afghanistan – in which alliances formed around the most extensive and mobile organizations, again largely in ethnoregional patterns. These new political formations superficially evoked traditional social structure but, in reality, the traditional "micro-societies" of Afghanistan, built on tribal, ethnic, and linguistic lines, had fractured in the chaos that beset the country – in some cases actively undermined by manipulative regional powerholders – and reconstituted into new sources of power for opportunistic warlords.[69] Sarah Chayes evokes this disintegration of order in her portrait of Afghanistan, vividly relaying the contemporary consequences of the traditional concept of *yaghestan*, the chaotic age that befalls Afghanistan in cycles of rebirth and destruction.[70] The consolidation of national institutions proved ephemeral in the face of the constant realignment of interests; instead, patrimonialism has served as the basis of authority.

In April 1992, the Northern warlords Massoud and Dostum took control of Kabul. An interim government composed of *mujahideen* parties was assembled, but the state was a hollow one. All of the major

[67] Rubin 2002: 270. [68] Ibid.: 265. [69] Saikal 2005.
[70] Chayes 2006.

revenue sources were controlled by regional councils that retained the income for their own purposes. Militias roamed the streets of the capital fighting, looting, and raping. Paradoxically, the arrival of the interim government did nothing but intensify the competition for power. Long-standing rivalries among the parties quickly escalated into a new civil war. In particular, Hekmatyar refused to recognize the agreement since it made Massoud defense minister and effectively recognized that Kabul was controlled by the northern coalition. Rubin argues that this mutual animosity quickly took on the character and dimensions of a Pashtun versus non-Pashtun battle for the control of Afghanistan, once again reinforcing the ethnicized character of post-Soviet Afghan political conflict, which had "come to be dominated by four ethnically identified armed forces:"[71] Uzbeks under Dostum, the Shia alliance Hizb-e-Wahdat including the Hazara and Ismail Khan, Pashtuns under Hekmatyar, and Tajiks under Massoud. Yet neither the strategic objectives of these factions nor the discourse around them were explicitly ethnic. Alliances were not dictated by ethnicity – cooperation between the various commanders shifted quickly and unpredictably in a cycle of continuous fighting for control of Kabul. Hekmatyar, for example, soon successfully isolated Massoud by joining with the latter's erstwhile allies, Dostum and the Shia Hizb-e-Wahdat. Interethnic atrocities mounted as the militias fought each other for control of the capital by neighborhood, shattering the city's infrastructure. Kabul still bears the scars of its physical devastation in clearly visible layers that, in 2002, residents could wearily identify with the various successive conflicts that had wreaked damage on their city.[72]

At the same time, regional centers of power continued to play a dominant role in the social and political structure of the country. Particularly in the non-Pashtun areas of the North, Northeast, and West, state apparatuses and armed forces remained in place – albeit now under the control of regional strongmen rather than that of Kabul and thus forming the basis of power for the non-Pashtun groups who for the most part focused on asserting their regional autonomy.[73] The Hazaras enjoyed a great deal of independence in the central highlands territory known as Hazarajat. In the North, Rashid Dostum maintained his

[71] Rubin 2002: 273. [72] Personal conversations; Kabul, Afghanistan, June 2002.
[73] Rubin 2002: 274–278.

powerful political niche; having amassed armed forces of 120,000 men he guaranteed the security of the northern capital of Mazar-i Sharif, where the UN and other diplomatic missions moved their headquarters during this period. Ahmad Shah Massoud retained control over most of the Northeast, including the famed Panjshir Valley. In the West, Ismail Khan turned Herat into a relatively peaceful center of economic and cultural revival.

Into this fragmented sociopolitical structure stepped the Taliban in late 1994. According to the founding legend, a group of *madrasa* teachers and students led by Mullah Mohammed Omar formed the movement in order to end the power of the warlords, regain security in the face of the chronic anarchy, violence, and extortion that persisted under the local militias, and establish a pure Islamic regime.[74] The Taliban thus stepped into a political and institutional space that had emerged as a result of the preceding twenty years: the inter-elite battles, in which modernizing intelligentsia destroyed itself; and the collapse of state institutions after the Russian invasion and the onset of the *mujahideen* battles. In this space, *madrasa* networks became increasingly salient among a new elite while other institutional ties were being destroyed. The Taliban received significant levels of initial popular support in Pashtun-dominated areas by presenting themselves as an Islamic solution to state failure, and by establishing authority and strict order through *sharia* law. In so doing, the Taliban echoed the rationale of earlier Islamist parties in Afghanistan. This same rationale has, in turn, over the past decade enabled the Taliban to reassert some legitimacy in the southern parts of Afghanistan where the international community has failed to restore order and security.

Rubin points out that had the Taliban stopped at bringing order to the Pashtun areas of southern Afghanistan, "they might have joined about five other ethnoregional coalitions that existed at that time in negotiating a decentralized form of Afghan statehood."[75] But they transformed their movement into a political and administrative organization and were backed by large amounts of military and tactical aid from Pakistan, which saw the Taliban as a new ally in place of its former Pashtun surrogate, Gulbuddin Hekmatyar, who had failed to hold onto power. From their stronghold in Kandahar province, the Taliban

[74] Rubin 2002: xii. [75] Ibid.: xiii.

rapidly conquered territory and political power, capturing Kabul in September 1996. The *mujahideen* groups, having failed to establish a stable government in the face of their infighting, abandoned the capital almost without a fight. By August 1998, the Taliban controlled about 90 percent of the country's territory, thereby achieving a broader reach of authority across the country than any previous administration had been able to establish.

Within a month, however, those groups that had lost to the Taliban met in northern Afghanistan to form what became known as the Northern Alliance. This group continued to hold Afghanistan's UN seat. It was initially dominated by the Tajiks aligned with Ahmed Shah Massoud – who served as its de facto military and political leader – but also included Uzbek and Hazara groups, and even some Pashtuns. Yet with political power embedded in local strongmen and their various armed groups rather than unified a state apparatus, it had no effective organizational counterpart to the Taliban's administrative structure and could not mobilize foreign fighters as could the Taliban.[76] Afghanistan remained divided between the Taliban-controlled south and capital city and the Northern Alliance-controlled northern part of the country, into which the Taliban continued to make advances. The Taliban's rhetoric, objectives, and alliances became increasingly pan-Islamic rather than nationalist, particularly in the face of growing ostracization by the international community. Al-Qaeda, the global jihadist terrorist organization led by Osama bin Laden, became increasingly integrated into the Taliban organization through the personal relationship of the two leaders and the military alliance between the two groups.

These patterns persisted until October 7, 2001, when the United States began its bombing campaign in Afghanistan to root out Al-Qaeda and its Taliban sponsors in response to the terrorist attacks of September 11, 2001. In strategic partnership with the Northern Alliance on the ground, the United States helped to quickly rout the Taliban, liberating Mazar-i-Sharif on November 9 and Kabul on November 13. The Taliban abandoned even their stronghold in Kandahar on December 6, one day after the selection of Hamid Karzai, a Durrani tribal chief and former *mujahideen* leader, as chairman of the Afghan Interim Administration under the Bonn Agreement.

[76] Ibid.: xix.

The Afghanistan Bonn Agreement

The speed of Operation Enduring Freedom, the US military campaign in Afghanistan, forced a diplomatic scramble to bring together the country's non-Taliban leadership. UN Secretary-General Kofi Annan named Lakhdar Brahimi as his special representative to shepherd the process and negotiations. Events on the ground moved quickly, precipitating political responses. The day after the Northern Alliance marched into Kabul, the UN Security Council passed a resolution affirming the UN's central role in supporting Afghanistan's political transition efforts and calling for a new government that would be "broad-based, multi-ethnic and fully representative of all the Afghan people."[77] The intense combined diplomacy of the United Nations and the United States got the main Afghan political parties to agree to convene in Bonn to choose an interim government and map out the political transition process.[78] Representatives from four key groups were present: the various factions of the Northern Alliance; supporters of the former king, Zahir Shah; Pashtun *mujahideen*, tribal, and religious leaders based in Pakistan; and a mixture of Shia factions with ties to Iran. As the Bonn Agreement acknowledged in its preamble, the grouping was not fully representative. Brahimi is reported to have stressed repeatedly in Bonn that few would remember that the meeting had been unrepresentative if those there successfully fashioned a process resulting in legitimate and representative government[79] – an assertion that appears mistaken in retrospect. Afghan civil society groups held a tandem forum near Bonn, in an attempt to have alternative voices heard in the political process. Most obviously, the Taliban was not included – nor was their loose ally, the Hezb-i-Islami faction led by the Pashtun Islamist Gulbuddin Hekmatyar. The lack of representation of such spoiler groups meant later that the "Bonn process was ill designed to cope with their resurgence through political means."[80]

The Bonn Agreement of December 2001 – officially, the *Agreement on Provisional Arrangements in Afghanistan Pending the Re-Establishment of Permanent Government Institutions* – was not a ceasefire agreement between belligerents. Rather, it represents a different type of peace settlement, providing the framework for further negotiations about how peace would be achieved in Afghanistan. It

[77] United Nations Security Council Resolution 1378, November 14, 2001.
[78] Thier 2004. [79] Rubin 2004: 7. [80] Ponzio 2011: 183.

left for future resolution through the transitional governance process many major and contentious decisions, including, for example, questions of political power-sharing – both at the central level and between the center and the provinces – and the very nature of the Afghan state and its constitution. Nonetheless, the agreement established a series of milestones to which parties would have to adhere when the time came. The Afghan factions and the diaspora political leadership meeting in Bonn agreed, under the supervision of the UN, to the creation of an Interim Administration, endowed with Afghan sovereignty. This Interim Administration would be the main counterpart of the UN and other peacebuilding and reconstruction partners during the course of the transitional governance period. In recognition of the not fully representative agreement, the Interim Administration was to last only six months before the selection of a Transitional Administration. The Bonn Agreement also stipulated a two-year window for a new constitution to be drafted. The chairman of the interim and transitional administrations was endowed with the power to make law by decree with his cabinet's agreement.

The composition of the Interim Administration was agreed at the conference: Hamid Karzai was named chairman, and the rest of its members represented a carefully assembled mosaic of different ethnic and tribal leaders. Rubin observes that the Bonn Agreement reflected the distribution of political power at the time, which in turn was a result of the US strategy to oust the Taliban.[81] The composition of the Interim Administration was widely viewed as lopsided, at best. It had a high – critics would say too high – representation of Tajiks from the Northern Alliance in control of the most powerful ministries. The three key ministerial portfolios of Defense, Foreign Affairs, and the Interior were allocated to the three Panjshiri leaders who had served as Ahmed Shah Massoud's lieutenants – Mohammed Fahim, Abdullah Abdullah, and Yunus Qanooni, respectively.[82] Triumphant and resurgent warlords such as Ismail Khan and Rashid Dostum, who had participated in the fighting against the Taliban, regained control in their regions through their appointment to governorships. As is the fate of most losers in civil war, the Taliban stood no chance of being included

[81] Rubin 2002: xxxii. See also Goodson 2003 and Chayes 2006 on how the US military strategy produced longer-term political ramifications in Afghanistan.

[82] Massoud himself had been assassinated by suicide attackers on September 9, 2001.

in a power-sharing arrangement – but it remained a force with considerable support and organizational strength in the Pashtun-dominated southern parts of the country. In the Taliban home base of Kandahar province, the governorship was given to another warlord, the Pakistan-affiliated Gul Agha Shirzai. Independent militias continued to receive funding and weapons from coalition forces that sustained the fight against the Taliban instead of disbanding and becoming part of a new civil society. Some factions reignited old internecine conflicts quickly after the Bonn conference, vying for power and the control of territory and toll revenue.[83] On the other hand, no widespread threat to the security and stability of the country emerged immediately, nor any major challenge or threat to the Bonn process itself.

Elite Settlements in Comparative Perspective

Although violent conflicts in Cambodia, East Timor, and Afghanistan were all sparked in some way by decolonization and Cold War politics and each lasted for just over two decades, this chapter has demonstrated that the three violent struggles had distinct motivations and features that are crucial to understanding the peacebuilding record that followed (Table 3.1).

Notwithstanding these important differences, the international community sought to pursue sustainable peace in each country by mandating a UN peace operation to implement the peace settlement, governing in partnership with domestic counterparts while pursuing simultaneous statebuilding and democratization. Chapter 4 picks up this story, examining how competing domestic and international interests and visions of political order played out over the implementation of those interventions. It demonstrates that the peace agreements are indeed best viewed as the momentary manifestation of an ongoing power struggle among elites, one that continues after the ink is dry. This dynamic is not restricted to the countries considered here. Analysts have noted, for example, that while outside actors viewed peace deals in the Democratic Republic of the Congo, Liberia, and Sudan as binding commitments among belligerent groups, the parties to conflict saw these settlements in more instrumental terms, such that they

[83] The militias had an estimated 200,000 soldiers, while the newly constituted Afghan National Army remained small and relatively weak.

Table 3.1 *The Cambodian, East Timorese, and Afghan conflicts and settlements in comparative perspective*

Country Cases	Antecedent Conflict	Peace Settlement
Cambodia	Twenty-one-year civil war (1970–1991) between three major, coherent factions opposed to each other on ideological grounds, each supported by external patrons during the Cold War.	1991 Paris Peace Agreement: the outcome of a mutually hurting stalemate between still hostile groups, ushering in an attempt at power-sharing governance.
East Timor	Twenty-four-year resistance struggle (1975–1999) against Indonesian occupation waged by a guerilla movement and a relatively incoherent national resistance front.	1999 independence referendum: marked a final end to occupation, with the umbrella revolutionary front seeing no major opposition in the transitional phase.
Afghanistan	Twenty-two-year anti-imperialist struggle and civil war (1979–2001) among many fairly coherent ethnotribal groupings with regional power bases.	2001 Bonn Agreement: enabled the international community to play kingmaker, while empowering specific ethnoregional groups in complex power-sharing compromises.

continually adapted their actions to the evolving context in ways that served their own conceptions of political order and adversely affected subsequent peacebuilding efforts in these countries.[84]

The political bargains represented by brokered peace deals typically obsolesce over time in post-conflict countries instead of representing a stable elite political settlement. How quickly and to what extent that obsolescence occurs depends in large part on the degree of credible commitment among parties to the deal, an issue this chapter has characterized. Also significant is which parties, if any, are marked as victors,

[84] On Congo, see Lemarchand 2012; on Liberia, see Reno 2004; and, on Sudan, see Srinivasan 2012.

and the power realignment that starts to take place in response. The Cambodian parties to the Paris Peace Agreement viewed their obligations as particularly limited because there was no credible sanction for any one group if it failed to follow through on its commitment. The ability of the different groups to enforce each other's agreement was especially asymmetrical in the Cambodian case: the weaker parties to the bargain had little leverage to penalize the State of Cambodia, which could rely on its grip on the government apparatus to act as it chose. The power-sharing compromise embodied in the Supreme National Council very quickly proved pyrrhic. In East Timor, by contrast, the settlement that ended the war was an independence vote achieved by domestic elites loosely united under the umbrella resistance front of the National Council for Timorese Resistance. There, elite factions did not have to conclude a brokered peace deal per se; instead they had to come together to govern the country with the UN-mandated transitional authority. At the outset, the Timorese elite factions were thus relatively united against more empowered international peacebuilders and the higher degree of international assistance acted as a check against any of the Timorese factions reneging from the settlement. Yet, there, too, as the peace operation unfolded, the distinct elite factional interests evident during East Timor's initial civil war at the time of Portuguese decolonization began to assert themselves with lasting consequences. The Afghan parties to the Bonn Agreement demonstrated a moderate degree of commitment to it, facilitated in part by a series of political deals or side-payments that ensured that different interests were served. The relatively dispersed power among different Afghan elites, with no one faction enjoying a high degree of asymmetrical power, also contributed to a relatively stable early peace process. The formal Bonn process, however, was increasingly compromised over the course of its implementation as the informal sources of power and conflict in the country began to reassert themselves.

In general, internationally brokered peace settlements appear better at conferring international legitimacy upon domestic elites who have a tenuous hold on domestic legitimacy than in achieving true compromise among competing elites. This is also a finding not restricted to the three countries considered here. Devon Curtis observes that the Arusha peace process of 1998–2000 that established Burundi's peacebuilding trajectory, similarly "conferred legitimacy on individuals and parties who otherwise had no popular support, leading to the charge that the Arusha process had international and regional, but not popular legitimacy."[85] Many of the most contentious issues in the Arusha peace process were in fact left explicitly for the parties to the agreement to negotiate during the transitional phase.[86] Like in Cambodia, the final power-sharing agreements in Burundi were the result of office trading among elites focused on sharing the spoils of power, in many cases the very individuals who had fostered conflict and who threatened continued violence when their interests were not met.

These elite settlements mark the first critical juncture on the peacebuilding pathway. The notion of path dependence rests on the insight that political and institutional dynamics are often self-reinforcing: the choices made at critical junctures – in this case the elite settlement as the terms upon which a peace operation is predicated – have a long-lasting effect on the political landscape. Pierson points to the "enduring consequences that often stem from the emergence of particular institutional arrangements."[87] In particular, power inequalities that are relatively modest to begin with can be reinforced and amplified over time in a feedback loop. Agreed upon institutional arrangements, in turn, can be manipulated and subverted by elites in various ways. The following two chapters illustrate how these processes play out over the remaining phases of the peacebuilding pathway – the transitional governance phase of an international intervention and its aftermath.

[85] Curtis 2013: 85. [86] Campbell and Uvin 2015; and Curtis 2007.
[87] Pierson 2004: 11.

4 International Intervention and Elite Incentives

Peacebuilding became a signature undertaking of the international community in the post-Cold War era. As the number of United Nations-led peace operations proliferated globally, so, too, did study of these interventions, which developed along three major avenues of analysis. First, there are numerous case study-based assessments of specific peacebuilding attempts. These are extremely rich in empirical detail, many penned by peacebuilding scholar-practitioners reflecting on their experiences in different countries.[1] The best of these accounts provide fascinating narratives of how domestic elites interacted with peacebuilders during implementation of particular interventions; however, they do not typically attempt to reach any broader generalizations about the patterns of peacebuilding. A second body of work focuses more on the machinery and mechanisms of peacebuilding approaches themselves, offering detailed interpretation of operational mandates that focus on how the specifics of intervention – such as mission scope, size, multidimensionality, mechanisms of implementation, and so on – affect outcomes.[2] These studies tend to be geared toward identifying the technocratic challenges associated with peacebuilding and thereby generating targeted and informed measures for improving practice. The third body of scholarly work on peacebuilding has focused on more theoretically motivated analyses of international interventions. Within this strand of writing, both case-oriented and quantitative empirical studies have aimed to offer generalized insights on the way in which specific components of interventions – such as the degree and scope of the mandate, often termed the "footprint" – and some consideration of the broader conditions under which they are implemented affect the relative success of peacebuilding

[1] Examples of such studies on the countries examined here include Doyle 1995 and Ratner 1995 on Cambodia; Martin 2001 and Smith 2003 on East Timor; and Ponzio 2011 on Afghanistan.

[2] For example, Caplan 2005; and Chesterman 2004.

interventions. The standard analytical approach is thus evaluative and variable-centered, based on a probabilistic logic – delving into what mission parameters and contextual factors condition the likelihood of success.[3]

Collectively, the scholarship treats peacebuilding interventions, in effect, as exogenous processes that are applied in post-conflict countries and thus measures governance outcomes in these countries against the yardstick of the modern political order that is sought through peacebuilding. The UN's transitional governance approach to transformative peacebuilding structures the pursuit of rule-bound, effective, and legitimate governance by guiding domestic political elites through a series of choices about institutional architecture. This process, as it is designed, results in new administrative structures and constitutional arrangements that are tailored to local contexts and aspire to the highest international standards of democratic governance. Accordingly, peace operations are extolled as relative successes if they end with some degree of effective and legitimate governance being successfully transplanted into their host countries via this method of institutional engineering.

Yet, in one post-conflict country after another, initial euphoria at the successful holding of elections and design of the formal institutions for democratic governance has turned over time into relative dismay at the poor governance outcomes that arise in the aftermath of intervention. The transitional governance approach achieves some important successes in establishing the formal institutional infrastructure of legitimate and effective governance. The part of the story that has been missing is that the domestic political dynamics set in motion by the peace operation itself hamper the meaningful longer-term consolidation of governance outcomes in specific patterns. This chapter, like other work before it, focuses squarely on the peacebuilding interventions implemented by the United Nations in tandem with domestic counterparts. It does so, however, through a historical institutionalist lens that identifies the patterns in how domestic political elites interact with peacebuilding interventions to iteratively reshape the transitional governance process and actively engage in building neopatrimonial instead of modern political order. The case-centered, conjunctural

[3] Exemplars of this type of approach include Doyle and Sambanis 2006; Howard 2008; Paris 2004; and Zürcher et al. 2013.

logic helps to better identify the causal mechanisms that contribute to longer term governance outcomes.

Moreover, this chapter's focus on the transitional governance experiences of the three countries demonstrates the significance of temporal sequence. The manner in which peacebuilding contributes to the building of political order is shown to be path-dependent. The phenomenon of increasing returns is clearly on display, such that previously available options and strategies – for both domestic elites and international actors – recede once certain choices are made. In turn, political actors can be seen to be reorganizing their strategies around the path taken. The fact that temporal location – when certain things occur or choices are made, relative to others – matters is also made especially clear in terms of the significance of the early selection of specific counterparts for the transitional governance process.[4] In short, this chapter highlights how decisions made for the sake of expedience and practicality have long-term political consequences. Foregone alternatives that may have been more desirable become increasingly difficult to reach as time passes and countries move along the peacebuilding pathway.

Peacebuilding through transitional governance rests upon two distinct characteristics that contribute to unintended governance consequences in post-conflict countries. Underpinning the transformative model, first, is the implicit assumption that statebuilding and democracy-building are mutually reinforcing processes that can be advanced fruitfully in post-conflict countries through external peace operations. Second, the transitional element of the intervention, by which the United Nations takes on some degree of executive state function for a two-to-three-year period to ensure basic governance needs are met, requires the identification of a domestic counterpart with which the UN can govern in tandem. This chapter demonstrates, through an examination of the interventions in Cambodia, East Timor, and Afghanistan, how the interplay between these two hallmarks of the transitional governance approach undermine the basic objective of transformative peacebuilding, which is establishing the basis for rule-bound, effective, and legitimate political order. The three cases illustrate how the transitional governance experience itself empowers specific domestic elites, conferring legitimate authority upon them and offering them financial resources and sources of patronage. The

[4] Thelen and Mahoney 2015: 20–24 discuss these features of temporal analysis.

elections that mark the end point of international interventions, in turn, empower these elites to occupy the legitimate political space even as they offer a focal point for the consolidation of hierarchical patron–client networks.

This dynamic becomes evident over the course of transitional governance, as the series of facilitated decisions it embodies alter the post-conflict political order in subtle, yet lasting ways. This chapter illustrates how the principles underpinning transformative peacebuilding are more deeply flawed because they also fail to take into account how domestic political elites will use the resources bestowed by the international community in their pursuit of forging neopatrimonial political order. It focuses on the international peacebuilding interventions in Cambodia, East Timor, and Afghanistan, splitting the analysis of each case into two sections. First, the transitional governance period is portrayed as, at heart, a process of institutional engineering, where the interaction between domestic elites and international peacebuilders takes place, in many respects, as a series of negotiations around these institutions. Second, the first post-conflict election in each country is discussed. Serving as the end point of intervention, these elections are crucial, externally imposed moments of open political contestation – and their results confer lasting political advantages to those elites who claim victory in them.[5]

The historical institutionalist lens offers a fruitful perspective to help make sense of what occurs over the course of these interventions. James Mahoney and Kathleen Thelen advance a theory of institutional change whereby actors motivated to change outcomes use different strategies to exploit the ambiguity in the interpretation of rules to their advantage by redeploying the rules to suit their own purposes or changing those rules outright.[6] "Insurrectionaries" take the most obvious and visible route to change institutions, actively mobilizing against them. But three other sets of strategies offer fine characterizations of the myriad more subtle and yet equally effective ways in which elites can and do operate within the neopatrimonial hybrid between patrimonial and legal-rational forms of authority. "Subversive" actors conform in the short run to the current system, while biding their time to achieve

[5] Pierson 2015: 133 points to the value of anchoring analysis around such moments of political contestation.

[6] Mahoney and Thelen 2010: 22–29.

their longer-term change goals. "Parasitic" actors exploit the current set of institutions even as they depend on those institutions to achieve gain. "Opportunistic" actors thrive in conditions of institutional ambiguity, successfully exploiting the numerous possibilities within the prevailing system to advance their goals. This chapter illustrates how the winning elites in the three cases considered here have used *all* of these institutional change agent strategies in obtaining their preferred form of political order.

Transitional Governance in Cambodia

The Cambodian transitional governance experience was the first of its kind, with the UN being responsible for holding a national election as well as governing the country in collaboration with counterparts.[7] With an outlay of $2.3 billion over five years and 22,000 people deployed to the mission, it dwarfed spending on any previous UN peace operation.[8] Two issues are evident when analyzing the United Nations Transitional Authority in Cambodia (UNTAC). First, the principle of power-sharing among the four Cambodian factions that was embodied in the Paris Peace Agreement and re-emphasized in UNTAC's mandate proved a red herring, since the various Cambodian factions were not truly reconciled to the agreement and refused to cooperate with UNTAC's attempts to implement its principles. Second, as a result, one particular faction – the State of Cambodia (SOC) governing regime, led by Hun Sen – was allowed to maintain its grip on the state apparatus. Thus entrenched, even defeat in the first election was not enough to dislodge this regime's hold on power. The UNTAC experience illustrates vividly the basic tension between statebuilding and democratization embodied in the transitional governance approach. The need to continue governing the country meant the UN had to rely on the SOC. The SOC, in turn, was able to parlay its control over the state into a set of political resources that enabled it to perform better than expected in the election and its immediate aftermath.

[7] The UN Transition Assistance Group (UNTAG) deployed in Namibia from 1989–1990 was responsible for some elements of election supervision and implementation – but under UNTAG the UN did not assume any dimension of host country sovereignty or share civil administrative responsibilities with the Namibian government.

[8] Zürcher et al. 2013: 60.

The Paris Peace Agreement signed by the four Cambodian factions in October 1991 established the two major features of the peace settlement. First, the agreement was the genesis of UNTAC, the peacebuilding operation mandated several months later to implement the peace settlement.[9] UNTAC's wide-ranging mandate gave the UN a brand new role and scope of action in a peacebuilding intervention. Second, the Paris accords also mandated a particular role for the Supreme National Council (SNC). This quadripartite body was created in the run-up to the final peace agreement to achieve binding consensus among the four Cambodian parties. With the peace settlement concluded, the SNC became the ongoing institutional manifestation of that temporary consensus. It comprised a membership of 13 individuals representing each of the four parties, with Prince Sihanouk named as the supposedly neutral president of the group; the six SOC delegates were loyal to Hun Sen's clique within the regime.[10] It was endowed with Cambodian sovereignty and authority and it would govern the country as UNTAC's parallel domestic counterpart, acting as an advisory body in the transitional governance period before elections were held. Doyle notes that the Security Council's endorsement of the SNC helped, in turn, to legitimize its delegation of authority for administrative and electoral affairs to UNTAC.[11]

UNTAC represented a new, transformative approach to peacebuilding. It was the first UN peace operation to be mandated with the organization and supervision of an electoral process from start to finish. Its roles on this front included promulgating electoral laws, organizing the polling and monitoring, educating Cambodians about their new electoral rights, and certifying the elections as free and fair. Along with its other responsibilities – including the civil administration component, discussed below; a military component monitoring the ceasefire and demobilization of the factions' armed wings; a civilian police component; a refugee repatriation component; and a human rights component – the electoral component made UNTAC larger than any previous peacekeeping operation and the most intrusive operation yet in the internal affairs of a member state.[12]

9 UNTAC was established by UN Security Council Resolution 745 on February 28, 1992.

10 Strangio 2014: 47.

11 Doyle 1995.

12 Doyle and Sambanis 2006: 213–217.

UNTAC also assumed an unprecedented degree of transitional administrative authority in Cambodia, granted with the formal consent of the four factions in the Paris Agreement in an attempt to ensure a neutral political environment for the conduct of the first elections. UNTAC's central mandate was to help control the governance of Cambodia in the transitional period. The large Civil Administration Component of the operation handled this dimension of the peacebuilding strategy by monitoring and supervising existing bureaucratic structures in five designated key areas of civil administration – defense, public security, finance, information, and foreign affairs.[13] This combination of administrative and electoral organization functions makes Cambodia the first post-conflict country in which the UN implemented a strategy of peacebuilding through transitional governance.

As UNTAC worked to implement its mandate, it became clear that the peacebuilding process was compromised by the competing conceptions among the four Cambodian parties as to the nature of the intervention. The true consent from each of those parties to the peace settlement and the intervention was tenuous at best. Those inconsistent commitments translated directly into problems for the institutional mechanisms of transitional governance in Cambodia. Each of the parties to peace, for example, viewed the relationship between UNTAC and the SNC in a different way.[14] A major point of contention was the role envisioned for Hun Sen's State of Cambodia (SOC) and how it would interact with UNTAC and the SNC in which it represented just one of the four distinct sets of Cambodian preferences. The SOC itself, relying on its control over the apparatus of both central and subnational government, essentially continued to emphasize its own domestic governing authority. By treaty, however, it was the SNC that officially embodied Cambodian sovereignty. For the Khmer Rouge, the KPNLF, and FUNCINPEC, the SNC – with their participation – was the only legitimate source of political power in Cambodia. In their conception, UNTAC would act on behalf of the SNC, thereby rendering Hun Sen's SOC relatively powerless. Prince Sihanouk was given special authority in the SNC under the peace accords in the hope that he could bolster UNTAC's stance and help push the factions toward compliance.

[13] Doyle 1995: 37–40 describes the manner in which UNTAC exerted this control function over these five key administrative areas, as well as monitoring and supervision of national and provincial administration.

[14] Ratner 1995: 159–160.

Yet he turned out to be mostly detrimental to the process, hesitating to break deadlocks but insisting that the UN defer to him. UNTAC, in line with the Permanent Five's initial design of the arrangement, envisioned the SNC as an important reconciliation body that would help it make and implement important decisions. When it was proven wrong on that front, UNTAC had to assume more of the responsibility itself.

These competing visions of how transitional governance would unfold meant that the concerned parties never reached agreement on how to implement the peacebuilding process as envisioned by the Paris Peace Agreement. Frederick Brown and David Timberman observe that UNTAC had essentially been "charged with the task of enforcing an extraordinarily complex, time-phased scenario predicated on an environment of conciliation and compromise among the Khmer parties that did not, in fact, exist."[15] Many have argued, in addition, that the Permanent Five did not give UNTAC the necessary teeth to achieve its objectives, especially in the realm of day-to-day administration. UNTAC was supposed to ensure a neutral political environment by supervising the five designated key areas of civil administration and thereby preventing any of the factions – particularly the SOC – from using government resources to influence the elections. The mandate was to "control" Cambodia and the four factions through supervision, rather than actually govern the country. Yet the framers of the Paris Peace Agreement and the UNTAC mandate did not specify how this should be done, leaving it to the discretion of UNTAC's command, led by the Special Representative of the Secretary-General (SRSG), Yasushi Akashi. Many in the United Nations felt that pushing the incumbent SOC regime too far on the issue of political neutrality would derail the peace process. In turn, the SOC refused to relinquish its control of the state – in practice, it "simply administered around UNTAC."[16] An UNTAC progress report found, for example, that high-ranking SOC officials gave the ministries and provincial administrations instructions in how not to cooperate with UNTAC.[17] This failure to pry away the SOC's grip on the state apparatus later fed into today's relatively poor governance outcomes in Cambodia. It became apparent closer to the elections that UNTAC's control over the other three factions was negligible as well.

[15] Brown and Timberman 1998: 17. [16] Doyle 1995: 35.
[17] Cited in Doyle 1995: 44.

The Cambodian Elections of 1993

In the face of these challenges with regard to transitional governance, UNTAC essentially abandoned its attempts to implement the comprehensive Paris peace settlement. Midway through the peace operation toward the end of 1992, supported by a series of UN Security Council resolutions, it reformulated its mandate to focus on the election and create a legitimate Cambodian government. UNTAC did indeed successfully hold Cambodia's first democratic national election in May 1993. Analysts assessing UNTAC close to the end of its tenure in 1993 concluded that of all its various dimensions its Electoral Component was probably the most successful.[18] Today it is clearer that while this may have been true in a technical sense – in terms of registering voters and holding a relatively conflict-free, high-turnout election, even in the face of a high degree of voter intimidation and harassment by the SOC and the Khmer Rouge – UNTAC failed, to a large degree, in reaching the objective of creating legitimate government as a central component of modern political order.

Subsequent problems of statebuilding and democratic consolidation can be traced back to conditions at the time of the first election and the fact that the effort dedicated to the electoral process masked the deep antagonisms in the Cambodian polity. In early 1993, the Khmer Rouge withdrew entirely from the electoral and peacebuilding process, leaving the capital city, refusing to disarm and demobilize as agreed, and preventing UNTAC from entering the zones of the country it controlled.[19] It mounted a campaign of obstruction against the other Cambodian parties and UNTAC and succeeded in generating an atmosphere of instability and violence around the electoral process. Perversely, the SOC's political fortunes rose as there was an increase in Khmer Rouge-perpetrated electoral violence – in a context of political instability, it was seen as the only party with the armed forces capable of containing the Khmer Rouge and maintaining political order. Indeed, it

[18] Doyle 1995; and Shawcross 1994.

[19] Early in the UN's tenure in May 1992, an UNTAC convoy carrying both its chief administrator and military commander traveling near the Khmer Rouge stronghold of Pailin came across a roadblock marked by a thin bamboo pole laid across the road – and simply turned around upon being refused access by the callow Khmer Rouge guards (Strangio 2014: 53–54). This widely reported incident was seen to represent the UN's capitulation to the Khmer Rouge and its broader unwillingness to press on the more difficult parts of its mandate.

used this reason to delay demobilizing its own armed forces. At the same time, however, popular resentment about the SOC's corrupt practices was brewing.[20] The Khmer Rouge's suspicion of the SOC – their expressed reason for reneging on the Paris Peace Agreement – was not entirely unreasonable, considering the trajectory taken by the CPP and Hun Sen to their later levels of political hegemony. At the time, however, UNTAC, and particularly Akashi, viewed the Khmer Rouge as the one true threat to the peace process, and proceeded to systematically marginalize the radical party from the elections to prevent it from derailing the entire peace.[21]

A successful election became Akashi's single-minded priority in the desire to be able to claim the UNTAC mandate had been achieved, especially in light of the relative failure to demobilize and adequately supervise the Cambodian factions.[22] Despite warnings from UNTAC officials and others, Akashi did not perceive the SOC as a potential spoiler and he was therefore caught entirely off-guard when it explicitly began undermining the peace process immediately after the first elections.[23] The SOC's participation in the elections was crucial to UNTAC's success as Akashi came to define it. Yet that meant that he failed to use the leverage granted to UNTAC in the Paris Peace Agreement to reduce the SOC's grip on the administrative organs of state, in retrospect the most intractable future impediment to legitimate governance in the country. The head of UNTAC's administration, Gerald Porcell, lamented as he resigned in protest in February 1993 that as long as UNTAC lacked "the political will to apply the peace accords, its control cannot but be ineffective."[24]

In effect, Akashi's strategy for dealing with the Khmer Rouge strengthened the hand of the SOC, making it by far the strongest faction on the Cambodian political scene, militarily, politically,

[20] Strangio 2014: 51–52.

[21] Stedman 1997 argues that Akashi used the elections effectively in managing the Khmer Rouge's spoiler behavior. This observation was corroborated in author interviews with donor officials and civil society leaders; Phnom Penh, Cambodia, May 2005.

[22] UNTAC also facilitated the opening of civic space for what began as a vibrant and promising NGO sector in Cambodia and oversaw the repatriation of some 360,000 Cambodians from the Thai border camps and their reintegration into Cambodian society. Strangio 2014: 60.

[23] Greenhill and Major 2007; Peou 2002; and Stedman 1997.

[24] Quoted in Stedman 1997: 33–34.

and administratively. As the UNTAC Commander John Sanderson observed, "it was not the Khmer Rouge, but rather the SOC, which had the capacity to undermine the election or to overturn the verdict of the people."[25] Even before the 1993 election, the SOC had manipulated the terms of the peace agreement to its own advantage: the separation of the State of Cambodia (SOC) and its political party, the Cambodian People's Party (CPP), was in name only and hardly enforceable. During this period, the SOC made continuous efforts to interfere with the campaigning of other parties and practiced widespread voter intimidation and buyoffs, as well as violence in the run-up to the elections that included the killing of political activists from the other parties.[26] UNTAC found it impossible to separate the government's resources, in the hands of the SOC, from the funds used by the Cambodian People's Party (CPP), the political party that the governing regime formed in 1991 just before the peace accords were signed. UNTAC investigations found that the SOC state apparatus was often used to campaign on behalf of the CPP, for example.[27] To those who controlled the State of Cambodia and the apparatus of government, defeat in the country's first election was unimaginable and they did everything they could to ensure victory.

The elections, held from May 23–28, 1993, although hardly held in a "neutral political environment," were successful in terms of the 90 percent voter turnout and were declared free and fair by UNTAC and other international observers.[28] The results were surprising and unambiguous: FUNCINPEC won 45 percent of the vote and the CPP came second with 38 percent, translating into 58 and 51 seats, respectively, in the 120-member constituent assembly that was to draft and adopt a new constitution before evolving into the national legislature. FUNCINPEC's leader, Prince Norodom Ranariddh, was Sihanouk's son and the heir to his political power base, and many observers attributed FUNCINPEC's victory to a nostalgic, nationalist vote for the monarchy. What followed immediately after the elections was extraordinary and yet a characteristic marker of the future direction of the Cambodian political scene – as well as a fascinating illustration of what

25 Quoted in Greenhill and Major 2007: 34.

26 Heder and Ledgerwood 1996.

27 Doyle 1995: 41.

28 UNTAC's radio broadcasts and civic education program are credited with convincing voters to ignore intimidation and come to the polls, with the secrecy of their ballots guaranteed. Shawcross 1994; and Strangio 2014.

happens when there is an imbalance between the formal writ of power and its informal, or actual, exercise. The CPP simply refused to acknowledge FUNCINPEC's electoral victory and actively subverted it. It took an elaborate series of steps to instead entrench itself in power, including accusing the UN of massive fraud, roping in Sihanouk, and blackmailing the opposition with a short-lived secession and increased violence. As Ranariddh realized that the CPP would never hand over full administrative power FUNCINPEC was forced to compromise and agreed, in a deal brokered by Sihanouk, to share power equally with the CPP in the new interim government. UNTAC was left a bystander in these domestic political maneuverings and, subsequently, the CPP's heightened power made UNTAC helpless to block its bid for hegemony. Akashi supported the power-sharing solution, believing at the time that failure to compromise would undermine the triumph of having held the election. Indeed, he believed the "practical wisdom" combined FUNCINPEC's political power and victory with the administrative power and experience of the CPP.[29]

While many, Cambodians and international officials alike, were dismayed that the final arrangement did not truly reflect FUNCINPEC's electoral victory, there was little question that "the compromise aptly reflected the administrative, military, and even financial muscle of the CPP."[30] Sihanouk and Ranariddh even agreed to the CPP's stipulation that all votes in the new Assembly be passed by a two-thirds majority, which ensured that the CPP's consent would be needed in any legislation and hence enabled it to continue to dominate the business of government. In practice, moreover, the CPP retained control of all the provinces, even those it had lost in the election. In many central ministries, the personnel and policies remained unchanged from those of the SOC. Although the process of army consolidation began, the CPP retained control over the police. The SOC/CPP regime thus maintained its stranglehold on the state apparatus and would soon leverage this essential arena of strength into an outright power grab. The Khmer Rouge, by this point completely marginalized in the political process, refused to accept the new government. Cambodia's new combined army attacked Khmer Rouge positions all over the country and

[29] Yasushi Akashi, 1993, "The Challenge of Peace-keeping in Cambodia: Lessons to be Learned." Paper presented at the School of International and Public Affairs, Columbia University, New York, November 29, 1993.
[30] Shawcross 1994: 29.

the government appealed to Khmer Rouge soldiers to lay down their arms, which many did. Although a rump Khmer Rouge insurgency continued for a few more years, its campaign for power was effectively ended with the 1993 electoral process.

The Paris Peace Agreement and the transitional process they initiated themselves shaped the consolidated governance outcomes to ensue in Cambodia. From the beginning, the international community seemed resigned to allowing the State of Cambodia regime to retain its control of the country. In the words of Brown and Timberman: "The implicit quid pro quo of the Paris Accords in 1991 . . . had been that the incumbent CPP would have a fair shot at political dominance if it would go along with the rules of the game of UNTAC and abide by the results of the election."[31] Even when the CPP did not win, however, its lukewarm and inconsistent participation in the UN transitional governance process was enough to convey upon it the stamp of legitimacy it had lacked during its previous period of rule. In turn, as the next chapter demonstrates, the convoluted power-sharing arrangement that resulted from the election created two separate governments led by Ranariddh and Hun Sen who had been named first and second prime ministers.

The CPP's push to restore its political dominance and subvert the unstable power-sharing arrangement became the defining characteristic of political jockeying in Cambodia over the next decade. Several Cambodia experts warned in the mid-1990s of the CPP's and Hun Sen's "creeping coup,"[32] which later proved prescient. Brown and Timberman blame the international community for "retreat[ing] from its commitment to establishing a genuinely legitimate government when it acquiesced to Hun Sen's demands for power sharing" after the 1993 election.[33] They go on to observe that by effectively allowing Hun Sen, with Sihanouk's complicity, to override the electoral results, the international community became party to an act that broadcasted the message that power politics would continue to prevail in Cambodia over the rule of law and the electoral process. Yet, at the time, the CPP–FUNCINPEC coalition seemed to many to be the only option in an environment in which FUNCINPEC had electoral legitimacy but the CPP had institutional and military strength.

[31] Brown and Timberman 1998: 19.
[32] For example, Doyle 1996.
[33] Brown and Timberman 1998: 27.

A Constituent Assembly committee drafted a constitution in almost total secrecy, with barely any consultation with either UNTAC or Cambodian civil society groups, resulting in a document that was written and favored by the CPP, albeit one that was liberal in spirit.[34] The new permanent government would include two co-prime ministers and the two-thirds voting majority was also retained, both at the demand of the CPP and against FUNCINPEC's wishes. Ministerial posts and governorships were divided among the two parties. In reality, however, the CPP's continued control over the bureaucracy, army, and police was a locus of political power that simply outweighed FUNCINPEC's electoral victory. In terms of democratic consolidation and how power was distributed across the political system, the elite bargaining over the interim and then permanent arrangements was far more important than the elections themselves. The CPP, having used its leverage to get a power-sharing compromise and stack the institutional architecture in its favor, waited for its chance to seize power outright.

Transitional Governance in East Timor

The United Nations Transitional Administration in East Timor (UNTAET) represents the high-water mark of the transitional governance approach and its transformative peacebuilding aspirations. The international community spent $2 billion on the first five years of the Timorese peace operation and deployed more than 10,000 military and civilian personnel there; extraordinary figures for a country of fewer than one million people.[35] UNTAET was designated as the repository of East Timorese sovereignty until the country was made fully independent, in a mandate that represents the greatest degree of executive, legislative, and judicial authority a UN mission has exercised in a post-conflict nation to date.[36] The Cambodian experience represented the

[34] Author interviews with Cambodian opposition legislators, donor officials, and civil society leaders; Phnom Penh, Cambodia, May 2005. Also, Marks 2010.

[35] Zürcher et al. 2013: 60. According to Zürcher et al.'s estimates, per capita spending on peacebuilding in East Timor was about ten times more than in Cambodia and Afghanistan.

[36] UNTAET, alone among UN peacebuilding missions, was even granted effective treaty-making powers, which it exercised in signing an assistance agreement with the International Development Association (World Bank) and in initiating talks on dividing the Timor Gap seabed oil and gas reserves with Australia.

dire difficulties associated with pursuing effective and legitimate governance in a country where the parties were not truly reconciled. East Timor represents the more subtle and yet equally real complexities of attempting to transplant modern political order in a context of apparent elite consensus and a relative alignment with the objectives of the international community.

The Security Council mandate for UNTAET instructed the peace operation to guide East Timor to a state ready for independence.[37] Yet it provided no roadmap – along the lines of the Paris Peace Agreement for Cambodia, for example – for how to proceed or how to incorporate East Timorese participation during the process. UNTAET first addressed the governance of East Timor by directly assuming the bulk of administrative and executive functions, moving only in mid-2000 to begin the process of sharing and passing on authority to its Timorese counterparts.[38] UNTAET defenders have argued in retrospect that the transitional governance exercise adopted gradually increasing levels of East Timorese participation in decision-making processes over time. Yet the Special Representative of the Secretary-General (SRSG), Sergio Vieira de Mello, himself acknowledged that increasing Timorese participation in the governance of the country was a process of "false starts and hard-won political accommodations."[39]

UNTAET's strategy was to emphasize regular consultations with a small group of core leaders from the National Council for Timorese Resistance (CNRT) – including, in particular, Xanana Gusmão, Bishop Carlos Belo, José Ramos-Horta, Mari Alkatiri (the leader of the FRETILIN cadre returned from exile in Mozambique), and Mario Carrascalão (a leading Timorese businessman who had served as governor of East Timor under the Indonesian authorities but was widely seen to have worked on behalf of the Timorese population during his governorship). These CNRT leaders were viewed by the UN as the authentic representatives of the people of East Timor and Gusmão was the undisputed first among equals. The head of the earlier UN Mission in East Timor (UNAMET), Ian Martin, wrote that the UN believed that Gusmão's direct participation was crucial: UN representatives saw that progress in the negotiations before the referendum was

[37] UNTAET was established by UN Security Council Resolution 1272 on October 25, 1999.

[38] Center on International Cooperation 2006.

[39] Goldstone 2004: 86.

made only when Gusmão was present and the UN itself took big steps forward only after consulting him in his Jakarta prison cell.[40] Vieira de Mello later acknowledged that this elite consultation system, albeit well intentioned, did not go far enough and that its Timorese partners should have been brought on board earlier and should have been consulted more thoroughly and substantively on matters of policy formulation and implementation.[41] In contrast, for example, the World Bank was seen as rather more successful at including Timorese in both needs assessment and policy formulation, most notably in the Joint Assessment Mission that took place in October and November 1999 immediately after the referendum violence was ended in order to identify reconstruction and development priorities.[42]

The timing and sequencing of the transitional governance process created some immediate challenges for future statebuilding and democratization prospects. Most observers agree that the slow pace of incorporating Timorese views and participation in government – a process that came to be called "Timorization" – was the most problematic aspect of the experiment, proving extremely troublesome for UNTAET's ability to govern and orchestrate a transition.[43] Here I contend, furthermore, that UNTAET's handling of the problem – especially the manner in which it chose its main counterparts – allowed the entrenchment of particular institutions and a certain pattern of political behavior that subsequently had adverse effects on democratic consolidation and governability in East Timor. Sue Ingram makes a similar argument, going so far as to contend that, in its lack of attention to forging a political settlement among Timorese elites, "UNTAET built the wrong peace."[44] From this perspective, two things went wrong: not enough Timorese participation in government; and, when Timorization occurred, too much emphasis on just the CNRT and its elites, which prejudiced the political process in favor of FRETILIN leaders. Furthermore, a third dynamic emerged that is at the core of the tension between state- and democracy-building: the East Timorese elites' near

40 Martin 2001. 41 Cited in Caplan 2005: 118.

42 Author interviews with World Bank, East Timorese, and NGO officials; Dili, East Timor, April 2005. Caplan 2005: 168–169 concurs.

43 Chesterman 2002; Chopra 2000; Goldstone 2004; and Suhrke 2001. This sentiment was also confirmed in author interviews with UN and other donor officials; Dili, East Timor, April 2005.

44 Ingram 2012: 4.

obsession with participation in the *political* arena meant that both they and UNTAET failed to emphasize the Timorization and renewal of the eviscerated state and administrative infrastructure.

No formal structures were built into UNTAET for East Timorese official or civil society participation – either in the electoral component or on the administrative side of the mission itself. The paradox surrounding participation was built into the very mandate of UNTAET.[45] Resolution 1272 stressed the need for UNTAET to "consult and cooperate closely with the East Timorese people";[46] yet only after first vesting full sovereign powers in UNTAET and the Transitional Administrator, who was "empowered to exercise all legislative and executive authority; including the administration of justice."[47] This formal contradiction could certainly have been resolved in practice, if Vieira de Mello and UNTAET had moved to build channels of participation into the mission – the mandate itself had given the Transitional Administrator the freedom to develop whatever necessary mechanisms for political consultation and even to move toward a dual-structure government. But Caroline Hughes notes that UNTAET's actions spoke for themselves when it acted first to organize itself and only then "reluctantly conceded the need to admit the Timorese elite to the circle of power," much later moving to incorporate political actors from the grassroots.[48]

UNTAET was thus originally extremely reluctant to incorporate East Timorese participation.[49] On the one hand, many UN and other expatriates working in East Timor came to the country believing the political system was a *tabula rasa*, and managed their dealings with the Timorese accordingly. This perception hardly did justice to the nuanced and freighted contemporary Timorese political landscape. On the other hand, there was a pervasive fear among UNTAET officials that by working too closely with specific Timorese political actors, they would prejudice the results of the all-important first election by privileging a particular group over others. In part due to the guiding principles

[45] Chesterman 2002: 64 makes a similar point in discussing the problems of Timorese consultation.
[46] UNSC Resolution 1272 (1999): para. 8.
[47] Ibid.: paras. 1 and 6. [48] Hughes 2009a: 96.
[49] Ingram 2012 and Suhrke 2001 note that the Security Council deliberately made no express provision to include the Timorese in administrative or executive decision-making.

and institutional culture of the UN Department of Peacekeeping Operations, UNTAET emphasized impartiality with respect to local contending factions over building local participation. On the ground, this translated into a great deal of ambivalence on UNTAET's part over its relationship with the CNRT and how deeply to include its participation in governing the country – in some instances UNTAET treated the CNRT as a political faction, in others as a vehicle for inclusive Timorese political participation.[50]

The UN Department of Political Affairs, which had originally managed the Timorese peace process, had planned to include more specific provisions for Timorese participation by giving the Timorese political authority while the UN assumed legal and administrative authority and served in an advisory role.[51] This system would have matched more closely the relationship between UNTAC and the Supreme National Council in Cambodia. The Department of Political Affairs even proposed a fully dual-structure administration along with a specific electoral timetable to emphasize the transitional nature of the administration. But the final Department of Peacekeeping Operations proposal sent to the UN Security Council included neither the dual-state structure nor the timetable; instead, only consultative principles with unspecified mechanisms made it into the UNTAET mandate.

The mission was hence launched as a fully UN-staffed operation with no formal counterpart. Yet UNTAET found, upon its arrival, a natural group to act as its local counterpart. The CNRT had acted as the umbrella pro-independence organization during the course of the decades-long resistance, enjoyed considerable legitimacy from its symbolic role at the head of a popular and successful national resistance front, and had been the organizational driving force behind the pro-independence victory in the referendum. Xanana Gusmão continued to lead the CNRT, endowing it with his charisma and popular support – although FRETILIN leaders within the organization increasingly challenged his claim to speak for a unified CNRT. It also benefited from the extensive non-military network that was developed throughout the towns and villages of East Timor during the course of the resistance. The survival of CNRT and FRETILIN had depended on this network, which now translated into a formidable organizational presence that reached throughout the country. UNTAET could not hope to meet this de facto control in the field, even though it had de jure authority at the

[50] Suhrke 2001. [51] Ibid.: 9.

center. After Indonesian provincial administrators left East Timor in the wake of the referendum, the CNRT was the one organization with nationwide political reach in an eviscerated institutional state structure and acted in many areas as a de facto governmental authority over the country.[52]

Furthermore, there was a natural political affinity between UNTAET and a major wing of the CNRT, in that both favored a "national unity" approach to politics and government that reflected their nervousness about open political competition.[53] CNRT elites, in particular, opposed political party development, fearing a return to the brief but violent civil war of 1975, which followed a period of nascent party development in East Timor and provided a pretext for Indonesia's invasion. Karol Soltan, the Deputy Director of UNTAET's Department of Political, Constitutional, and Electoral Affairs, remarked that he came to think of the fear of 1975 "as the greatest enemy of democracy in East Timor."[54] The CNRT was predisposed toward a transitional arrangement before full independence: in the mid-1990s it had proposed as a political compromise a UN-supervised transition to independence as long as 11–13 years. Even in the wake of the August 1999 referendum, some CNRT leaders, including Gusmão himself, were still in favor of a relatively long, five-year UN-assisted transition to independence, and other East Timorese leaders were amenable to the final two- to three-year solution as designed.[55] Yet while the CNRT did become UNTAET's de facto interlocutor in a number of different ways, the relationship was a complicated one and was never formalized. My interpretation is that UNTAET in fact did rely heavily on the CNRT for Timorese political participation. It proved such an attractive initial counterpart precisely because it was an umbrella Timorese organization that was explicitly not a political party; in other words, the fear of unduly influencing political outcomes led UNTAET to rely on the CNRT. In the longer run, however, this reliance on an umbrella organization masked the lack of consensus about what the institutional arrangements of the new country should look like.[56] It also had

[52] Author interviews with East Timorese, UN, and other donor officials; Dili and Viqueque, East Timor, April 2005.

[53] Goldstone 2004: 89. [54] Soltan 2002.

[55] Author interviews with East Timorese and donor officials; Dili, East Timor, April 2005.

[56] Ingram 2012. She argues that the CNRT's national unity message masked deep and long-standing disagreements among the Timorese political elite.

precisely the effect UNTAET feared, both by empowering FRETILIN leaders within the CNRT and by compounding the resistance-era, elitist nature of Timorese politics.

From the start, nevertheless, UNTAET attempted to avoid the politicization of the administration. Collaboration came initially through the newly created National Consultative Council, a small body with an East Timorese majority and a handful of senior UNTAET staff. In response to complaints about the delay in consulting the Timorese about political options for transition to self-governance, this morphed in July 2000 into the larger and entirely Timorese National Council, which comprised members of the CNRT as well as the Catholic Church and other civil society organizations. The National Council was intended to operate as a national legislature but it was appointed rather than elected, its members received little support in the way of financial or human resources, and Vieira de Mello retained absolute executive powers, including a veto.[57] At the same time, a coalition cabinet of transitional government was created, the East Timor Transitional Administration (ETTA). ETTA introduced Timorese proto-ministerial counterparts for the core UNTAET executive staff and the eight main cabinet posts were split – with four posts assigned to Timorese elites (Internal Administration, Infrastructure, Economic Affairs, and Social Affairs) and four to international staff (Police and Emergency Services, Political Affairs, Justice, and Finance).[58] Many believed that Gusmão himself chose the four Timorese cabinet members – two from FRETILIN, one from the more conservative Timorese Democratic Union (UDT), and one from the Catholic Church – reflecting UNTAET's reliance on CNRT in general and on Gusmão in particular, as well as the continued importance of Timorese political allegiances dating to 1975.[59] Together, the coalition government and the National Council were intended to provide "democratic institutions before democracy that could be the setting of democratic learning-by-doing at the national level."[60]

Yet these compromises on Timorization were too little and too late. By this time, Timorese elites were unsatisfied with even the National

[57] Author interviews with donor officials; Dili, East Timor, April 2005.

[58] The National Council and coalition cabinet were established by regulation on July 14, 2000. Another Timorese leader, José Ramos-Horta, was sworn in as Cabinet member for Foreign Affairs in October 2000.

[59] Chesterman 2002: 66. [60] Soltan 2002.

Council and ETTA co-governmental arrangements. The flawed relationship between UNTAET and ETTA was indicative of a fundamental transitional governance problem: the tension inherent in the UN's dual role as both government and transitional peace operation. ETTA, which was to assume the responsibility to deliver essential public services from UNTAET, was resource-starved in comparison. International cabinet members enjoyed a great deal of infrastructural support and much higher salaries, for example, than their East Timorese colleagues. Richard Caplan notes that the result of such inequities was "resentment and compromised effectiveness on the part of East Timorese administrators, who were already executing their responsibilities with serious handicaps."[61] The UN's role as government compromised the institutional and human capacity-building necessary to construct an effective state infrastructure to take over at transition.

By 2001 Timorese elites had reached the consensus that the relationship with UNTAET was counterproductive and should be ended as soon as possible. In December 2000, the Timorese Cabinet members threatened to resign, using one of the few measures actually available to them in the absence of genuine political power, as Simon Chesterman observes, in "an attempt to challenge UNTAET's legitimacy by threatening its consultative mechanisms."[62] They expressed their frustration in a letter to Vieira de Mello: "The East Timorese Cabinet ministers are caricatures of ministers in a government of a banana republic. They have no power, no duties, nor resources to function adequately."[63] Xanana Gusmão expressed his and the CNRT's disappointments with UNTAET in his New Year address of December 31, 2000, echoing, in particular, the East Timorese leadership's irritation over their lack of political participation. In turn, the Timorese leadership's frustration over their exclusion from decision-making in the political arena meant that they fixated on political participation, rather than broadening their desire to govern into also calling for Timorization of the state apparatus and emphasizing capacity-building in that arena. Indeed, when offered the choice by UNTAET in mid-2000 between a "technocratic" solution that would accelerate Timorization of the state administration and a "political" solution to more quickly transfer political power to the Timorese, the country's leaders opted for

[61] Caplan 2005: 103. [62] Chesterman 2002: 68.
[63] Cited in Beauvais 2001: 1130, fn. 111.

the latter.[64] This had the effect, parallel to the dynamic in Cambodia, of failing to bolster the state as a countervailing center of governing authority.

While a process of Timorization was at least attempted at the national political level, the development of parallel community empowerment through political institutions at the district level faltered. International staff continued to dominate governance at the subnational level: even as late as March 2001, only 2 of the country's 13 District Administrators were Timorese. Caplan argues that one reason UNTAET was so hesitant to devolve authority to the subnational units was because of the lesson from the Kosovo experience, brought to East Timor by Vieira de Mello and some of his deputies, that it was essential to establish unchallenged authority over the entire territory. Yet the circumstances were different in East Timor, where the local leadership was at first entirely supportive of the UN's aims and the mission itself, and could have been entrusted with more authority much sooner. The other issue was that District Administrators were constrained in performing their jobs because of excessive centralization in Dili. UNTAET's head of the Office of District Administration, Jarat Chopra, resigned very publicly in March 2000 and a month later all 13 District Administrators signed a memo to protest the centralizing tendencies of UNTAET.[65] The one exception to the lack of Timorization within UNTAET was the Division of Health Services, which had a dual international–Timorese authority structure from the beginning and was very successful in delivering essential public services as a result. This cooperation was made possible by the existence of an organized cadre of Timorese health professionals along with senior UN health officials who understood and believed in the importance of working together with their domestic counterparts.[66]

Other international organizations operating in East Timor had a very different position on Timorization and state capacity-building. Suhrke argues that the United Nations Development Program approach was based on the alternative assumptions that there were East Timorese with valuable administrative skills to be mobilized from

[64] Goldstone 2012.

[65] Caplan 2005: 119; also Beauvais 2001; and Chopra 2000.

[66] Author interviews with former UNTAET health officials, donor officials, and current East Timorese officials; Dili, East Timor, April 2005. See also Anderson 2014a.

the outset and that transition to an independent government would require the incorporation of Timorese into important positions.[67] The World Bank, in contrast to UNTAET, had early in the process attempted to conduct a skills inventory to identify those Timorese who could be brought into the transitional process.[68] It included East Timorese from the start in its November 1999 Joint Assessment Mission, rejecting UNTAET's view of a skills vacuum in East Timor.

UNTAET's slow moves toward the Timorization of government at the national level were matched by its reluctance to foster political participation at the subnational level, a pattern that was reinforced by the view of politics held among the Timorese elite. The story of the Community Empowerment and Local Governance Project (CEP) is telling in this respect.[69] The CEP was the first joint project between the World Bank and UNTAET as the sovereign government of East Timor. It was intended to support the creation of elected village and subdistrict councils so that block grants could be provided to the subdistricts, which would then decide on development priorities by adjudicating among village proposals. The project was designed to promote local-level participation in development and reconstruction decisions, and was intended in part to be an introduction to democratic and accountable governance. Many have observed that although the CEP was ambitious, it fit within the decentralized design of district administration that UNTAET and the World Bank had planned for East Timor. Yet UNTAET balked at the basic concept of the project proposed by the World Bank, arguing that local participation and formal recognition of local authorities by UNTAET could come only after formal elections. The CEP thus confirmed "the worst suspicions of the East Timorese: that the UN has no inclination to share power with them during the transition, or to include them in any decision-making beyond perfunctory consultation."[70] UNTAET officials' opposition to the CEP in early

[67] Suhrke 2001: 15.

[68] Author interviews with World Bank and other donor officials; Dili, East Timor, April 2005.

[69] The following discussion of the CEP draws on author interviews with East Timorese, World Bank, and other donor and NGO officials; Dili, East Timor, April 2005. For further details on the contentious CEP experience see also Chopra 2000: 30–31; Suhrke 2001: 16; and Mark Dodd, 2000, "UN staff battle over East Timor independence policy," *Sydney Morning Herald*, March 13.

[70] Chopra 2000: 31.

2000 placed a severe strain on their relations with senior Timorese leaders, including Gusmão, and even with other international organizations and NGOs. The inter-agency rivalry over the project also revealed the different approaches to Timorization during the process, highlighting that there were other possible avenues toward increasing political and administrative participation that UNTAET simply did not take.

UNTAET was not the only organization to have trouble broadening political consultation. The CNRT itself was criticized by elements of Timorese civil society for failing to be inclusive, relying too much on past political currencies and traditional elites, and not paying enough attention to the current landscape of East Timorese politics and society. Timorese NGOs, for example, were dismayed at Gusmão's December 2000 suggestion that the CNRT would prepare a draft of the constitution that the elected Constituent Assembly would only need to "fine-tune" before its passage[71] – this was hardly the genuine participatory constitution-writing process that the UN had promised. Gusmão later favored the idea of deeper popular consultation but the idea of a national constitutional commission was rejected by the National Council.

The East Timorese Elections of 2001

As UNTAET moved slowly toward further Timorization, the CNRT umbrella was beginning to fracture in the face of differing elite viewpoints and objectives and FRETILIN re-emerged as the dominant party on the Timorese political scene. This core element of the CNRT was dominated by members of the East Timorese diaspora who had remained active in the resistance movement from afar – from Mozambique, in particular. They decided after returning to East Timor in 1999 that they would seek to be the party of government on their own and FRETILIN began the dissolution of the CNRT when it withdrew in August 2000. It thereby freed itself from the agreement among the parties that formed the umbrella organization not to set up branches below the district level and immediately began rebuilding its formidable organizational structure at the village level, a feat the other parties simply

[71] Gusmão used this language in his New Year's Eve speech of December 31, 2000.

could not match. Gusmão spoke bitterly against this political mobilization and the fracturing of the identity of national unity underpinning the CNRT.[72]

Political fragmentation increased as all the parties began to gear up for the Constituent Assembly elections of August 2001 – what one donor official called the "checkered flag" for political parties to start forming.[73] The guerrilla resistance leaders of FRETILIN's armed faction FALINTIL saw themselves as marginalized by the FRETILIN leaders who had returned from exile, whom the FALINTIL forces viewed as having sat out the long and arduous guerrilla battle in relative comfort. Gusmão remained unaffiliated with a political party, projecting an image of himself as above factional politics. A handful of small political parties formed: some appealed to labels and affiliations from the era of party formation in 1975, such as the Timorese Democratic Union; and others channeled newer voices on the Timorese political scene, such as the Democratic Party representing Timorese youth, many of whom had studied abroad and had become increasingly resentful of the old-guard politicians and their resistance-era governing plans.

FRETILIN was indisputably the most powerful and best-resourced party and it advocated early elections in the knowledge that it would triumph handsomely. It had governed East Timor briefly in 1975 and established a deep bond with the Timorese people over the course of the Indonesian occupation and the guerrilla insurgency it led. It had served as the organizational backbone behind the CNRT's ability to step into the institutional vacuum created by the attenuation of political and institutional development under Indonesian rule, during which no political, administrative, or professional class was allowed to emerge in East Timor. FRETILIN, however inaccurately, self-consciously took on the CNRT's mantle as a political umbrella organization. As East Timorese independence drew near, it shared some characteristics with other independence movements that morphed into political parties, such as India's Congress Party or South Africa's African National Congress. Perhaps most significantly, these umbrella political fronts tend to begin their elected political careers by attempting to mediate national sociopolitical cleavages internally rather than allowing them to play out in an electoral arena.

[72] Ingram 2012: 9.
[73] Author interview with donor official; Dili, East Timor, April 2005.

Reflecting their concern not to bestow undue legitimacy on any one party, many UNTAET officials feared that FRETILIN would win an overwhelming majority of the vote in the first elections and lead the country toward becoming a one-party state. They encouraged the Timorese to adopt a mixed voting system – combining first-past-the-post district representation and national party-list proportional representation – hoping that this would give smaller parties more representation.[74] FRETILIN nevertheless scored a large victory in the Constituent Assembly elections of August 2001, winning 55 of the available 88 seats. Although it won 57 percent of the overall vote, it secured 63 percent representation in the assembly by also winning 12 of the 13 district seats. The Constituent Assembly replaced the National Council; and a new Transitional Government, with a fully Timorized cabinet, was chosen. Although this cabinet was selected to present an image of national unity, FRETILIN's victory was reflected unambiguously in its hold over the most important and powerful cabinet positions.[75]

Partnering with a small like-minded party, FRETILIN had the votes necessary to push through its draft constitution for approval with no need for compromise. It had been working on the task since first coming to government in 1975, while the other parties had not even begun to tackle the issue; furthermore, FRETILIN paid minimal attention to the results of the popular consultation conducted.[76] An Asia Foundation survey in 2004 reported that the Timorese citizenry was divided over whether genuine public participation had taken place: 44 percent responded that it did compared to 41 percent who felt that it did not. The FRETILIN-controlled proto-legislature thus defined the scope of its own powers, particularly vis-à-vis the other organs of government. Although numerous CNRT leaders favoured a pure presidential system for East Timor, the Maputo clique within FRETILIN that oversaw the design of the constitution explicitly subordinated the president to the government in a move that observers believe was intended to marginalize Gusmão on the political scene.[77] The final constitutional arrangements essentially neutralized the non-affiliated Gusmão's overwhelming mandate, over 82 percent of the vote, in winning the presidency in

74 Chesterman 2002: 69. 75 Ingram 2012: 9.

76 Author interviews with East Timorese legislators and donor officials; Dili, East Timor, April 2005; Baltazar 2004.

77 Chesterman 2002: 69.

April 2002.[78] Ingram observes that, in effect, two rival centers of power were created – with the prime minister and government empowered to make policy, while the president retained enormous moral authority with the population – thus setting the scene for "fierce political contest over the following years."[79] Finally, at the end of the transitional period, FRETILIN was also instrumental in transforming the Constituent Assembly into the National Parliament on independence, obviating the intended second election that other parties had anticipated would increase their own showing in the legislature.[80] The clique of returned FRETILIN diaspora leaders formed the core of East Timor's first Council of Ministers. It was not long before the political dominance of this group, with its uncompromising governance style and unilateral set of political priorities, was challenged as the new political landscape of East Timor evolved and matured.

Transitional Governance in Afghanistan

The transitional governance challenge in Afghanistan was very different from both the lack of consent involved in the peace settlement in Cambodia and the increasingly heated demands for local participation in East Timor. In Afghanistan, a dilemma shaped the political landscape and dominated the immediate peacebuilding challenge. On the one hand, governing the country required, as it had for centuries, the centralization of authority in Kabul. On the other hand, stabilizing the country in the aftermath of the civil war and the rout of the Taliban required the distribution of power to regional strongmen.

The United Nations Assistance Mission in Afghanistan (UNAMA) became operational in early 2002 to support the implementation of the peace framework as laid out in the Bonn Agreement.[81] Over the first five years, an estimated $8 billion was spent on the peacebuilding operation in Afghanistan, with almost 30,000 military and civilian personnel deployed to assist the effort.[82] UNAMA was similar to

[78] Author interviews with donor representatives and civil society leaders; Dili, East Timor, April 2005. Also, Aucoin and Brandt 2010.

[79] Ingram 2012: 18.

[80] Author interviews with East Timorese legislators and journalists; Dili, East Timor, April 2005.

[81] UNAMA was established by UN Security Council Resolution 1401 on March 28, 2002.

[82] Zürcher et al. 2013: 60.

UNTAC in that it was established to assist with a peace settlement, but it is telling that UNAMA was not designated a transitional authority by the Security Council; rather, it is a "special political mission" and is led by the UN's Department of Political Affairs, in contrast to the more traditional peacebuilding operations led by the UN's Department of Peacekeeping Operations.[83] The Security Council mandate did not explicitly endow UNAMA with any dimension of the Afghan government's sovereignty or executive authority, as it had the UNTAC and UNTAET mandates in Cambodia and East Timor, respectively. Furthermore, the United States was heavily involved in the Afghan political transition, particularly through its influential ambassador, Zalmay Khalilzad, who had Hamid Karzai's ear and served as one of his most trusted advisors.

UNAMA, however, was the focal point of the international community's assistance in the process of peacebuilding through transitional governance in Afghanistan. Indeed, although the Bonn framework envisioned the international community playing an "assistance" role, UNAMA in practice took on much more of a "partnership" role in governing with counterparts in the Afghan Interim and Transitional Administrations.[84] Entrusted with the bulk of donor reconstruction funds, instead of the interim government, UNAMA effectively operated for some time as a parallel administration, hence it qualifies as a transitional governance vehicle as defined in this book. It was responsible for many of the same state- and democracy-building activities as were the more formal transitional authorities (such as UNTAC and UNTAET), including particularly capacity-building and governing assistance for the Afghan Interim and Transitional Administrations. It also assisted the process by which the Transitional Administration was selected, followed by a constitution-drafting process and the holding of elections at the end of the transitional governance period.

UNAMA was explicitly intended to be a swing of the pendulum away from the broadly expanded scope of the two immediately preceding UN peacebuilding missions in Kosovo and East Timor.[85] Lakhdar Brahimi, the Special Representative of the Secretary-General

[83] Other such UN special political missions operate currently in Iraq and Libya, for example.

[84] On this partnership role, see Thier and Chopra 2002: 894 and fn. 1; also Chesterman 2004: 87–92.

[85] Chesterman 2004.

for Afghanistan, was extremely influential in determining the mechanics and substance of the Afghan political transition. Indeed, the design of UNAMA was based on the recommendations of a review of UN peacekeeping operations that came to be known as "the Brahimi report" after its chair.[86] Brahimi articulated the need for a "light footprint" in Afghanistan in terms of the UN and international presence in order to emphasize Afghan ownership of the process.[87] In practice, however, UNAMA was "arguably the most institutionally and normatively advanced integrated mission fielded by the United Nations in one of its most high-profile interventions."[88] The international community, led by UNAMA, was intimately involved in both the transitional political process and day-to-day governance and state functions. In turn, it is evident that the Afghan Interim and Transitional Administrations, and later the elected government, derived their legitimacy from the UN-led transitional governance process originating in the Bonn Agreement and culminating in elections.

The Bonn Agreement provided a roadmap, complete with milestones, for a process of further negotiations among Afghans about political transformation and state reconstruction in their country. The Interim Administration and the UN adhered to the timetable stipulated in the Bonn Agreement to hold an Emergency *Loya Jirga* in June 2002, within six months of the peace settlement. The use of the grand council meeting, a centuries-old, traditional Pashtun consensus-building and conflict resolution mechanism, was considered an effective way to incorporate traditional forms of governance and thereby build domestic legitimacy into the political process. *Loya jirgas* had in the past made key governance decisions during periods of turmoil when no legitimate ruler was recognized by all Afghans, and the Northern Alliance agreed to a UN-monitored Emergency *Loya Jirga* as "the legitimating device for the process of building a more representative government."[89] The key output of the forum was to decide on "a broad-based transitional administration, to lead Afghanistan until such time as a fully representative government can be elected through free

86 Brahimi 2000; also Thakur 2001.

87 UN Special Representative of the Secretary-General for Afghanistan briefing to the UN Security Council, February 6, 2002.

88 Donini, Niland, and Wermester 2004: 4. See also Donini 2004: 136–139; and Freeman 2007: 1.

89 Rubin 2004: 7.

and fair elections to be held no later than two years from the date of the convening of the Emergency *Loya Jirga*."[90] In a general atmosphere of optimism about the future of their country, the assembled leaders reached agreement on the Afghan Transitional Administration (ATA) that would lead the country and its reconstruction.

The realities of constructing political order in post-conflict Afghanistan became more apparent, however, as the process of determining the composition of the ATA began to reflect the political challenges ahead. In effect, the *Loya Jirga* was hampered in fulfilling its mandate seriously because of the many unresolved power struggles going into the conference – and its outcomes perpetuated these conflicts rather than tackling them directly. According to the Bonn Agreement, the central objective of the Emergency *Loya Jirga* was to approve the key personnel who would govern the country as part of the ATA. Hamid Karzai was named the Transitional President, as expected. The composition of the rest of the ATA was not debated within the *Loya Jirga* forum, however. It was decided upon by key power-brokers after intensive behind-the-scenes negotiations over key portfolios, in a contentious debate that kept the delegates waiting in Kabul beyond the planned timeframe. The ATA slate was finally presented to the delegates as a *fait accompli* on the last day of the meeting, when Karzai announced the names of key cabinet members without providing a written slate or opportunity for discussion, let alone asking for a formal vote. There had been a widespread expectation among the delegates that the *Loya Jirga* would provide the chance to correct the factional and ethnic imbalances created at the Bonn conference.[91] But the composition of the cabinet remained much the same as in the Interim Administration, continuing to reflect the exigencies of informal power-sharing in an ethnically fragmented and centrifugal country: Tajiks retained the most powerful portfolios, including defense and foreign affairs, while Pashtun representation was increased slightly.

In short, many of the decisions made ostensibly by the *Loya Jirga* were reached behind the scenes in the interests of short-term stability and power considerations rather than for the longer-term purposes of strengthening the central state or boosting democratic participation and legitimacy and weakening traditional, unaccountable strongmen. Simon Chesterman observes: "Few people deluded themselves into

[90] Afghanistan Bonn Agreement 2001. [91] Thier 2004: 54.

thinking that the *Loya Jirga* was meaningful popular consultation – the aim was to encourage those who wielded power in Afghanistan to exercise it through politics rather than through the barrel of a gun."[92] Critics of the Emergency *Loya Jirga* argued that it represented a missed opportunity to instill democratic practices in Afghan political culture, especially failing to assert civilian leadership and draw power away from the warlords.[93] Widespread reports surfaced immediately after the *Loya Jirga* of a series of backroom deals, outright intimidation, debate-stifling, and vote-packing on the floor that combined to prevent elected delegates from exercising their full authority and decision-making power as representatives of the people.[94] Many of the most notorious *mujahideen* leaders were treated with deference, sitting in the front row of the *Loya Jirga* and displaying full opportunistic behavior in exploiting the evolving political landscape to continue to suit their own ends. The most powerful were elevated into roles as vice presidents and provincial governors: Marshal Mohammed Qasim Fahim, who became leader of the Northern Alliance in September 2001 after Ahmed Shah Massoud was assassinated, served as Defense Minister and Vice President; Ismail Khan was made provincial governor of his stronghold of Herat; Haji Mohammed Mohaqeq, the former *mujahideen* leader of the Shia Hazaras became Minister of Planning; Gul Agha Shirzai, strongman in the south, was made governor of Kandahar. Karzai and his foreign backers thus demonstrated their intent to pursue a co-optation strategy that ignored past transgressions, a strategy that many human rights advocates criticized.

The tensions at the heart of constructing a workable political order in Afghanistan, so clearly on display in the outcomes of the Emergency *Loya Jirga* of 2002, continued to manifest themselves as UNAMA worked with the new ATA to implement a process of peacebuilding through transitional governance. Richard Ponzio describes how the international community struggled to reconcile divergent elements of

[92] Chesterman 2004: 92.

[93] For example, Goodson 2003; International Crisis Group 2002; and Thier 2004.

[94] In a particularly egregious example of behind-the-scenes orchestration, the US Ambassador, Zalmay Khalilzad, announced that the former king, Zahir Shah, would not seek election as head of state but would support Hamid Karzai's candidacy – prior to the announcement made on behalf of the king himself. Many Pashtuns were incensed by what appeared to be a combination of Northern Alliance strong-arm tactics and foreign interference. International Crisis Group 2002.

authority in the country, observing that the need to incorporate traditionally legitimate sources of authority was often at odds with liberal democratization ideals.[95] At the heart of the peacebuilding challenge was "competing interpretations of what constitutes legitimate political authority."[96] The clash of these distinct visions of political order is represented by Afghan warlords who, in continuing to assert their traditional forms of authority, have remained a serious obstacle to the consolidation of effective and legitimate government in Afghanistan. During the transitional governance period, large areas of the country remained dominated by private militias under the control of various anti-Taliban commanders, particularly those of the Northern Alliance. Many of the warlords and local strongmen assigned key posts in central and regional government resisted the demobilization of their personal forces and continued to enrich themselves with customs revenues and illegal financial flows. Karzai tried, from the Interim Administration period onward, to neutralize their independent power by incorporating them into his cabinet and provincial government structure, a strategy that worked with some (such as Ismail Khan and Mohammed Fahim) and less with others (such as Rashid Dostum and Gul Agha Shirzai).

Each of these strongmen pledged their allegiance to the government, but their willingness to submit to the authority of the central government was not truly tested during the transitional governance process.[97] These political realities met with mixed reactions from the Afghan people. Most understand that building post-conflict political order by co-opting some warlords was better than the instability that would be generated by excluding them – but these strongmen continued to be seen with blood on their hands. Ponzio's focus group of Afghan citizens revealed warlords and militia leaders to be among the least trusted groups in Afghan society, in contrast to tribal elders, who are viewed highly.[98] The political reality was simple, however: having accommodated and co-opted these regional power-holders into the new political

[95] Ponzio 2011: 164–169. [96] Ibid.: 165.

[97] Karzai removed Ismail Khan as governor of Herat in late 2004, appointing him Minister of Energy and Water in Kabul. In early 2006, however, Khan was sent to Herat to help calm Sunni–Shia clashes there, which some believe were stoked by Khan himself to demonstrate his power in Herat. After running for president against Karzai and losing, Rashid Dostum was appointed Karzai's top military advisor; at the time Dostum ostensibly "resigned" as head of his armed faction. Katzman 2007.

[98] Ponzio 2011: 172–173.

order, it became increasingly difficult to diffuse the extent to which they were able to retain their political advantage and manipulate outcomes in their favor.

As with the other two cases, the transitional governance process in Afghanistan suffered from a mismatch between the realities of the domestic political scene and the international community's governance and statebuilding objectives. The milestones established by the Bonn process, as well as UNAMA's mandate and light footprint, meant that the international community was preoccupied mostly with the central government. This bias was exacerbated by the poor security situation outside Kabul, which hamstrung institution building activities, let alone any meaningful civic engagement, at the subnational level. The National Solidarity Program (NSP) is an exception that proves the rule: it was created by the ATA in 2003 as an integrated rural development and community empowerment program to improve development outcomes at the community level and thereby enhance the Afghan state's legitimacy across the country. Through the elected community development councils that are created to select and implement small-scale development projects, the NSP has proven perhaps the most successful way of building linkages between the government and Afghan society.[99] Ironically, it relies essentially on nongovernmental organizations for implementation.

The ATA faced its own problems in consolidating its authority outside Kabul. Alexander Thier points out both failures and relative successes on this front.[100] On the security side, the government remained a factional entity among other armed factions; it could not assert its monopoly over violence in the territory. On the executive front, by contrast, Karzai was quite successful, with the backing of UNAMA and the international community, at inserting into positions of authority in the ATA a group of technocrats who were few but relatively powerful. Ashraf Ghani, who became Afghanistan's president in 2014, was one of these key technocrats, serving as Karzai's Finance Minister in the ATA. One difficult yet effective strategy for demonstrating the authority of the central state as an alternative to traditional strongmen was an attempt to tie back to the center the cadres of provincial civil servants who were functioning in surviving subnational government bureaucracies and remained loyal to the concept of a central state.

[99] Nagl, Exum, and Humayun 2009. [100] Thier 2004.

Yet UNAMA's substantial international presence in Kabul and deep involvement with the business of the central government faded quickly outside the capital, as did the authority of the central government. During the transitional governance period, regional leaders continued to assert their own authority in the provinces, often with resources supplied to them by foreign patrons – aid agencies often carried out their own agendas in the provinces with little consultation with either central or provincial governments.[101] A World Bank survey team found in 2002–03 that subnational administrative structures were surprisingly robust and cautioned that the central government would have to act immediately to ensure that particular source of state strength was not quickly eroded.[102] Yet the ATA found it difficult to truly connect with the provinces – for example, it had trouble disbursing even meager funds and, in turn, subnational administrations received small budgetary allocations and remained extremely weak.[103]

In short, while the political dimension of reconstruction was progressing along the Bonn milestones, state capacity-building was foundering in the absence of a robust, functioning Afghan administrative apparatus to guide reconstruction work.[104] On the statebuilding front, a telling dispute developed between the United Nations agencies coordinated through UNAMA on the one hand, and the Afghan Assistance Coordination Authority (AACA) – the government's coordinating representative to the donor community – on the other. The Interim Administration had created AACA by executive decree almost immediately after the Bonn Conference in order to orient international aid through a nationally owned program that prioritized direct assistance to the state. In parallel, the government wrote a National Development Framework (NDF) for the first donor conference to take place inside Afghanistan in April 2002, a comprehensive and integrated framework of development and reconstruction priorities. The NDF

[101] Donini 2004: 138. [102] World Bank 2004.

[103] Author interviews with government officials and World Bank, UNDP, and other donor officials (Kabul, Afghanistan, June 2002) indicated that this was a serious problem that was clearly recognized as a major statebuilding challenge in 2002; very little progress has been made in remedying the issue to date. See also Rubin 2006: 26.

[104] Author interviews with officials of the Afghanistan Assistance Coordination Authority (AACA), the United Nations Development Program, and the World Bank; Kabul, Afghanistan, June 2002.

was widely viewed by donors as a strong statement of the government's vision as well as a structure to direct aid programming in the country. Yet many donors were skeptical that the government could effectively and cleanly execute direct budgetary support, with particular concerns being raised about the lack of functional administrative connection between the center and provinces. As a result, the international community continued to channel its financial assistance through the UN agencies and other external actors instead of directly to the government.[105] AACA officials, led by Ghani who oversaw the writing of the NDF, wanted a single channel of aid financing, through the government budget, and struggled against what they saw as the UN agencies' attempts to undermine government ownership and streamlined statebuilding processes.[106]

Responding to the increasingly contested transitional governance environment, UNAMA established an integrated coordination structure in mid-2002 to bring UN programs more in line with the government's capacity-building and reconstruction priorities. UN agencies were assigned to work as "secretariats" within ministries, providing personnel and technical assistance in support of the government's program, and UN programs became increasing embedded with those of the state.[107] For example, the United Nations Development Program (UNDP) was the lead agency assigned to work with the Ministry of Finance and the Office of Administrative Affairs to manage the civil service payroll and establish new human resource management procedures; the UNDP then coordinated other donors' work in this area. This more integrated system was beneficial in that it kept the Bonn process moving forward, especially facilitating the necessary dimension of international engagement in governance and capacity-building. The drawback, however, was that UNAMA became involved in internal debates over aid allocation authority and, as a result, coordination between UNAMA and the government was placed under constant strain. Alexander Costy observes that what became clear from such debates was that the UN had still not developed a strategy for incorporating greater national control over the management of aid

105 Costy 2004.

106 Author interviews with AACA, UN, and World Bank officials; Kabul, Afghanistan, June 2002.

107 Author interviews with UNDP and World Bank officials; Kabul, Afghanistan, June 2002.

resources as part of a peacebuilding operation.[108] This issue remained contentious in Afghanistan, resulting, after the transitional governance period, in the Afghanistan Compact, a renewed commitment to coordinated assistance under a government program negotiated between the Karzai administration and international donors in London in December 2006.

The Afghan Elections of 2004 and 2005

The political timeline established in the Bonn Agreement, including some of the mechanisms of informal power-sharing, worked toward a measure of democratic consolidation in Afghanistan. The ATA was to govern the country, in tandem with UNAMA, until a new constitution was adopted within 18 months, followed by national elections. A Constitutional *Loya Jirga* met in December 2003 and January 2004, as planned, to draft and ratify a new Afghan constitution.[109] Some degree of popular consultation took place: the drafting commission consulted Afghans in every province in the country and in the refugee communities in Pakistan and Iran. Yet the government and the UN also decided to keep the substance of deliberations confidential and chose not to publish the text of the proposed constitution even during the public consultation phase. As a result, behind the scenes maneuvering among power-brokers bore more responsibility for the final result than any genuine consultation.[110] The final draft was published only a month before the scheduled opening of the Constitutional *Loya Jirga* and featured extensive executive-made revisions to the document completed by the Constitutional Review Commission. Rubin concludes that the constitution "reflected to a considerable extent the agenda shared by Karzai and those cabinet members who considered themselves 'reformers.'"[111] The government even had an active lobbying team on the floor of the *Loya Jirga* and successfully defused

108 Costy 2004: 156.
109 The *loya jirga* institution featured, albeit with varying degrees of independence, in the creation of each of the country's five previous constitutions. Rubin 2004: 7. Details on the process of constitution-drafting and consultation are from International Crisis Group 2003; Rubin 2004; and Thier 2010.
110 Thier 2010.
111 Rubin 2004: 10; also International Crisis Group 2003; and Thier 2010.

many of the competing requests emanating from various groups there.[112]

There were two particularly salient issues during the constitution-drafting process – presidentialism and the status of Islam.[113] The drafting commission originally envisioned a semi-presidential system, in which a prime minister would share power with the president. The intention was that this would institutionalize ethnic power-sharing between a Pashtun president (expected to be Karzai) and a non-Pashtun prime minister (likely to be a Panjshiri Tajik).[114] The decision to move to a fully presidential system came late in the game, at the stage of joint review of the proposed constitution by the drafting committee and the government's National Security Council. Karzai and his allies in Kabul had a strong desire for the establishment of a purely presidential system and, although this had been strenuously resisted by the drafting commission, they prevailed over the Northern Alliance bloc, which had begun to see splits among its leaders in the cabinet. The debate about the role of Islam explicitly involved balancing the domestic demands of Islamic parties and clerics with the desire of international actors on standards of governance – the latter made it clear that they did not want any reference to *sharia* law although they accepted that the constitution would declare Afghanistan an Islamic state.

Both the presidential election of October 2004, which returned Hamid Karzai to the head of government and the parliamentary elections of September 2005 were held successfully and were declared to be free and fair by the international community. There was, nevertheless, significant criticism of the choice of the single non-transferable vote (SNTV) electoral system for the September 2005 parliamentary elections and the primary outcome to which it led – a fragmented parliament full of non-aligned legislators at the expense of established parties.[115] A brief discussion of why and how the SNTV system was chosen in Afghanistan and its consequences illustrates sharply how

112 Rubin 2004: 16. 113 Ibid.: 12–14.

114 This outcome is what transpired, de facto, after the 2014 presidential election, where the victorious Ashraf Ghani, a Pashtun, agreed to create a new chief executive officer post to govern in collaboration (at least in theory) with the runner-up, the Tajik Abdullah Abdullah.

115 Reynolds 2006.

governance choices made for the sake of expediency and advancing the entrenched elite's own interests hampered the establishment of the effective and legitimate political order sought by the international community. The norm for the electoral system chosen in most post-conflict countries since 1989 has been list-based proportional representation (PR). The many advisors and constitutional experts consulted in the Afghan case favored a PR system there too. Most of them believed that the right way to deal with the factionalized nature of Afghan politics would be to give all major power contenders a stake in the system and therefore concluded that some form of geographically rooted proportionality was the means to achieve that goal.[116] The major benefit of a list-based PR system is that it supports the building of political parties and encourages the articulation of programmatic platforms, elevating policy discourse over the attributes of individual politicians.

Under the SNTV system, by contrast, voters cast ballots for a single individual rather than choosing from a party-determined list and candidates are elected by winning the greatest number of votes instead of through proportionality. Andrew Reynolds explains that the main intended benefit of the SNTV system is to promote representation and accountability: it enables voters to select independent candidates whom they know and trust, rather than favoring members of nascent parties with undefined platforms.[117] On the other hand, analysts believe the system loses its attractiveness when the districts are too large because it tends to fragment the vote, even creating a lottery-like effect among independents and minority party candidates in larger districts – and Afghan districts had, on average, a high number of seats. An SNTV system also creates a difficult strategic problem for parties, since there can be a large disproportionality between votes cast for party members and actual seats won by these candidates.[118]

[116] For example, Johnson et al. 2003; and Reynolds and Wilder 2004.

[117] Reynolds 2006: 105.

[118] Under SNTV, a party can win the majority of votes in a district and yet not necessarily win the majority of seats. For example, if a voting district has five seats, it is simply the top five vote-getters who win those seats. If the top candidate from Party A wins 80 percent of the vote and the next four candidates from Party B win 20 percent of the vote among them, Party A gets one seat in the assembly while Party B gets four. A PR system would assign Party A four out of five seats in this example.

Overall, an SNTV system can result in a confusing ballot for voters and lead them to wonder where their vote led in terms of actual representation. These disadvantages are particularly problematic in post-conflict environments, where it is arguably essential for buy-in to a new democratic system that votes cast are clearly translated into seats won.

The constitution ratified by the *Loya Jirga* in January 2004 did not explicitly describe the voting system to be used for the national legislature, but an appendix noted that a decision had been reached to use some form of list-based PR. The Transitional Administration, together with the Joint Election Management Body (JEMB) and UNAMA, originally worked out the details of the system, agreeing on a closed-list PR system with multi-member districts, allowing party leaders to decide on candidates and their ordering on the ballot. Yet this proposal faltered when, as Reynolds reports, Karzai's legal advisor gave a confused presentation of the system to the transitional government cabinet, opening the way for critics to argue that the system was far too complicated for Afghan voters to understand.[119] Criticism was fueled by a generalized distrust of political parties, based on the chaotic multiparty period of the 1960s and subsequent Communist and Soviet rule.[120] Faced with these objections, Karzai asked for other alternatives that would allow Afghans to vote for individuals rather than parties. The SNTV system simply emerged as the least bad alternative.

Yet there was widespread concern about the choice of SNTV in Afghanistan, with lobbying efforts persisting even after President Karzai signed the SNTV electoral law. Three of Karzai's main challengers – Rashid Dostum, Yunus Qanooni, and Haji Mohammed Mohaqeq – stated that they supported PR and not SNTV for the electoral system, as did UNAMA officials, international organizations, and emerging Afghan progressive political and civil society activists.[121] Zalmay Khalilzad, the US ambassador and close confidant of Karzai, was one notable exception: it was reported that he had pushed for a firm decision to allow elections to proceed quickly above all else and that

119 Reynolds 2006: 106–107.

120 A similar distrust of political parties existed in post-conflict East Timor, also stemming from a chaotic earlier party-based period that had ended in civil war.

121 Reynolds 2006: 110.

he did not believe the electoral system to be particularly important.[122] What finally tipped the decision was that a new objection to list-based PR had emerged from Karzai's co-ethnic Pashtun allies in his cabinet: they feared that a list system would benefit non-Pashtun leaders and would lead to fewer Pashtun supporters for Karzai in the legislature. Reynolds concludes, "without much theoretical basis, the president and his advisers determined that SNTV was the system that would best serve their interests."[123]

Things did not turn out the way the Karzai clique hoped. The SNTV system splintered the Pashtun base and turned what was Karzai's absolute majority in the presidential election into a disjointed supporting bloc in the national assembly, holding less than one-third of the seats. The fragmentation was more general, with more than thirty different parties and factions winning seats, few of them on the basis of any identifiable platform. Almost half of those elected had fought as *mujahideen* and parliamentary alliances started to form on the basis of alliances with traditional power-holders and strongmen.[124] Thus, the electoral system led to a parliamentary outcome that made it even more challenging to govern the country. Karzai found it increasingly difficult to cobble together ad hoc coalitions to support his programs. Reynolds reported in 2006 that the new legislature had "already shown itself to be a place of wheeling and dealing, of clientelism and shifting alliances, where men with tainted pasts hold significant sway over the future of Afghan democracy."[125] This dynamic is made possible since the legislature in its nascent stages lacks a formal role for political parties that could mediate intra-assembly tensions. Without such organized blocs – their absence a result of the SNTV system and Karzai's attempts to marginalize those parties that do exist – traditional power-brokers have tried to dominate proceedings.[126] Finally, it was the case, as expected, that the SNTV system would prove unsatisfying to Afghan citizens searching for true representation and accountability: only about one-third of the six million votes cast were for winning candidates, with two-thirds cast for candidates who lost. The SNTV decision reflects, in microcosm, how choices made for elite

[122] A similar push for quick elections in Cambodia led Special Representative of the Secretary-General Akashi to make a series of decisions regarding the Khmer Rouge that also had unforeseen long-term consequences.
[123] Reynolds 2006: 111. [124] Ibid.: 111–112.
[125] Ibid.: 116. [126] International Crisis Group 2006.

political expediency in Afghanistan set the country on a path along which the major governance challenges of a hamstrung central government and fragmented political power were compounded rather than resolved.

Transitional Governance in Comparative Perspective

Post-conflict Cambodia, East Timor, and Afghanistan – the differences in the nature of their conflicts, brokered peace settlements, and evolving political landscapes notwithstanding – underwent remarkably similar transitional governance attempts at peacebuilding led by the United Nations. The sequence of formal institutional choices engineered by the transitional governance process and the core milestones obtained in each country are captured in Table 4.1.

Over the course of this sequence of interventions, the pendulum swung back and forth with regard to the perception of the "right" degree of UN peacebuilding presence. After UNTAC's experience in Cambodia, observers concluded that UN peace operations typically had less than satisfactory impact because they were underresourced, in both financial and personnel terms, because their mandates were too circumscribed and failed to give them enough teeth to change the game on the ground, and because they were not coordinated appropriately. Responding to early critiques that UNTAC was not given enough of a mandate or resources in Cambodia, UN peace operations in East Timor (and Kosovo) a few years later were much larger, more comprehensive in terms of mandate remit, and even more encroaching on the sovereignty of their host countries. A few years later, however, responding to criticisms of heavy-handedness in East Timor, the UN elevated the importance of "country ownership" in preparing for the reconstruction process in Afghanistan and rolled out a "light footprint" UN presence that did not impinge so directly on the country's sovereignty.[127] At UN headquarters, reforms since the turn of the century have attempted to remedy earlier pathologies created by the organizational make-up of the various departments involved in peace

[127] In a similar vein, UN transitional administrations in Kosovo and East Timor did not establish a timeline to exit at the outset of those missions because senior peacebuilding officials believed that the explicit timetable of the ongoing Bosnian peace operation led to adverse consequences that eventually, and paradoxically, delayed exit. Zaum 2012: 147.

Table 4.1 *Transitional governance milestones in Cambodia, East Timor, and Afghanistan*

Milestone	Cambodia	East Timor	Afghanistan
Peace Settlement	**Paris Peace Agreement** October 23, 1991	**Independence referendum** August 30, 1999	**Bonn Agreement** December 5, 2001
UN SC resolution creating transitional authority	**United Nations Transitional Authority in Cambodia** (UNTAC) UNSC Resolution 745 February 28, 1992	**United Nations Transitional Authority in East Timor** (UNTAET) UNSC Resolution 1272 October 25, 1999	**United Nations Assistance Mission in Afghanistan** (UNAMA) UNSC Resolution 1401 March 28, 2002
Domestic counterpart for transitional government mechanism	**Supreme National Council** Quadripartite arrangement to share Cambodian sovereignty between the four factions to the conflict. Established in 1990, leading to the Paris Accords; became UNTAC's sovereign counterpart.	**National Consultative Council** (CNRT leaders + senior UNTAET staff) Followed in July 2000 by **East Timor Transitional Administration** (international–domestic coalition cabinet) AND **National Council** (broader Timorese representation)	**Afghan Interim Authority** Established at Bonn December 22, 2001 **Afghan Transitional Authority** Selected at Emergency *Loya Jirga* June 10–21, 2002
Presidential election	N/A	April 14, 2002 Xanana Gusmão 83 percent	October 9, 2004 Hamid Karzai 55 percent
Parliamentary elections	May 23–28, 1993 FUNCINPEC 58 seats CPP 51 seats Other opposition 10 seats Power-sharing compromise reached between CPP and FUNCINCPEC	August 30, 2001 FRETILIN 55 seats Democratic Party 7 seats Other opposition 16 seats	September and November 2005 High degree of fragmentation (>30 parties and factions) but three roughly equal blocs: pro-government; opposition supporters; unaligned
Constitutional assembly	Cambodia constituent assembly June–September 1993	East Timor constituent assembly Approved constitution on March 22, 2002	Afghan Constitutional *Loya Jirga* December 14, 2003–January 4, 2004
Independence	September 24, 1993	May 20, 2002	January 26, 2004

operations, establishing in 2005 a new intergovernmental UN Peacebuilding Commission to exercise strategic oversight across hitherto bureaucratically separated peacebuilding functions.[128] Overall, the effect of these reforms has been limited.

The evidence examined in this chapter should be taken as a firm warning that this type of attention to mandate scope and implementation as the route to improving peacebuilding is blinkered at best and, more likely, dangerously misguided. The cases examined here illustrate that none of the attempted policy shifts or nuances in the precise type or degree of transitional governance really mattered. In reality, it is the fact of transitional governance itself and its two hallmark characteristics – joint international–domestic governance and the simultaneous pursuit of statebuilding and democratization – that yields the perverse outcomes we see in practice. Interestingly, the latter feature is problematic even in cases where executive governance remains in the hands of domestic elites. René Lemarchand argues, for example, that the results of UN peace operations in Burundi, the Democratic Republic of the Congo (DRC), and Rwanda also illustrate the "contradictions between statebuilding and democracy promotion, the two principal goals of peacemaking."[129] Transitional regimes in Burundi and DRC – brokered and designed by outside actors but without an element of international governance – shared power among domestic elites, in interim arrangements preceding elections. Devon Curtis echoes the dynamics identified in this chapter in demonstrating how these transitional arrangements led to the entrenchment of certain actors and their consequent ability to develop an elite-centered system to share the political–economic spoils of power.[130]

The characteristics of peacebuilding through transitional governance enabled the winning elites in all three cases considered here to use (and continue to use, as the next chapter demonstrates) the full suite of institutional change agent strategies identified at the beginning of the chapter – insurrection, subversion, parasitism, and opportunism[131] – in obtaining their preferred form of political order. I do not wish to imply an instrumental rationalist logic to the process of institutional

[128] United Nations 2004; UN Security Council Resolution S/RES/1645, 20 December 2005; and UN General Assembly Resolution A/RES/60/80, 30 December 2005.

[129] Lemarchand 2012: 228. [130] Curtis 2007.

[131] Mahoney and Thelen 2010.

change. It does not necessarily have to be intentional; it can come as the unintended consequence of distributional struggles in which no actor sought the transformation that actually occurs. The balance of authority between the international operation and its domestic counterparts is a crucial piece of the institutional change story – and that balance shifts over the course of a transformative peacebuilding intervention. From the moment a transitional governance mandate is signed, it becomes an obsolescing bargain: as soon as the intervention begins, the balance shifts so that the UN becomes dependent on its domestic counterparts for success and the bargaining power of the latter increases.[132] At the outset of an intervention, the ability of international peacebuilders to impose and enforce a particular set of institutional rules is relatively high; in turn, domestic elites have less discretion in interpreting those rules. As the intervention progresses, its ability to enforce a particular set of institutions – formal rules, policy structures, and norms – wanes quite quickly. At the same time, the discretion of domestic elites increases in making formal institutional choices and in developing informal strategies for operating within existing institutions. In the aftermath of interventions, those who advanced the rules and institutions in the first place – the international community through the peace operation – are left able only to turn a blind eye as long as the rules are not being opposed outright.

The international community's model of peacebuilding through transitional governance has achieved only limited success because of a lack of systematic attention to the domestic political games in which it unfolds. A critical analysis of the transitional governance approach demonstrates that it transforms the political landscape in unintended ways, especially by making state- and democracy-building an elite project and thereby serving elite interests. Joint international–domestic governance and the simultaneous pursuit of statebuilding and democratization result in a domestic political dynamic that co-opts the peacebuilding intervention and systematically thwarts the consolidation of legitimate and effective governance. The following chapter extends this narrative by demonstrating how this dynamic continues to play out in the aftermath of intervention. In essence, the state becomes a pawn in the struggle for political power as domestic elites use their resources

[132] Doyle and Sambanis 2006: 309; and Vernon 1971.

as patronage to cement their preferred neopatrimonial political order in place – with the result that state effectiveness is hampered and legitimate authority compromised. Governance outcomes come to reflect not the modern political order sought by international interventions but neopatrimonial political order instead.

5 Neopatrimonial Post-Conflict Political Order

Patrimonialism has been the prevailing form of political order that must be overcome in constructing rule-bound, effective, and legitimate government. Post-conflict countries are no exception to this pattern. In Cambodia, East Timor, and Afghanistan, international interventions that sought to establish one particular conception of political order found themselves in competition with the neopatrimonial practices preferred by domestic elites. The dynamic contest between these two visions of political order is especially apparent in the aftermath of a peacebuilding presence, when domestic elites and their supporters reassert patrimonial forms of politics that undermine the formal institutions of governance transplanted by interventions. As a result, a decade and more after the transformative peacebuilding missions in the three countries considered here, what is apparent is that patrimonial and rational–legal authority coexist in a quintessential neopatrimonial hybrid form – with personalized politics practiced within the institutional trappings of Weberian bureaucratic effectiveness and electoral democratic legitimacy.

Neopatrimonial political order operates through a system of rent-seeking and rent distribution through patronage.[1] Patron–client relationships form and persist on the basis of these distributional strategies, which bind elites to each other as well as to their social sources of support. In the liberal ideal associated with modern political order, by contrast, elites endowed with legitimate authority through the vote should

[1] Fukuyama 2011: 336–343, explains that the term "rent" derives from *ancien régime* France, where in the fifteenth to eighteenth centuries, the monarchy grew strong by co-opting elites. It did so by offering them the ability to purchase small pieces of the state or public assets, such as the right to collect specific types of taxes, that would generate a continuous stream of revenue and that could be handed down to descendants. The monarchy gave local power-holders these various privileges in return for cash ("*rente*"), thereby mortgaging itself to these power-holders who, in turn, served as a concerted bloc defending the status quo and preventing reform. See also Ertman 1997: 98–99.

use the rationalized bureaucracy to deliver programmatic public policies and collectively oriented goods and services. It is apparent from the experiences in Cambodia, East Timor, and Afghanistan that post-conflict elites, like their counterparts across the contemporary developing world, find that it is both easier and more profitable for them to focus, for the most part, on distributing narrowly targeted public rents and patronage goods to their clients in exchange for political support. One major insight of historical institutionalist theory is that actors use a variety of strategies to achieve change in political outcomes "beneath the veneer of apparent institutional stability."[2] One such process is that of "conversion," whereby actors can reshape institutions and policies to achieve objectives very different from the purposes for which they were originally created.[3] Thus, the characteristically hybrid nature of neopatrimonialism suits their ends very well: they perform their major functions in the formal institutional realms of state administration and electoral politics while maneuvering in more hidden and less risky ways to represent their own interests and those of their major client groups.

Analytical approaches that rely on more short-term measures of peacebuilding success and evaluate interventions as exogenous treatments are unfortunately restricted in seeing these gradual and endogenous processes of institutional change that continue to unfold. This chapter addresses this blind spot by tying international interventions to their aftermath, viewing the creation of post-conflict institutions as the beginning of the next phase of political contestation. It thus devotes further attention to the consequences of the institutional decisions made during the transitional governance process and the unfolding domestic political dynamics, as I assess the degree of state capacity and democratic consolidation in Cambodia, East Timor, and Afghanistan. Hewing to the historical institutionalist perspective, I examine how governance power shifts and settles through the institutional system, paying particular attention to the manner in which domestic elites use the institutional infrastructure to their advantage in consolidating their own grip on power. Two core elements of the nature of neopatrimonial political order in the three cases are highlighted. First, I emphasize that the effects of the transitional governance strategy last into the final phase of the peacebuilding pathway. Political elites thus continue to use

[2] Thelen and Mahoney 2015: 23.
[3] Hacker, Pierson, and Thelen 2015: 185–186.

the strategies of institutional change on display during the transitional governance period as they work to consolidate their preferred neopatrimonial political order in the aftermath of intervention. Second, the chapter recognizes that post-intervention Cambodia, East Timor, and Afghanistan vary in the extent to which they can be characterized as peaceful, democratic, and well-governed. The governance qualities of the specific hybrid order that forms in each country rest on the particular system of rent extraction and distribution that emerges in each, which results, in turn, from how transitional governance interventions interacted with antecedent conditions in each case. The consequences of these peacebuilding attempts can only truly be understood when they are viewed as pivotal points in time.

Power dynamics evolve in ways that can be hidden unless enough time has elapsed to view their outcomes, especially when path-dependent feedback loops are involved.[4] The previous chapter emphasized that because UN peace operations must govern, they asymmetrically empower one group of domestic elites to dominate the transformative peace process and its aftermath. This has lasting consequences. Paul Pierson identifies five mechanisms through which power can beget power: the transfer of a stock of resources to victors; their subsequent access to a stream of resources over time; the signal that political victory sends about relative political strength and capability and the alignment of other actors to these signals; shifts in political and social discourse, or the cultural power to change society's preferences; and the inducement of preference changes that benefit those in power through targeted investments, institutions, and policies.[5] The evidence presented in this chapter shows that these mechanisms apply as much to those elites conferred power by the international community as to those who win it under their own steam.

Post-Intervention Cambodia: Exclusionary Neopatrimonialism and the Threat of Violence

The United Nations Transitional Authority in Cambodia declared victory and left the country having held free and fair elections in May 1993 and having overseen the process of constitution-drafting in the months that followed. On the ground, however, the power-sharing

[4] Pierson 2015. [5] Ibid.: 134–141.

coalition between FUNCINPEC and the Cambodian People's Party that resulted from the 1993 elections created legislative and executive gridlock. The CPP continued to hold power across the organs of government and to administer the country just as it had before the elections, as the State of Cambodia, and, before UNTAC itself, as the Vietnam-installed regime known as the People's Republic of Kampuchea. The co-governing arrangement between Ranariddh and Hun Sen, nominally the first and second prime ministers respectively, was a fiction from start to finish. The latter wielded true power while the prince spent much of his time enjoying the perks of office and the two men intensified their competition to win power outright for their factions. Formal institutions and arenas of political contestation were stripped of meaning as they were used by Cambodian elites to do nothing more than mask the real political competition under the surface.

The power-sharing agreement concerned the top strata of government and, in practice, FUNCINPEC's authority was restricted to the cabinet level while the CPP retained its monopoly on administrative power exercised through the state hierarchy. In the ministries, FUNCINPEC found itself in a weak position – although it appointed many party functionaries to senior ministry and provincial positions, it simply lacked the bureaucratic capacity to have the necessary presence further down the hierarchy. Until 1993, FUNCINPEC had been a resistance movement rather than a political party and it proved unable to quickly develop any deeper institutional strength. In the provinces, FUNCINPEC-appointed governors and senior officials found that rank-and-file bureaucrats simply ignored their bidding and followed the instructions of their CPP leaders instead. Finally, the security apparatus was brought entirely under the control of the CPP and, increasingly, Hun Sen's faction within it – who portrayed the incorporation of the other Cambodian factions into political life as a threat to the nation.[6] Overall, the government bureaucracy and the military, ostensibly two organs of the state, became organs of the party. The CPP achieved this result by extending and strengthening the patron–client network within and among the state, party, and military apparatuses.

Continuing bureaucratic factionalism has prevented the development of national institutional capacity to this day. Institutions such as a neutral and effective bureaucracy, a nonpartisan army, an independent

[6] Hughes 2009a.

judiciary – let alone precedents for peaceful power transfer – have not taken root in Cambodia. A promising sign under UNTAC and immediately after the first election was the flourishing of NGOs and media outlets, and growing subnational political participation. UNTAC was innovative in helping to establish Cambodian NGOs dealing with human rights, democracy, and development, even giving them start-up advice and funding.[7] But these advances could not amount to much in the broader political environment.

In effect, it had already become clear by 1995–96 that the Cambodian political system fell far short of the pluralist, representative, accountable, and efficient government envisioned by the framers of the Paris Peace Agreement and the UNTAC mandate. Institutional capacity aside, Ashley points out that Cambodia's post-electoral power-sharing system did not emerge from, nor contribute to, the desire for reconciliation on the part of the country's elites and thus, unsurprisingly, did not lead to a political transformation of the type sought by the international community.[8] Not only did the power-sharing system fail to foster reconciliation among the factions and build a new political system based on compromise and inclusion. Worse still, the power-sharing system created dual governments as FUNCINPEC brought its supporters into the already bloated state structure. This deadlocked effective decision-making and governance and perpetuated parallel crony-based political networks. Having failed to secure electoral legitimacy or an administrative power base, FUNCINPEC leaders instead mimicked the CPP in rent extraction and distribution networks, entering into "a tenuous compact among competing patronage systems."[9] The power-sharing system thus failed to foster true reconciliation among the factions. More perversely, it served in replacing outright elite conflict with a dual system of rent-seeking and predation. Operating both within and outside the state, these "[h]ierarchical patron–client networks . . . have expanded and subsumed the formal state structure."[10]

These patronage conditions have underpinned an ever-expanding dynamic of elite rent-seeking and rent distribution that undermines democracy and state capacity. The CPP and FUNCINPEC were united in their desire to protect their patronage resources and sought to ensure

[7] Author interviews with donor officials and civil society leaders; Phnom Penh, Cambodia, May 2005.

[8] Ashley 1998. [9] Gottesman 2003: 353. [10] Ashley 1998: 55.

that their interests were not threatened through reforms. Both parties, for example, were anxious to ensure that their own supporters survived a process of civil service reform, which prevented a necessary retrenchment program; and attempts to modernize the public financial management system and increase state revenues also stalled since they were seen as a threat to the ability of the two patronage networks to extract off-budget rents.[11] The consensus principle of the coalition government endowed the CPP in particular, with its control of the state, de facto veto power over any reforms that threatened its political, financial, or institutional interests. The capacity of the state to deliver public goods and services had been weak under the State of Cambodia. Post-UNTAC administrative reforms became increasingly unlikely. The state had no nonpartisan, technocratic constituency to support institutional reform and the building of state capacity and to defend itself against the elite's desire to cement the patron–client networks upon which its popular support depended. UNTAC, in emphasizing elections over statebuilding, missed the window of opportunity to build that coalition for the reform and strengthening of the state, which, in turn, has hampered the international community's efforts to build state capacity and improve Cambodian governance into today.[12] Caroline Hughes observes that the government has, in particular, prevented development partners from having any real influence over the civil service, judiciary, and natural resource sectors in order to maintain these core elements of the administrative apparatus as "a sphere of discretionary political action and an instrument of political control."[13] Measures of government effectiveness in Cambodia demonstrate that while state capacity may have improved slightly in the late 1990s, it has since declined and has stagnated at a relatively low level in comparison to its per capita income peers.[14]

[11] Author interviews with donor officials and civil society leaders; Phnom Penh, Cambodia, May 2005. See also Nunberg et al. 2010; Nunberg and Taliercio 2012; Turner 2013.

[12] Author interviews with donor officials; Phnom Penh, Cambodia, May 2005 and October 2005.

[13] Hughes 2009a: 139.

[14] Such measures include, for example, the World Bank's Country Policy and Institutional Assessment (CPIA) public sector management and institutions cluster score for government effectiveness, as well as the "government effectiveness" measure in the Worldwide Governance Indicators dataset. Kaufmann, Kraay, and Mastruzzi 2010.

The capture of the state apparatus, a hallmark feature of neopatrimonial political order, doomed Cambodia to an inevitable backslide in terms of democratic consolidation and it also hampered statebuilding. UNTAC's failure to move the CPP toward depoliticizing the state structure was its true legacy for post-1993 Cambodia, having much more of an impact on the country's later course than UNTAC's success in holding elections. The international community lost the opportunity to build a countervailing locus of authority in the Cambodian state apparatus that could potentially prevail against a corrupt, violent, and cynical political elite and form the basis for a genuine political settlement to come out of peacebuilding through transitional governance. The power-sharing coalition, viewed by the international community as an encouraging move toward legitimate governance, was a mismatch for Cambodia's zero-sum, "winner-takes-all political culture."[15] The consolidation of two parallel patron–client networks embedded in the state also affected internal party dynamics, concentrating power in the hands of Hun Sen and Ranariddh. The two leaders managed to work together for the first three years of their coalition government, avoiding contentious issues and pursuing enough economic liberalization to satisfy foreign reform demands. Indeed, Cambodia scholars have argued that the privatization and marketization reforms introduced in the country in 1989 made the expansion of dual party-based clientelist networks easier and more profitable.[16] In this regard, too, the international community's policy preferences enabled post-conflict elites to achieve their own objectives more effectively.

Yet, even as they cooperated in rent extraction and distribution, Hun Sen and Ranariddh continued to jockey for absolute power in the still-evolving political context. Tensions quickly mounted between the two leaders; by 1996, Ranariddh began to complain vocally about inequality in the coalition and the imbalance between the two prime ministers and their parties became increasingly obvious. The Khmer Rouge still managed to exert an influence on governance in the country even as a spent military and political force, when Ieng Sary, one of the faction's top leaders, announced that he would defect to the government and bring with him both a large proportion of Khmer Rouge troops and the resource-rich territory around his stronghold of Pailin. Hun Sen and Ranariddh, each eager to decisively tip the power balance their

[15] Chandler 1998: 43. [16] Hughes 2009a; and Springer 2009.

way, both offered large sums of money and the promise of future rent streams to entice Ieng Sary to join their respective sides. In the end, this was another political battle won by Hun Sen.[17]

Anticipation of the 1998 national elections set off a series of events through which Hun Sen and the CPP were able to consolidate their political power. The three main opposition parties – FUNCINPEC, the Buddhist Liberal Democratic Party, and the new reformist Sam Rainsy Party (SRP) – formed a coalition to contest the elections and challenge the CPP's grip on power. In turn, the CPP became increasingly concerned about the increased attractiveness to voters of the opposition coalition. Violence erupted in the charged political atmosphere when an opposition rally led by Sam Rainsy was bombed in March 1997. In July of the same year, troops loyal to Hun Sen and the CPP staged a coup d'état, bringing tanks onto the streets of Phnom Penh, skirmishing with and defeating royalist troops, and forcing Ranariddh, Sam Rainsy, and other non-CPP politicians into exile. Hun Sen's pretext for this move to oust Ranariddh from the political scene was the oft-invoked specter of renewed civil conflict, based on the accusation that Ranariddh was about to strike a reintegration deal with the Khmer Rouge. This coup marked the breakdown of the attempt to share power between elite groups and the emergence of a de facto one-party system led by the hegemonic CPP.[18]

More broadly, the 1997 coup and the series of elections that have followed represent a sequence that has returned Cambodia to the often-violent, inherently undemocratic, and traditionally clientelist manner of asserting political order in the country. The expanding and tightening grip on Cambodia's administrative and political systems exerted by the CPP and Hun Sen has thwarted any meaningful progress in either state capacity-building or democratic consolidation. A new election was held in 1998 with the exiled politicians returning to Cambodia to participate after almost a year of post-coup negotiations and pressure from the international community. Yet FUNCINPEC and the SRP did not have the deep party roots at the subnational level that were necessary to challenge the CPP's organizational strength and claim to state authority across the country. In the announced election results, decreed free and fair by international observers, the CPP won a plurality, while

[17] Strangio 2014: 75–76.

[18] Barma 2006; Brown and Timberman 1998; Croissant 2007; and Roberts 2009.

Table 5.1 *Electoral results in Cambodia, 1998–2013*

July 1998 Parliamentary	July 2003 Parliamentary	July 2008 Parliamentary	July 2013 Parliamentary
CPP 64 seats FUNCINPEC 43 seats Sam Rainsy Party 15 seats	**CPP** 73 seats FUNCINPEC 26 seats Sam Rainsy Party 24 seats	**CPP** 90 seats Sam Rainsy Party 26 seats FUNCINPEC + royalist party 4 seats	**CPP** 68 seats CNRP (merger of Sam Rainsy Party + Human Rights Party) 55 seats

FUNCINPEC and the SRP split the majority. (Official electoral results from 1998–2013 are presented in Table 5.1.) It was common knowledge that the CPP controlled this election, dominating new oversight institutions such as the National Election Committee and restricting opposition politicians' access to the media.[19] In another ostensibly power-sharing arrangement, Hun Sen was renamed prime minister and Ranariddh was made the president of the National Assembly. Some space for the representation of opposition parties was made at subnational levels of governance, but the CPP continued its entrenched hold on the structures of the state. In practical terms, little changed "the view that FUNCINPEC and SRP representatives took part in government essentially on the sufferance of the CPP."[20]

This familiar pattern was repeated in the July 2003 elections: after an electoral process marked by voting fraud and violence, the CPP won over half the seats in the national assembly, although it did fall short of the two-thirds majority needed to form a government. One year of stalemate followed, with negotiations to form a government beginning in July 2004 and culminating in yet another deal on paper with FUNCINPEC. In practice, the control exercised by the CPP and Hun Sen on the country's levers of power simply became more concentrated, even as the CPP continued to gain a veneer of international legitimacy from these elections, which it has prided itself in organizing efficiently. Although international observers have certified all of Cambodia's series of post-conflict elections as free and fair, the CPP's electoral strategy is

[19] Gottesman 2003; Hughes 2003. [20] Hughes 2009b: 55.

common knowledge: in 2003, its guidance to party representatives was to offer clear voting instructions and easy poll access for their supporters, combined with misdirection for other parties' supporters.[21]

Within a decade of UNTAC's withdrawal, the formal institutional and electoral space was simply no longer the true arena of political contestation. As he further consolidated political power, Hun Sen continued to strengthen the CPP's control over the state and its lucrative patronage networks. The CPP-dominated Royal Government of Cambodia has created and reinforced a system of resource generation and distribution for paying off rivals and supporters that runs parallel to the formal trappings of government through access to large off-budget "slush funds." What should be public goods and services for the rural population – such as schools, health clinics, roads, and bridges – are branded as targeted "gifts" provided by the CPP and its senior leaders to the population, instead of being presented as programmatically delivered government outputs.[22] Villages across the country thus receive "Hun Sen schools" and health centers bearing the names of Hun Sen's wife and other prominent CPP elites. From 1998 onward, this particularist approach was a pillar of the CPP's electoral strategy and proved crucial in their increasing vote share in the 1998 and 2003 national elections and the 2002 and 2007 local elections. Through its clientelist strategy, the CPP has claimed for itself the mantle of being the only party that could effectively deliver public services – notwithstanding the need to rely on personal networks or bribes to access these services. In 2003, for example, the CPP's electoral message was, "We are the party that gets things done; don't bite the hand that feeds you."[23]

The patronage machine has also been indispensable to the processes of elite accommodation within the country – and has, in turn, freed the government and party elites, to a great extent, from the need to be accountable to the Cambodian population. With the CPP hegemonic, a "shadow state" system developed, with elites focusing on developing predatory and exclusive control over high-rent economic activity, thereby assuring their hold on power.[24] The army and police have been complicit in the patronage system, relying upon the valuable resource

[21] Ibid.: 51–53.
[22] Author interviews with donor officials, Cambodian analysts, and civil society leaders; Phnom Penh, Cambodia, October 2014.
[23] Hughes 2009b: 50. [24] Barma 2012a; Hughes 2009a; and Le Billon 2000.

concessions they have been granted by the political elite to enrich individual officials and strengthen their bureaucratic power through an array of illegal and predatory activities.[25]

Cambodia's political elites have expanded their patronage networks both vertically, to accumulate uncontested power at the subnational level, and horizontally, to include wealthy business interests and military leaders, who control, together with politicians in mutually beneficial arrangements, access to most of the country's lucrative natural resources, including timber and now oil.[26] An elite strata of Cambodian businessmen accrue rents in partnership with government and party officials, through channels such as preferred access to government procurement contracts and government-brokered land grabs in anticipation of lucrative development projects. Cambodian newspapers are filled with reports of protests about evictions in Phnom Penh and other towns.[27] Rural areas are also affected by this phenomenon: Hughes reports that what was a fairly egalitarian land-holding system in the countryside in 1989 was transformed into a highly unequal one by 2006, where 70 percent of the land was owned by the richest 20 percent of the population, resulting in a considerable "dispossession of the poor" in the context of the rural subsistence economy.[28] Overall, a process of privatization of state assets – forestry, fisheries, minerals, water, petroleum, and land – has generated revenues for the government to distribute as clientelist payments for political support; and has fortified a mutually symbiotic relationship between Cambodia's political and economic elites.

As these predatory patterns have increasingly permeated the country's political economy, the role of violence and intimidation in influencing election results gave way, for over two decades, to an increasing reliance on patronage distribution aimed toward uncontested political dominance. In this way, elite predation has replaced outright conflict

[25] Hendrickson 2001: 72. [26] Barma 2012b.

[27] The notorious Boueng Kak Lake development is one such example. What used to be a major freshwater lake in central Phnom Penh that served as a source of food and income generation for about 4,000 households living in the villages around the lake, as well as an important element of the urban ecology, was granted in a concession to a CPP senator in 2007. In a joint venture with a Chinese property developer, his company began filling in the lake and evicting residents, offering them minimal compensation, in order to prepare the land for a luxury development. See Kent 2016.

[28] Hughes 2009a: 158.

as the main avenue through which Cambodians experience insecurity and vulnerability in everyday life – but "the threat of violence [remains] an ever present prop to the system."[29] In addition to patronage distribution, the CPP's other core electoral strategy has been the mantra that it alone can ensure security and order in the country and prevent it from descending again into conflict; when, ironically, the only real insecurity in Cambodia emerges from within the CPP and as a result of its tactics. Hun Sen and other party leaders regularly raise the specter of renewed civil war in the event that the CPP's governing legitimacy were to be challenged. Yet the opposition persists – in the elections of 2013, even in the face of the typical widespread enticements for CPP voters and the intimidation of opposition supporters, Cambodian voters delivered surprising gains at the polls to opposition parties on the back of high levels of expressed discontent with poor government services, corruption, land grabs, and poor economic opportunity. Still dominating oversight and executive functions within government, the CPP persuaded Sam Rainsy and his new opposition party, the Cambodia National Rescue Party (CNRP), to end a boycott of parliament and enter into a working relationship with the governing regime. By late 2015, what appeared to be a promising rapprochement had ended, with a bitter stand-off between Hun Sen and a newly self-exiled Sam Rainsy in full force. Opposition leader Kem Sokha marked the twenty-fourth anniversary of the Paris Peace Agreement in October 2015 by denouncing the CPP government for having failed to deliver on the promises set out in the peace deal.[30] Hun Sen, in turn, reverted to his dire warnings of the return of civil strife and violent conflict if voters fail to support the CPP.[31]

It may be the case that the logic underpinning the neopatrimonial political order provided by the CPP in post-conflict Cambodia is in the process of changing from one of enforcing internal security to one in which the regime will need to deliver a greater measure of public services and some level of collective goods in order to retain political support for itself. The 2013 election results were viewed as a watershed in this respect, especially since the basis for the regime's legitimacy

[29] Hughes 2009a: 156; also Hughes 2003; and Un 2005.

[30] Kuch Naren. 2015. "CNRP Says Peace Accords Not Yet Fully Implemented." *The Cambodia Daily*, October 24.

[31] Alex Willemyns. 2015. "Hun Sen, Pondering Defeat, Has War on Mind." *The Cambodia Daily*, October 26.

appears to be shifting as an older generation scarred by the civil war and genocide becomes superseded politically by a new generation with little direct memory of war and more modern demands of government. In 2014, it seemed that the CPP regime recognized that it would have to start doing something differently or else be at real risk of being voted out.[32] Perhaps, twenty-five years after the end of the Cambodian civil war, post-conflict incentives are finally being truly reoriented. In the immediate post-conflict environment, it was apparent that the time horizons were extremely short, orienting the country's elites toward high levels of extractive behavior – and even collusion if necessary, as evidenced in the CPP's and FUNCINPEC's dual rent networks. Now, with some degree of demand for accountability, government performance in terms of service delivery, and renewed attention to electoral legitimacy, the time horizon may finally be lengthening – and it appears likely that the CPP will have to better deliver some measure of public goods in order to get the minimal level of public support necessary to stay in power legitimately. If this were to become true, it will not have been the international peacebuilding intervention that achieved these results; the changes will have been the outcome of a more organic process of evolution in governance.

Post-Intervention East Timor: Inclusionary Neopatrimonialism and Latent Conflict

After East Timor attained independence, the UN designated two successive missions, the United Nations Mission of Support in East Timor (UNMISET, 2002–2005) and the UN Office in Timor-Leste (UNOTIL, 2005–2006), to assist with the program of continued reconstruction. The central dimension of both those mandates was to provide continued capacity-building assistance to the East Timorese administration. Although by September 2001, UNTAET had established the East Timor Public Administration as part of an all-Timorese transitional government, this embryonic civil service had only a very limited capacity. The civil administration was highly dependent on international assistance to make up for a low level of professional skills, particularly in the central government functions of human resources and public

[32] Author interviews with donor officials, Cambodian analysts, and civil society leaders; Phnom Penh, Cambodia, October 2014.

financial management.[33] Timorese political leaders' emphasis on political incorporation had meant that little attention was paid to the state-strengthening dimension of the peacebuilding program. Measures of government effectiveness in East Timor demonstrate that state capacity did not much improve after the transition to independence and has remained at low levels.[34]

FRETILIN's domination of the political process after the transitional period – facilitated by UNTAET's slow moves to incorporate broader political participation and the sequencing of the Timorization of government – proved problematic for the strengthening of the state and the longer-term consolidation of democracy in East Timor. FRETILIN, in essence, "placed the new National Parliament in clear subordination to a government intent on using its majority to push through its ambitious legislative program."[35] It also quickly began to consolidate its patronage networks throughout the country by politicizing civil service hiring in district administration, ensuring positions were filled by FRETILIN cadres.[36] By mid-2005 it became apparent that, notwithstanding its grassroots support and dominating organizational presence throughout the country, the population at large did not necessarily share FRETILIN's goals for the country.

The FRETILIN leadership's particular history and contemporary policymaking style and content increasingly compromised the party's political legitimacy. The party compounded a pattern of Timorese elitist political behavior that threatened true democratic consolidation. In an oft-cited example of what was viewed as the FRETILIN leadership's political tone-deafness and elitist orientation, it chose Portuguese as the official national language, marginalizing the Indonesian-educated

[33] Author interviews with East Timorese government officials in civil service human resources management and public financial management; Dili, East Timor, April 2005.

[34] Such measures include, for example, the World Bank's Country Policy and Institutional Assessment (CPIA) public sector management and institutions cluster score for government effectiveness, as well as the "government effectiveness" measure in the Worldwide Governance Indicators dataset. Kaufmann, Kraay, and Mastruzzi 2010.

[35] Goldstone 2004: 84.

[36] Author interviews with academics, East Timorese provincial officials, and donor officials; Dili, East Timor, 2005. One Timorese official reported that FRETILIN was the only party that had a presence in his (relatively large) province.

and Bahasa-speaking urban youth who were in the process of forming their own increasingly significant political constituency. Timorese civil society representatives have criticized the country's hierarchical and closed political culture, pointing out that although it may have contributed to the success of a national resistance movement it has since been detrimental to democracy.[37] The opposition began to mobilize – the Catholic Church, for example, began to take on a more activist and populist role, opposing the government over certain pieces of legislation.[38]

Politically motivated violence erupted in April 2006, reflecting deep and long-standing political animosities among the elite, emerging state capture and competing patterns of patronage behavior, and an absence of elite efforts to engage with community and customary forms of governance.[39] This conflict turned violent as FRETILIN proved unable to assert legitimate control over armed groups – the breakdown in authority resulted in an episode of arson and looting in Dili and its environs. Over the course of several months of severe political instability, 38 people were killed and 69 wounded, 1,500 houses were destroyed, and 150,000 people were internally displaced.[40] Eventually, the majority of the population had their wishes fulfilled when FRETILIN Prime Minister Mari Alkatiri was forced out of office at the behest of Xanana Gusmão and other revolutionary leaders.

The 2006 conflict marked the onset of internal strife and political instability, distinct from both the decades-long resistance and the 1999 conflict associated with the independence vote. It revealed deep-seated social tensions in East Timor and some saw it as an outcome of UNTAET's failure to broker a domestic political settlement at independence.[41] The "crisis," as it became known, was triggered by rising tension between factions in the armed forces and police. There was some truth to the notion that this dispute reflected long-standing

[37] Author interviews with East Timorese NGO representatives and journalists; Dili, East Timor, April 2005. At the time, Gusmão escaped criticism of elitist political decision-making. Also, Bowles and Chopra 2008.

[38] In April 2005, the Catholic Church trucked in tens of thousands of unemployed youth from the provinces to Dili in order to stage a demonstration against the government's plan to make religious education in schools optional rather than mandatory.

[39] Boyle 2009; Brown 2009; and Scambary 2009.

[40] Figures from Hughes 2009a: 154.

[41] For example, Ingram 2012.

animosities between the Western and Eastern factions within the armed forces – more Western commanders were killed during the Indonesian occupation and Western soldiers complained that their treatment under mostly Eastern commanders was unfair. The tension was a concrete manifestation of decisions made during the transitional governance period: when the East Timor Defense Force was created at independence, the first of its two battalions was recruited from the ranks of the FALINTIL guerrilla fighters in a process that disproportionately favored Gusmão loyalists and troops from the eastern districts of the country.[42] Some of this tension was also the outcome of political intrigue: the Minister of the Interior Rogério Lobato, with the implicit consent of Alkatiri, established loyalist groups inside the armed forces as a counterweight to those troops loyal to Gusmão. A UN Security Council assessment mission found that Lobato also supplied an irregular paramilitary group involved in the violence with arms intended for the police and that he instructed the group to use the weapons against political opponents.[43] Yet the crisis quickly spiraled to encompass a number of sociopolitical grievances and dimensions – escalating because it became a vehicle for key groups, particularly resistance veterans and Dili residents, to rally against the unpopular Alkatiri government.[44]

Overlaid on the political scene was the fact that during this period East Timor had rapidly become one of the most petroleum-dependent countries in the world, with oil and natural gas revenues providing about 90 percent of government revenues, on average, since petroleum production commenced in 2004. In retrospect, observers point to the role played by petroleum revenues in lubricating the 2006 civil conflict and political fight.[45] At the time of independence the FRETILIN government had to operate with a very small budget and refused to borrow to finance more spending. As the country began to reap its first hydrocarbon revenues in 2004, the opposition disapproved of the continued austerity measures in the face of this windfall. By 2005–06 FRETILIN's decision not to spend the country's petroleum

[42] Ingram 2012: 11. See also Rees 2004.
[43] United Nations Security Council 2006.
[44] Scambary 2009 provides a detailed examination of this crisis. See also United Nations Security Council 2006; United States Library of Congress 2009.
[45] Barma 2014.

Table 5.2 *Electoral results in East Timor, 2007–2012*

May 2007 Presidential, second-round runoff	June 2007 Parliamentary	April 2012 Presidential, second-round runoff	July 2012 Parliamentary
Jose Ramos-Horta (independent) 69 percent (22 percent first round) Francisco Guterres (FRETILIN) 30 percent (28 percent first round)	**FRETILIN** 21 seats CNRT (National Congress for Timorese Reconstruction) 18 seats PSD-ASDT 11 seats Democratic Party 8 seats Other 6 seats **Result:** CNRT-led coalition government	**Taur Matan Ruak** (independent) 61 percent (22 percent first round) Francisco Guterres (FRETILIN) 39 percent (29 percent first round)	**CNRT** 30 seats FRETILIN 25 seats Democratic Party 8 seats Other 6 seats **Result:** CNRT-led coalition government

wealth to relieve poverty, kick-start growth, and create much-needed employment had contributed substantially to the population's widespread disaffection with the party.

New presidential and parliamentary elections were held in May and June 2007, respectively. Xanana Gusmão stepped aside as president to run for prime minister, the real seat of power in the country, and his ally José Ramos-Horta easily won the presidential election against the FRETILIN candidate. In the parliamentary elections, FRETILIN received the largest number of votes but, in a serious rebuke from the voters, it saw its tally slip from 57 percent in the 2001 elections to 29 percent and it was unable to form a coalition government. (Official electoral results from 2007–2012 are presented in Table 5.2.) Gusmão's new National Congress for the Reconstruction of East Timor or CNRT – conveniently the same acronym of the enormously popular national resistance front under whose banner the independence referendum was won in 1999 – won 23 percent of the vote, the next highest share after FRETILIN's. In a contentious decision, President Ramos-Horta exercised his constitutional right in selecting the CNRT to form the new government – but Gusmão was only able to do so at the head of a volatile new coalition.[46]

A precedent for the peaceful transfer of power was thus set relatively early in East Timor's post-conflict years. Yet this was still a government where authority was concentrated in the hands of a small group of revolutionary-era political elites. The crisis had also clearly thrown the country into a serious constitutional and political crisis, the resolution of which was not uncontentious. For example, observers criticized Gusmão for having initially compromised the constitution by demanding Alkatiri leave office; yet there is no legal process in East Timor for determining the constitutionality of his actions as president. There appeared to have been a reversal of some degree of earlier behavioral democratic consolidation among core political elites – but public attitudes toward democracy remained encouraging. In a more promising sign of renewed political institutionalization, smaller parties were proliferating and growing in strength, capitalizing on the frustration of young, urban, and educated East Timorese with the older, Portuguese-speaking, conservative leaders of FRETILIN and attempting to better channel the political participation of the East Timorese population. On the statebuilding front, the insistence on political participation and development on the part of both the UN and the Timorese elite continued to overshadow responsibility being undertaken for reconstructing the still-eviscerated structures of state. Although the formidable statebuilding challenge may have been obscured by the attempts to repair the country's fragile democracy, the lack of attention to institutional and human capacity-building contributed in no small part to the political instability experienced in 2006.

Under the Gusmão-led coalition government, the neopatrimonial nature of politics in East Timor has become increasingly apparent. Political elites began to benefit from the oil price spike and the significant stream of petroleum revenues in the late 2000s, distributing the patronage made possible by these fiscal receipts and gaining political support on that basis. East Timor thus began to follow a pattern familiar to rentier states, with public sector hiring and pay increasing along with growing concerns over elite capture of petroleum

[46] Politically motivated violence continued after the election, with rebel soldiers undertaking coordinated, unsuccessful assassination attempts against President José Ramos-Horta and Prime Minister Xanana Gusmão in February 2008.

concessions and lucrative procurement contracts.[47] The new governing coalition viewed the Timorese population's dissatisfaction upon failing to see some immediate benefits emerging from the country's newfound peace and its petroleum wealth as a key dimension in the downfall of FRETILIN. The electoral campaign run by Xanana Gusmão's CNRT thus pledged to increase social spending rapidly in order to deliver a peace and petroleum dividend. Once in office, Gusmão's administration delivered on that promise by initiating social transfers to specific groups in the population and opening up decentralized mechanisms for rapidly increasing public infrastructure spending – with immediate and sustained results. Capital spending climbed from less than $25 million in 2005 to about $180 million in 2008 and $600 million in 2011.[48] Cash transfers constitute a very large share of the budget – $234 million, or 13 percent of the 2012 budget, and a great deal more than the $153 million spent on the health and education sectors.[49] These spending increases were made possible through the government's repeated annual requests to Parliament to exceed the legally prescribed level of petroleum revenue spending established to prevent the short-term squandering of resource wealth.[50]

In short, since the 2007 elections, it has become both legitimate and relatively easy for the government to engage in the neopatrimonial distribution of ever-higher shares of the country's petroleum rents. Viewing the various public spending measures in the best possible light, the new coalition government acted in the aftermath of the 2006 crisis to "buy the peace" with the country's best interests in mind. From this viewpoint, the government fulfilled its campaign promises and perceived mandate to distribute rents in the form of public expenditures to key constituencies – thereby maintaining post-election political stability by pacifying the social dissent and controlling the internecine elite

[47] Barma 2014; and Blunt 2009. [48] International Monetary Fund 2009, 2013.

[49] República Democrática de Timor-Leste, "State Budget 2012: Budget Overview – Book I." Dili, October 2011.

[50] East Timor's Petroleum Fund Law of 2005 established a concept known as Estimated Sustainable Income (ESI) that is intended to ensure intergenerational saving. ESI is defined as the maximum amount that can be appropriated from the fund in any given fiscal year, such that enough revenue is left in the fund for the same value to be appropriated in all subsequent years. The Petroleum Fund Law sets ESI at 3 percent, on the assumption that the Petroleum Fund will generate an annualized 3 percent return on investment. República Democrática de Timor-Leste, *Petroleum Fund Law*, Law No. 9/2005.

conflict that had together led to the 2006 crisis. A preliminary analysis of the geographic allocation of public spending in East Timor found that the government was spending more – in terms of both cash transfers and public investment allocation – in those districts most strongly supportive of the coalition partners in the 2007 election.[51] The coalition was rewarded with another victory in the 2012 elections, in which FRETILIN failed to make an expected comeback in the polls; and there has been no return to widespread conflict since 2006.

Yet this is an equilibrium underpinned by a neopatrimonial political order, rather than the effective and legitimate governance envisaged by the international community and the major UNTAET intervention. A small group of political–economic elites has cemented its place in authority by dispensing patronage in exchange for broad political support. The coalition government, for example, has targeted its major clientelistic practices to very deliberately and very successfully co-opt the veterans of the clandestine resistance. High-level veterans are best understood as being still-armed militia leaders who represent a substantial threat to political stability. They are the specific individuals dispersed throughout the country who still have the capacity – and, if their demands are unmet, the expressed willingness – to mobilize civil conflict and even violence against the regime.[52] Of the aggregate spending on cash transfers, $85 million – a full 5 percent of the total 2012 budget – went to veterans.[53] The official annual veteran payment averaged just under $3,200 per beneficiary in 2011, representing 137 percent of the Timorese average total household budget.[54] These transfer payments to veterans have been framed as recognition for past service to the country rather than as a form of social assistance and outpace and crowd out other social spending. Veterans have also been explicitly targeted as the beneficiaries of the government's decentralized public investment efforts. Several interviewees in 2013 urged me to imagine the counterfactual – asking, in particular whether political stability would have persisted had major patronage distribution

[51] Catherine Anderson, Naazneen Barma, and Douglas Porter, 2009, "The Political Economy of Natural Resource Management in Timor-Leste: A Value Chain perspective," Unpublished report, Washington, DC: The World Bank.

[52] International Crisis Group 2011.

[53] República Democrática de Timor-Leste, "State Budget 2012: Budget Overview – Book I." Dili, October 2011.

[54] Dale, Lepuschuetz, and Umapathi 2014: 292.

through government spending channels not been initiated and targeted to veterans.[55]

A different dimension of the neopatrimonial political order has manifested itself at the national level, through elite rent-seeking and the capture of significant elements of the government's public investment program and recurrent public sector contracts. In contrast to the distribution of government spending to different groups of the population, this latter channel of rent distribution benefits only an extremely small and concentrated political–economic elite and their clients. Reports abound of well-connected contractors – especially the family members and business partners, both Timorese and foreign, of senior government officials – winning single-sourced contracts, in contravention of the procurement law, with extremely high profit margins.[56]

This type of predatory rent capture by elites is a typical rentier state syndrome – but the East Timor experience exhibits an interesting twist. During the term of the first coalition government from 2007 to 2012, there was the sense that individuals and companies with particular ties to the coalition partners were capturing the lion's share of the contracts, thereby excluding those connected with the opposition from the lucrative rent streams. Since the government's re-election in 2012, however, there have been signs that opposition elites are also being incorporated into the system of rent-sharing. In one sign of this increasingly collusive elite behavior and capture of petroleum rents, the CNRT government and FRETILIN opposition in February 2013 came to a budget agreement behind closed doors that led to an unprecedented unanimous budget vote in Parliament. Many surmised that the implicit quid pro quo for the opposition's agreement was their increased access to rents through preferred procurement channels.[57] As in Cambodia, it appears that neopatrimonial practices may be as important, if not even

[55] Author's interviews with government officials and donor and civil society representatives, Dili, East Timor, November 2009 and February 2013.

[56] Author's interviews with government officials and donor and civil society representatives, Dili, East Timor, February 2013. A number of interviewees mentioned a recent Deloitte audit of procurement in East Timor, circa 2012, that catalogued specific irregularities and sources of leakage. During my visit to Dili in February 2013, newspapers focused on the particularly egregious case of the award of a lucrative hospital provisions contract to the husband of the Minister of Finance.

[57] Author's interviews with opposition politicians and donor and civil society representatives, Dili, East Timor, February 2013.

more important, to establishing inter-elite compromises and accommodation as they are to bolstering popular support for the governing party and the reigning political order. At the same time, the Timorese population has also demanded cleaner and more efficient government. In February 2015, Gusmão stepped aside as prime minister to make way for a new generation of leadership. In a sign of a continuing thaw in elite political rivalries – combined with a move toward a more technocratically inclined executive – Gusmão and his ruling CNRT party recommended FRETILIN member Rui de Araujo, the country's successful health minister at independence, to be prime minister.

Elite collusion in neopatrimonial governance is unsurprising in the context of East Timor's contemporary political history. Leaders across the political spectrum in the small country come from a small slice of society – being primarily drawn from three main groups: the *mestiço* elite; smaller groups of Indonesian-Chinese-affiliated businessmen; and a handful of "Timorese–Timorese" leaders of the clandestine resistance, many of whom come from indigenous royal houses. The current generation of leaders for the most part grew up together while attending one of two major Portuguese seminaries near Dili; divided themselves into opposing factions in the 1975 civil war; and then came together again, albeit playing diverse roles, during the resistance and the post-independence UN transitional period. Their political–economic incentives are, for the most part, aligned – especially in the context of the relatively short time horizons in place as a result of the known end circa 2022 of the revenue stream from the country's only operational major gas field and the projected depletion at current spending rates of the country's petroleum revenues by 2028.[58] The number of politically and economically powerful families in East Timor has certainly multiplied since independence, with the Indonesian–Chinese-affiliated group particularly in the ascendant. Nevertheless, the core political–economic elite in East Timor represents, in essence, a very small winning coalition necessary to remain in power.[59] Over the past five years, moreover, through a deliberate

[58] La'o Hamutuk, "How Timor-Leste Got Ten Billion Dollars . . . and How Quickly We Will Spend it All." Dili, May 30, 2012. Blog posting accessed at: http://laohamutuk.blogspot.com/2012/05/how-timor-leste-got-ten-billion-dollars.html.

[59] Bueno de Mesquita et al. 2003.

neopatrimonial strategy, this elite has elicited and reinforced the political support of the only real potential spoilers, veteran leaders, by distributing just enough of the gains to pacify dissent and secure an element of legitimacy across the country.

Post-Intervention Afghanistan: Competitive Neopatrimonialism and Persistent Insecurity

The inauguration of the new Afghan national assembly on December 19, 2005 marked the official conclusion of the Bonn peace process as Afghanistan met its milestones. UNAMA's role in the aftermath of the Bonn process was to support the new government of the Islamic Republic of Afghanistan in its various dimensions of peacebuilding, including the identification of a new security framework, the improvement of governance, and the promotion of development. A new roadmap, known as the "Afghanistan Compact," was drawn up at the London Conference on Afghanistan held in early 2006. At this gathering over sixty countries and international agencies committed themselves, in partnership with Afghan government leaders, to the principles and targets laid out in the Compact, which was to guide the international community's support to Afghanistan in state capacity-building and the institutionalization of democracy. The express goal of the compact was to rely more heavily on Afghanistan's nascent institutions, with pledges of financial support from the international community.

Political stabilization, implicitly the international community's overarching goal in Afghanistan, has proceeded in fits and starts. Many have guessed that the fragmented parliament that resulted from the single non-transferable voting system adopted for the 2005 parliamentary elections was what Karzai intended in order to keep the executive stronger than the legislature: the elections led to three roughly equal-sized blocs in the assembly – one pro-government, one comprising the opposition parties, and one unaligned.[60] Even for the supposedly empowered executive, however, a fragmented parliament can make the formation of government and legislative politics very hard to handle. Legislative gridlock is undesirable everywhere and in post-conflict

[60] "Multi-multi-party Democracy." *The Economist*, October 22, 2005. See also Reynolds 2006.

situations can even be dangerous given the immediate need for effective governance to underpin political stability. Constitutional experts consider a stable party system to be an asset in post-conflict democracies. The SNTV system typically impedes party-building, making electoral alliances personality-driven and beholden to regional and other particularist power bases rather than being formed on the basis of programmatic and collectivist appeals articulated by ideologically coherent parties. The parliamentary fragmentation induced by the SNTV system impeded Karzai's reform agenda, since in practice it meant that for each executive initiative he had to assemble anew a legislative coalition through piecemeal deals and logrolling.[61] Moreover, since Karzai was unable to maintain a coalition of support for his program, the Afghan parliament was able to assert itself vis-à-vis the government. In May 2006, for example, the legislative body approved most of Karzai's proposed cabinet – but only after refusing to rubberstamp the whole body and insisting on individual hearings for each member.

Power tussles with parliament aside, Karzai acted to make the cabinet more his own by dropping the powerful trio of Panjshir Valley leaders who dominated the political and military scene after the Taliban's defeat and finally freeing himself from accusations that his government was under the control of the Northern Alliance faction. The move was seen as a step away from the "compromise government" that Karzai and his foreign allies built initially as a power-sharing mechanism. Later iterations of the cabinet included more technocrats as well as some remaining leaders of ethnic and political groups from around the country. Bringing local leaders to govern in the capital had the added benefit of neutralizing their influence in their regional strongholds. Thus, in the mid-2000s, it seemed that the Karzai administration was making progress in curbing the most egregious displays of patronage – for example, by moving Ismail Khan out of the governorship of Herat and into the post of Minister of Energy and Water, by demoting Gul Agha Shirzai from the governorship of Kandahar province to that of Nangahar province, and by removing Marshal Mohammed Fahim from his post as defense minister. By later in the decade, however, more ominous patterns of neopatrimonialism had asserted themselves.

Core choices made about Afghanistan's institutional architecture during the Bonn process and under UNAMA's supervision have had

[61] Reynolds 2006.

lasting effects on both state capacity-building and democratic consolidation in the country. Analysts have argued that the international community's preference for a "broad-based," compromise government over the course of the Bonn political process had the drawback of setting aside the pursuit of federalism, which many believed would have been a more natural fit for delivering public services and building governing legitimacy in the ethnoregionally diverse country. Federalism proponents argued that political contestation could have been transferred fruitfully to places other than Kabul, thereby recognizing the true loci of power – military, political, economic, and administrative – in the country. In attempting to create a strongly centralized national-unity government – which grew, in turn, out of UN efforts to solve the civil war dating back to the 1990s – critics argued that the international community fell prey to wishful thinking rather than designing appropriate institutions for the fissiparous reality of Afghan politics.[62]

Others have maintained that the appropriate solution to state collapse in Afghanistan was indeed a centralized state that could build effectiveness and maintain a credible monopoly on violence. In this view, decentralized or federal systems create insurmountable center–region tensions.[63] The highly centralized, unitary state model was intended to bring the provinces, once and for all, firmly under Kabul's political, administrative, and financial control – something that had not been achieved in modern Afghanistan. Many Afghan policymakers and observers themselves preferred the strong central state model, believing that persuading local strongmen to incorporate their power bases into a Kabul-led statebuilding process was an effective way to neutralize their extralegal power, and that decentralization or devolution could come later if still desired. Amin Saikal, for example, emphasized that meaningfully incorporating Afghanistan's "micro-societies" into the new fabric of the state was essential but possible within either a centralized or devolved state structure.[64]

One of the key aims of the broad-based coalition idea advocated by the international community was to ease fears that Pashtuns, who accounted for two-fifths of the Afghan population, making them the largest single ethnic group, would grow too strong. Pashtuns, on the other hand, believed that the concept of broad-based government

[62] Goodson 2005; and Reynolds 2006. [63] Cramer and Goodhand 2002.
[64] Saikal 2005.

was actually "code for rule by non-Pashtun figures from the old anti-Taliban coalition, the Northern Alliance,"[65] and that the Interim and Transitional Administrations overly represented these other groups. During the transitional period precisely the ethnic dynamic that national unity government proponents were trying to avoid was set in place, whereby Pashtuns, with the encouragement of Karzai, reasserted themselves politically and aroused the suspicions of Afghanistan's other major ethnic groups. The October 2004 presidential elections took on a significantly ethnic cast as a result of this ethnic electioneering, with Tajik, Hazara, and Uzbek leaders leading the vote in provinces dominated by their own ethnic groups.

In a promising sign for political institutionalization, some of these leaders – the Tajik Yunus Qanooni and the Uzbek Rashid Dostum foremost among them – would later form political parties in the run-up to the September 2005 parliamentary elections in order to broaden their appeal across ethnic lines. Despite the reluctance of Karzai and other senior officials to see the formation of parties for fear that they would deepen ethnic divisions, more than fifty parties registered prior to those elections. A few months ahead of the parliamentary elections, Qanooni announced the formation of an opposition front to compete in the elections, intended to forge a serious opposition bloc to Karzai's government.[66] Such moves toward party-building and other elements of political institutionalization could represent important advances in terms of behavioral consolidation of democracy among core political elites.

Yet the perception of corruption and personal empowerment and enrichment has also been a constant in the narrative of contemporary Afghan democracy. In August 2009, Hamid Karzai failed to secure an outright majority in the presidential election, being dogged by accusations of corruption in his administration and concerns about his attempts to secure victory by allying with unsavory warlords with documented human rights abuses. He nonetheless won re-election when the runner-up, Abdullah Abdullah, refused to participate in the second-round run-off due to widely acknowledged problems of voter intimidation, media censorship, and electoral fraud perpetrated by government

65 Goodson 2005: 31.

66 Carlotta Gall. 2005. "Afghan Parties Form Opposition Front to Oppose Karzai in Elections." *New York Times*, March 31.

Table 5.3 *Electoral results in Afghanistan, 2005–2014*

September 2005 Parliamentary	August 2009 Presidential	September 2010 Parliamentary	June 2014 Presidential, second-round runoff
High degree of vote fragmentation due to SNTV system; three roughly equal-sized blocs: one pro-government, one supporting opposition parties, and one unaligned	**Hamid Karzai** (independent) 50 percent Abdullah Abdullah (United National Front) 31 percent *Second-round runoff vote scheduled for Nov 2009 canceled after Abdullah refused to participate.	High degree of vote fragmentation due to SNTV system; three roughly equal-sized blocs: one pro-government, one supporting opposition parties, and one unaligned	**Ashraf Ghani** (independent) 56 percent Abdullah Abdullah (National Coalition of Afghanistan) 44 percent *Abdullah was a clear leader in the first round of voting and alleged voter fraud in the second round.

supporters. (Official electoral results from 2005 to 2014 are presented in Table 5.3.)

Even in the face of elite acrimony around elections, the consolidation of democratic attitudes among the Afghan public showed early signs of progress, in that Afghans quickly embraced the concepts of elections and democracy. Over the course of successive elections, voter turnout has remained quite high, although it fell from 84 percent in the 2004 presidential election to just about 60 percent in the 2014 presidential election, in part due to increased Taliban intimidation in the run-up to the latter. Richard Ponzio's 2005 public opinion survey also found significant internalization of democratic norms.[67] But, in a sign that power is still bifurcated between formal and informal, Afghans' voting behavior does not necessarily match with their views on where power lies in their society. Ponzio's survey data also revealed that

[67] Ponzio 2011.

religious leaders were seen as having the most power and influence in local communities, followed by roughly equal perceptions of militia commanders, provincial and local government administrators, and tribal leaders, with elected officials coming in a relatively distant last in power and influence perceptions.[68]

The need to neutralize or incorporate alternative loci of power in the political system continues to be the major obstacle besetting both state-building and democratic consolidation in Afghanistan. While provincial governors and district officers are appointed by the center, most governors received their posts in the interim, transitional, and subsequent administrations because of their independent and traditional power bases. Andrew Reynolds noted that of the 249 legislators elected to the first national assembly 40 were commanders still linked to militias;[69] moreover, nearly half of all the original crop of MPs were *mujahideen* veterans of the war against the Soviets in the 1980s.[70] The persistent and instrumental patron–client culture associated with the militias has yet to be replaced by government and civil society institutions that offer public services in an accountable and programmatic manner. A frequent complaint of Afghans living in Kandahar, for example, is that life has reverted to the chaos under warring *mujahedeen* factions.[71]

Most subnational leaders, initially appointed in recognition of their power and granted renewed legitimacy through the transitional governance process, have further entrenched their predatory activities and bolstered their patronage networks. These warlords have developed sophisticated political–economic strategies to sustain their power bases, managing their own resources and position in regional economic networks, both licit and illicit, while also tapping into international support.[72] Dipali Mukhopadhyay notes, however, that there is important variation in terms of the behavior of local strongmen and their strategy for governing provincial areas, when granted formal power by the central government to do so.[73] She observes how some of the government's most formidable would-be competitors, the regional warlords, have turned into valuable partners in governing the country and

[68] Ibid.: 158–159. [69] Reynolds 2006: 112.
[70] "Let's Make a Deal: A Democracy Arrives, Afghan Style." *New York Times*, December 4, 2005.
[71] Chayes 2006. [72] Goodhand 2008; and Mac Ginty 2010.
[73] Mukhopadhyay 2014.

establishing a political order that, albeit suboptimal in comparison to the modern political order sought by the international community, is certainly better than what came before. Even as they practice traditional clientelist politics, some local strongmen are delivering an important measure of provincial governance on that basis.[74]

The political accommodation choices made over the course of the Bonn process exposed two major political consolidation challenges in Afghanistan. On the one hand, the Karzai government has not been able to extricate its reliance – sometimes problematic, sometimes surprisingly beneficial – on the successful warlords, among the winners at the end of the conflict, who have since posed problems for the representativeness of democracy and the legitimacy and authority of the central government. On the other hand, the political process in Afghanistan has been unable – because of the unwillingness of successive Afghan governments and their foreign backers – to incorporate the Taliban, the losers of the conflict. Violent clashes increased in the run-up to the 2004 and 2005 elections, with Taliban militants stepping up attacks against soft government targets, particularly in Afghanistan's majority Pashtun southern and eastern provinces; these intensified again around the 2009 and 2010 elections.

These attacks increasingly undermined the government's legitimacy and, by the end of the decade, the steadily mounting clashes also compromised the government's authority, resulting in large swaths of territory in those provinces being ceded to the control of the Taliban and its allies. In short, the question of how to handle the Taliban re-emerged with pressing urgency after 2006, when the movement stepped up its campaign of instability and attacks against the governing authorities, both central and provincial. The Bonn Agreement was clearly a winners' deal – but it was not necessarily the case that the longer-term political arrangements that emerged from the transitional process had to exclude the Taliban. By 2007, the Karzai government was holding informal talks with Taliban insurgents about bringing peace to Afghanistan, yet neither side has met the other's conditions to begin formal peace talks.

The challenges of political consolidation and government effectiveness that resulted, in part, from the narrowness of the Bonn peace deal threatened the stability of the Karzai government on dual fronts. While

[74] See also Migdal 1988 on the everyday realities of such strongman politics in the developing world.

the deal itself probably needed to be narrow to be struck, the Bonn process and international involvement subsequently continued to constrain the outcomes of the political transition in specific ways, especially because the United Nations and the United States were concerned with political expediency and having a government counterpart they could rely on. One manner in which both the warlord and the Taliban problem could have been dealt with outside the political process would have been through a substantial, focused effort on structuring a political economy as well as a political and civil society arena in which the benefits of participation were clearly more rewarding than continued opposition. Afghanistan has the ingredients for a robust and vibrant civil society, made up of interlocking layers of tribe, religion, ethnic, and linguistic networks – what Saikal terms "micro-societies."[75] The transitional governance process through which the international community instinctively pursued political stabilization failed in many ways to tap into the sources of legitimacy embedded in these micro-societies in a meaningful manner in order to leverage their salience and their power for central governance purposes.

Instead, it seems clear, as Hamish Nixon and Richard Ponzio argue, that the international community's peacebuilding strategy "resulted in the privileging of elections and institutions – however fragile and ill-prepared – over a coherent and complete vision for statebuilding and democratization."[76] Nixon and Ponzio observe that key international players, including the United States, and Karzai wanted power strengthened in the president's hands in order to be able to co-opt or defuse regional strongmen – hence, in order to fulfill political stabilization goals, the parliament was deliberately kept weak and the broader democratization and statebuilding agendas were adversely affected. They provide another example with the story of the Provincial Councils, which are intended to provide local representation and bottom-up development coordination and planning. Although these have been hailed as an essential part of the Afghan statebuilding process, they have yet to be endowed with the resources or competency to perform their stated functions.[77]

Progress on the statebuilding front has proven even more disheartening, although this is perhaps unsurprising since political stabilization was prioritized regardless of its longer-term impact on state capacity or

[75] Saikal 2005. [76] Nixon and Ponzio 2007: 29.
[77] Ibid.: 32–33.

effectiveness.[78] Measures of government effectiveness in Afghanistan demonstrate that state capacity may have improved somewhat in the last few years of the Taliban regime and the first few years of international presence, the latter probably due to the large amounts of service delivery and even central governmental functions carried out by aid organizations, but government effectiveness declined quite quickly once international attention drifted away from the country and it remains extremely low to this day.[79] A key measurable dimension of state capacity is the government revenue to budget ratio, an indicator of the ability of a state to finance its governing priorities and activities. In Afghanistan, Astri Suhrke reports, the government's 2002 tax revenue was less than 10 percent of the national budget and there was no change by 2004–05, when domestic revenues were expected to cover only 8 percent of the total national budget and the gap to be financed by donor funds; furthermore, this pattern was projected to continue for five years.[80] Based on this heavy dependence on external resources, Suhrke goes so far as to diagnose Afghanistan as a rentier state. Continued reliance on these external aid flows, no matter how efficiently handled, hampers the government's ability to strengthen its own legitimacy and authority vis-à-vis the population. Moreover, the Afghan government did not have the capacity necessary to absorb large inflows of aid – much of the money went to financing international consultants, who were not focused on transferring skills to their few Afghan counterparts and hence did not contribute to long-term capacity-building in the Afghan government.

Recognizing the immense reconstruction challenges still ahead of the country at the close of the Bonn process, the Afghan government and international donor community signed the Afghan Compact in December 2006. This strategy framed international assistance, tying it to government planning over five years; and follow-up meetings have since been held. In an equally promising development, alternative visions have begun to emerge in the country as the government attempts to

[78] Freeman 2007; Rubin 2006; and Rubin and Hamidzada 2007.

[79] Such measures include, for example, the World Bank's Country Policy and Institutional Assessment (CPIA) public sector management and institutions cluster score for government effectiveness, as well as the "government effectiveness" measure in the Worldwide Governance Indicators dataset. Kaufmann, Kraay, and Mastruzzi 2010.

[80] Suhrke 2009. This echoes Barnett Rubin's diagnosis of the Daoud regime of the 1970s as a rentier regime. Rubin 2002.

continue the logic of the Bonn process. An opposition group formed in April 2007, the National Front, called for changes to the constitution to elevate the post of prime minister to share governance responsibilities with the president and demands direct elections of provincial governors, who are currently appointed by the president. This new opposition front, which included some members of Karzai's cabinet, formed to challenge the president amid growing frustration with his rule and the government's progress.

A decade after the conclusion of the Bonn Process, however, the deep elite power struggles at the heart of Afghanistan's political instability persist, continuing to manifest themselves in a center–periphery contest over political order and stability. Early successes in constitution-making and elections through the transformative peacebuilding approach gave way to a deteriorating security environment and setbacks in the international community's pursuit of modern political order in the country. Many hoped that the 2014 presidential elections would mark a turning point for post-conflict Afghanistan, as it began the transition away from Karzai's weak and fractious regime, which was also regarded as increasingly petulant in the eyes of the international community. The new president, Ashraf Ghani, is viewed widely as a modernizing technocrat. Yet the 2014 presidential election was, like the one preceding it, marred by widespread allegations of voter fraud and intimidation. Abdullah Abdullah, the Northern Alliance leader and then foreign minister under Karzai, was a clear leader in the first round of voting and insisted that he was the victim of large-scale electoral fraud in the second round – an assertion later confirmed by European Union election monitors. The standoff threatened to boil over into violence until the two politicians eventually came to a co-governance compromise, with the Pashtun Ghani taking the presidency and the Tajik Abdullah assuming the newly created position of the government's Chief Executive Officer.

Since taking office, however, Ghani has acted to centralize power in the office of the presidency, marginalizing both Abdullah and his own vice president, the Uzbek warlord Rashid Dostum. Albeit in the guise of fighting endemic administrative corruption, Ghani has undermined state capacity in several ways. He has, for example, brought billions of dollars of government procurement under the direct purview of his office, bypassing the line ministries that are supposed to handle this state business; his aides, too, are taking policy formulation and implementation into their own hands, sidelining appointed officials. Even those who support Ghani's consolidating reforms are reported to be concerned about the effects of his changes on the prospects for sound governance.[81]

Afghanistan's foremost challenge to the consolidation of effective and legitimate governance comes from the continued salience of the traditional neopatrimonial equilibrium – a political order organized around subnational strongmen at the head of complex patronage networks endowed with alternative sources of authority, legitimacy, and wealth that empower them vis-à-vis the central government. Having failed in the first instance to incorporate their resources into the central government, the Karzai regime then acted to neutralize the salience of these patrimonial networks by competing with them at their own game: it attempted to build its own clientelist base in the provinces by distributing government positions to allies. Timor Sharan describes how, in return, this strategy delivered the quid pro quo of electoral support for the Karzai regime, which warned tribal leaders that if they failed to support the Kabul administration they would be excluded from local government and its attendant patronage spoils in the form of jobs, aid, and other privileges.[82]

The international community's strategy of prioritizing the stabilization of the country through a combination of democratization and political deal-making appears to have acted against the peacebuilding imperative by reinforcing traditional fragmentary loci of power, many of which have now come to operate in zero-sum opposition to the central state rather than in cooperation with it.[83] Antonio Giustozzi argues that, compared with previous periods of political development in Afghanistan, political parties in the country are now intent on securing for themselves a system of electoral support in exchange for patronage distribution. Examples of such political mobilization include parties associated with the Uzbek leader Rashid Dostum and the Hazara leader Haji Mohammed Mohaqeq: in both cases, organizational development took place around the logic of securing and distributing patronage instead of along the lines of ideological or programmatic

81 Azam Ahmed. 2015. "Afghan Leader Said to be Centralizing Power as Unity Government Plan Stalls." *New York Times*, March 15.

82 Sharan 2011.

83 Importantly, by contrast, some warlords have become able and willing governors on behalf of the state. Mukhopadhyay 2014.

goals.[84] This system of patronage is fed, in turn, by internationally provided resources, such that the post-conflict intervention in Afghanistan can itself be said to have cemented in place a rentier-driven neopatrimonial political economy in the country.[85] William Maley goes so far as to argue that flaws with the peacebuilding enterprise, including decisions to put in place a presidential and centralized political system, have driven Afghanistan from "institutionalization in the direction of neopatrimonialism."[86]

Those dynamics – which have resulted both from the narrowness of the Bonn peace deal and from the transitional governance strategy itself – have contributed to a lack of consolidation of modern political order. The transitional governance process privileged and legitimized Karzai at the center and subnational elites in the provinces, many of whom are now enmeshed in a predatory political economy equilibrium where state structures are fragmented and captured. The drug economy and other avenues of patronage and corruption have both created pockets of stability in some parts of the country and fuelled sociopolitical breakdown and violent conflict in others.[87] As Barnett Rubin predicted, the criminalized peace economy has expanded rapidly in the country, leaving power-holders as unaccountable as they were under previous governing regimes.[88] Jonathan Goodhand notes, for example, that the Afghan Independent Human Rights Commission reported that an estimated 80 per cent of parliamentary candidates in the provinces had some form of contact with drug traffickers and armed groups.[89] Poppy cultivation reached an all-time high in 2014, "stoking corruption, sustaining criminal networks, and providing significant financial support to the Taliban and other insurgent groups."[90] Pervasive corruption, drug-related and otherwise, has undermined both state capacity and the government's legitimacy; political groups out of power, including the Taliban, use the widespread patronage and corruption to perpetuate a sense of injustice and legitimize continued fighting against

[84] Giustozzi 2013: 328–330.
[85] Suhrke 2013; and Wilde and Mielke 2013. [86] Maley 2013: 255.
[87] Rangelov and Theros 2012 argue that conflict persistence in Afghanistan can be explained by the emergence of a hybrid governance regime where the exercise of power – by various international and domestic political actors at all levels of the state – is defined by its abuse.
[88] Rubin 2000: 1799–1780. [89] Goodhand 2008, fn. 34.
[90] Special Inspector General for Afghanistan Reconstruction, 2014, "Poppy Cultivation in Afghanistan," Special Report SIGAR-15-10-SP, October 2014.

the government.[91] The transitional governance process through which the international community instinctively pursued political stabilization was co-opted by domestic elites into this conflictual neopatrimonial environment. The Afghan state remains splintered, both politically and administratively – in turn making the quest for sustainable peace in the country elusive.

Neopatrimonial Political Order in Comparative Perspective

Francis Fukuyama cautioned, in his sweeping study of political order, that patrimonialism "constantly reasserts itself in the absence of strong countervailing incentives."[92] Neopatrimonial political order has been reasserted in post-conflict Cambodia, East Timor, and Afghanistan, despite the enormous resources devoted to achieving modern political order through transformative peacebuilding interventions. The political elites in the three countries who were empowered by the transitional governance approach to peacebuilding are, unsurprisingly, as motivated to retain control over the state as they were to seize it initially. Through their control of the administrative apparatus of government, these elites have access to sanctioned streams of rent creation and distribution, which underpin, in turn, the clientelistic networks of support that keep them in power. But neopatrimonialism is a hybrid form of political order – the elements of rational-legal authority that behoove elites persist. Patron–client relationships are not coercive – they are instrumental and centered on reciprocal exchange, such that the patron uses his influence and resources to provide benefits or protection to the client, who reciprocates with political support and personal services.[93] Hence elites build and support some minimal degree of state capacity and continue to rely on the legitimacy bestowed upon them by elections, both of which are necessary to retain support from the population and international community and to continue a strategy of rent extraction.

At the same time, however, the institutional trappings of modern political order can feed into the neopatrimonial equilibrium. The

[91] The Taliban has had an inconsistent approach to the poppy economy. Its leader, Mullah Omar, banned its cultivation in 2000 on religious grounds yet the Taliban has benefitted greatly, both before and after that decree, from farming taxes and illicit financial flows related to opium smuggling.

[92] Fukuyama 2011: 17.

[93] Scott 1972. See also Stokes et al. 2013; and Gans-Morse, Mazzuca, and Nichter 2014.

pursuit of electoral democracy increases the size of the selectorate, or the fraction of society that is allowed to choose the political leadership, without meaningfully affecting the size of the winning coalition, or the fraction of the selectorate that enables the leadership to stay in power.[94] The resulting elite incentives mean that narrow patronage distribution to key supporters will be relatively high and broad-based public goods provision correspondingly low. The demand for effective government and public goods and services in the absence of the strong institutions to deliver them, similarly, only exacerbates the reliance on particularist distributive strategies as the source of legitimacy and political power. The survival or demise of political elites in a newly institutionalizing neopatrimonial system depends on the success of their network at tapping patronage resources for distribution. Thus, once entrenched, and fearing the consequences of losing power, elites face short time horizons that lead to a vicious circle in terms of the quality of governance. Elites with high discount rates increase rent extraction and distribution in the present time period; they also have less incentive to invest in institutional capacity for the future, thus failing to lengthen time horizons and intensifying the current stakes.

There are clear differences in the nature and patterns of neopatrimonialism across the three countries studied, especially in the degree to which elites collude in rent-seeking and distribution. Cambodian elites across the political spectrum appear to be enmeshed in a system of mostly exclusionary and competitive clientelism where patronage has replaced outright violence in seeking electoral support but the threat of violence looms large. In East Timor, with the group in power controlling the levers of patronage distribution, intra-elite schisms and underlying sources of conflict persist but there are signs that elite groups are increasingly colluding with one another. In Afghanistan, patterns of rent-seeking and neopatrimonialism manifest themselves in a more conflictual manner, with multiple patron–client networks engaged in persistent conflict. The varied levels of stability, government effectiveness, and democratic legitimacy in the post-intervention phase in each country can be understood through a historical institutionalist lens on the long-term challenge of constructing political order. Particular governance outcomes depend especially on the time horizons facing post-conflict elites, which, in turn, are determined by pathways into conflict and the critical juncture represented by transitional

[94] Bueno de Mesquita et al. 2003.

governance. Where institutions are weakest, i.e., Afghanistan, short time horizons make politics a zero-sum game, hence elites concerned with making the most of their time in power develop a predatory relationship with society. Where formal institutions and informal norms extend the shadow of the future, as in East Timor, elites are more likely to orient some elements of policymaking to the provision of collective goods for society. Intermediate outcomes are also possible, as seen in Cambodia, where systemic patronage practices along with low-level violence still permits the delivery of economic growth and collective social services and public goods.

The neopatrimonial political order that has emerged in post-conflict Cambodia, East Timor, and Afghanistan is typically viewed with unease and disappointment by the international community. It does indeed reflect the fact that international peacebuilding fails to achieve the lofty ultimate goal set for it, framed as a sociopolitical transformation to underpin lasting pace. Yet the hybrid order depicted here is, in reality, a neopatrimonial equilibrium that achieves in post-conflict countries a certain measure of political stability along with particular forms of governing effectiveness and legitimacy. The final phase of the peacebuilding pathway examined in this chapter – the ongoing aftermath of intervention – illustrates two major patterns, both of which are apparent in examining how post-conflict institutions evolve. The first is the gradual whittling away and undermining of the institutional forms preferred by the international community – rationalized bureaucracy and electoral democracy. The institutional forms of these modes of governance may persist over time but the evidence suggests that they become hollowed out quite quickly in terms of the functions they are supposed to serve once international peacebuilders have left the scene. While formal institutions become empty scaffolding, true political contestation takes place in the arenas I have identified in this chapter. That contestation, moreover, can be seen to be a dual battle to gain political authority *and* to use that power to continue to perpetuate political advantage into the future. This fits perfectly Paul Pierson's observation on the path-dependent nature of power: "The exercise of authority is not just an exercise of power; it is potentially a way of generating power."[95] The second pattern offers cause for rather more optimism. Even as they unravel, to different degrees, the institutional

[95] Pierson 2015: 130

fruits of peacebuilding interventions, domestic elites in Cambodia, East Timor and Afghanistan have established and reinforced a stable political order that underpins their ability to deliver some measure of collective benefit to their populations. Assessed against the yardstick of modern political order, this neopatrimonial system is suboptimal – but it is, at least, a relatively secure equilibrium.

If we accept that peacebuilding must be improved, rather than discarded – as I argue in the conclusion – then we must fully apprehend how it has unfolded to date, which means seeing its results not simply as falling short of modern political order. The post-conflict neopatrimonial equilibrium constitutes a set of outcomes that we can fruitfully understand and explain. It is a political order, lying between the Hobbesian state of nature and the modern liberal ideal, that benefits elites while being suboptimal for the rest of society. Only if post-conflict elite incentives can be reoriented toward building institutions and state capacity to lengthen the shadow of the future and alleviate the commitment problems that perpetuate neopatrimonialism will moves toward more effective and legitimate governance be possible.

Conclusion

The Paradoxes of Peacebuilding

There is a paradox at the heart of the international community's approach to transformative peacebuilding. Modern political order – rule-bound, effective, and legitimate government – is asserted theoretically and known practically to be optimal for achieving political stability, economic productivity, and collective social welfare. Yet the two essential components of modern political order – a capable state and a democratically chosen government – cannot be built at the same time and certainly cannot be transplanted from the outside over a short time period. This is true in the theoretical sense: state formation and democratization are long-term, messy processes, subject to reversals and contradictions. It is also true in the empirical sense, as demonstrated by the intervention experiences of post-conflict Cambodia, East Timor, and Afghanistan.

The simultaneous pursuit of statebuilding and democratization through the transitional governance approach embodies this paradox – and, as a result, this peacebuilding strategy has resulted in a great deal of disappointment in the countries in which it has been applied. The UN's peacebuilding approach is derived from international norms surrounding appropriate forms of statehood and governance, and holds that a stable and lasting peace is made possible specifically by the creation of the core administrative and political institutions of democratic governance. On the administrative front, the theory of peacebuilding privileges the construction of the rationalized bureaucratic state; on the political front, the theory emphasizes the construction of the institutions of representative electoral democracy. Most centrally, the international community's implicit theory of peacebuilding assumes that statebuilding and democracy-building can and should be undertaken in tandem toward the goal of consolidated peace. A great deal of formal institutional change takes place in post-conflict countries during interventions, through the exertions of the international community. In the aftermath of intervention, however, the cases of Cambodia, East Timor, and Afghanistan demonstrate that powerful domestic elites reassert a neopatrimonial political order. These elites subvert the effective and legitimate governance sought by the international community, in large part by using the very resources bestowed upon them by peacebuilding interventions.

This conclusion reviews the core causal logic that underpins these findings and discusses its implications for the practice of peacebuilding and its future study. After a brief recap of the causal dynamics that play out over the peacebuilding pathway in Cambodia, East Timor, and Afghanistan, I probe the broader validity of the argument with some brief discussion of other peacebuilding interventions. Although this book has described and explained troubling outcomes for an endeavor as inherently optimistic as transformative peacebuilding, it should not be read as an outright indictment of the peacebuilding enterprise, nor should the evidence provided be seen as justification for simply dismissing peacebuilding out of hand. The bulk of this conclusion is devoted to a discussion of how peacebuilding might be improved upon to achieve more effective and more legitimate governance in post-conflict states. It does so by first disentangling the statebuilding and democratization imperatives that have been linked together in the pursuit of transformative peacebuilding. It then builds a series of targeted policy implications, along with one caveat, for improving peacebuilding practice. Finally, I reflect on the implications of the historical institutionalist framework applied here – with its emphasis on viewing "in time" the incentives facing domestic elites and the way they interact with internationally supported reforms – for research on peacebuilding and other issues central to the study of developing and fragile countries.

The Mirage of Modern Political Order in Post-Conflict States

Transformative peacebuilding attempts fall short of achieving their core objective of effective and legitimate governance in post-conflict countries because the interventions themselves enable, and are co-opted by, post-conflict elites intent on forging a neopatrimonial political order. This book has explained the disconnect between the formal institutional engineering undertaken by international interventions and the governance outcomes that emerge in their aftermath. It has done so through the lens of the incentives motivating domestic elites in those countries over the temporal sequence of three peacebuilding phases: the elite peace settlement; the transitional governance period; and the aftermath of intervention. The international community advances certain forms of institutional design at each phase in order to achieve the goals of effective and legitimate governance. Yet, over the course of the peacebuilding pathway, powerful domestic groups co-opt the process to shape formal institutions and dominate the practice of governance within those institutions to their own ends. Subsequently, these elites consolidate their holds on power by both working through and actively subverting the very institutions intended to guarantee modern political order, thereby damaging the prospects for effective and legitimate governance. The significant resources brought to post-conflict settings via the liberal peacebuilding model – foremost among them legitimacy and enormous sums of foreign aid – become a new source and site of power for domestic elites.[1] One of the core insights of historical institutionalism is that "incremental shifts often add up to fundamental transformations."[2] This study has demonstrated, in a subtle twist, that the incremental shifts pursued by post-conflict elites undo what are intended by the international community as fundamental sociopolitical transformations to build lasting peace.

In undertaking peacebuilding through transitional governance, the UN acts on an implicit theory about how best to change the domestic political game in order to create the foundations for sustainable peace. Yet, in practice, at each phase of the peacebuilding pathway domestic political realities trump international objectives. The international community has pursued elite peace settlements through a process of institutional engineering without grappling adequately with the fact that this phase simply initiates the hyperpolitical experience of peacebuilding for those countries going through it. Peace settlements are viewed by the international community as elite pacts to end conflict and embark upon the business of post-conflict governance. Post-conflict elites, by contrast, treat these agreements as simply delimiting the grounds and terms of continued struggle. They do not bring an end to long-term conflict; instead they move it into the political arena.

In turn, the transitional governance phase of peacebuilding requires a domestic counterpart to help govern the country while embarking upon a time-bound process of statebuilding and democratization. This approach, paradoxically, enables certain domestic elites to take an

[1] Richmond 2006. [2] Mahoney and Thelen 2010: 2.

iterative series of actions to lock in their power and bestows legitimacy upon them through democratic elections along with the other power and patronage resources that come with control of the state.[3] As David Roberts observes, "Victorious elites are routinely overwhelming in postconflict spaces"[4] – such that an attempt to create a new, improved power balance usually comes up short. At the same time, the emphasis on consensus and power-sharing typically embodied by the intervention approach comes at the cost of governance efficacy. In the implementation of transitional governance, a specific tension lies between the statebuilding and democratization components of the peacebuilding model: whereas democratization involves the inclusion of many actors and, ideally, the construction of bottom-up representative institutions, statebuilding focuses on top-down efforts to strengthen the bureaucratic apparatus, including instruments used to control citizens. Neither political rebalancing nor improved governance is fully achieved through the transitional approach – let alone both together.

In the post-intervention phase, a neopatrimonial political order that rests on pervasive patron–client networks fortifies itself, blocking the effective and legitimate governance sought through interventions and forming a low-level political economy equilibrium. The institutions engineered through transitional governance are manipulated by domestic elites intent on remaining in power. The patterns of clientelism and even predation are familiar to observers of developing countries – especially those where there are large and exclusive benefits to holding power.[5] Time horizons are short in an environment where institutions are weak and the shadow of the future is of uncertain length. Elites benefit from neopatrimonial practices while in power – and, fearing the consequences of losing office, are motivated even further to distribute the resources of the state as patronage in exchange for political support. The hybrid political order becomes even more pronounced as leaders intent on such practices prevent the consolidation of autonomous state structures. The state, instead of becoming an arena of rational-legal authority and legitimacy, comes to mirror the clientelist political balance.

[3] Barma 2007. [4] Roberts 2011: 70.
[5] Hutchcroft 1997; Le Billon 2003; and Robinson 2001.

A neopatrimonial political order is a self-reinforcing and suboptimal equilibrium that is quite simply the norm in newly democratizing developing countries suffering from low commitment credibility and weak institutions. Yet transformative peacebuilding purports to build modern political order – and this book demonstrates that it fails to do so because domestic elites are intent on something else entirely. The resources conferred by international peacebuilding interventions upon these elites are co-opted in a neopatrimonial order that is extremely resilient to the attempts of the international community to achieve rule-bound, effective, and legitimate governance. Brief examples from two additional cases illustrate the generalizability of this causal logic. The US-led nation-building endeavor in Iraq re-emphasizes the inherent tension between statebuilding and democratization. The peace process negotiated by the international community in Burundi, in turn, reiterates the manner in which steady elite interests reassert themselves over the institutional trappings of the liberal peace, with post-conflict elites using the resources and legitimacy conferred by the peace process to reinforce a neopatrimonial political order.

Transformative Peacebuilding Elsewhere

It is a striking comment on the persistence of the international norms represented in the strategy of peacebuilding through transitional governance that the Bush Administration, having invaded and occupied Iraq in March 2003 without the consent of the UN Security Council, nevertheless implemented a transitional governance sequence parallel to that the UN pursued in the three cases examined in this book. Following its military victory in Iraq, the Bush Administration in April 2003 installed the Coalition Provisional Authority (CPA) overseen by Paul Bremer, vesting it with full executive, legislative, and judicial authority in Iraq and thereby making it the country's transitional government. Just like the UN transitional authorities examined in this book, the CPA consulted and worked with a handpicked semi-sovereign domestic counterpart, the Iraq Interim Governing Council headed by Ayad Allawi, which was intended to represent Iraq's various political, ethnic, and tribal groups. In June 2004, the CPA transferred sovereignty to the Iraqi Interim Government, also led by Allawi. National Assembly elections were held in January 2005 and a few months later the Iraqi Transitional Government assumed the reins of power in the country, headed by Ibrahim al Jaafari. One of its main responsibilities – akin to those of the Afghan Transitional Administration – was to draft a permanent constitution for Iraq. After a constitutional referendum and new national elections, the first permanent government of Iraq, headed by Prime Minister Nouri Al-Maliki, came to power in May 2006.

In Cambodia, East Timor, and Afghanistan it is at least possible to point to some successes of the UN's peacebuilding operations. In Iraq, however, the overall failure of the reconstruction strategy and the decade-long civil war that followed overshadow small victories such as the ratification of a constitution or the holding of elections. The failure of peacebuilding in Iraq was over-determined and a complex causal chain led to deteriorating security and civil war.[6] Nevertheless, the Iraq experience also illustrates how the state- and democracy-building processes pursued simultaneously in peacebuilding acted at cross-purposes to each other and contributed to reinforcing a neopatrimonial political order. In post-invasion Iraq, too, the most powerful political elites – those at the head of the Shia parties – designed institutions that guaranteed the inclusion of their own support bases without acting to broaden political participation. The transitional governance arrangements meant, for example, that it was possible for Shia elites to avoid incorporating the Sunni voice meaningfully in the constitution-drafting process. Sunni negotiators walked out of the constitutional drafting committee and refused to be present at the signing ceremony of a document they viewed with deep suspicion; Sunni insurgents, in turn, used the noninclusive process as a pretext for ratcheting up their attacks against Shia civilians and the Shia-governed state.

In both the UN-led cases and in Iraq, furthermore, viewing elections as a primary sign of progress and a potential exit strategy led to a shortening of time horizons that further empowered those groups with pre-existing political organization, rather than focusing on broad political inclusion. The *ex post* power outcomes – conceived as "who governs?" – came, in each case, quite quickly to reflect the political and organizational power balance in place at the end of the conflict, instead

6 A great deal has written about what went wrong in Iraq. Chandrasekaran 2006 and Galbraith 2006 provide nuanced and persuasive accounts of the transitional government phase.

of a deliberated and elected outcome. Like the CPP's grab for the reins of government and political power in Cambodia, the political and administrative dominance of the de facto one-party FRETILIN government in East Timor, and the strength of regional power-brokers vis-à-vis the Karzai government in Kabul, organizationally powerful groups in Iraq – such as the Supreme Council of Islamic Revolution in Iraq (SCIRI), one of the two main Shia groups – managed quite easily to consolidate their hold on power through elections and subsequently to dominate the constitution-drafting process. The prior, much-criticized, Bush Administration policy of de-Ba'athification had previously stripped the Sunnis of representation in the state apparatus as a countervailing source of leverage as well as leeching the state of much of its institutional capacity.

Finally, as with the choice of the single non-transferable vote system in Afghanistan, a precipitous path toward elections in Iraq led to the choice of an electoral system with serious adverse consequences that were foreseeable. Many experts argued that the electoral system that likely made most sense for the January 2005 Transitional Assembly elections in Iraq was one of proportional representation (PR) in multi-member districts. This would have given constituencies strong ties to the assembly, with meaningful local connections for governance; and it would have been a worthwhile attempt to transcend the substantial sectarian identity divisions in Iraq. Yet party elites were writing the electoral laws and, in order to hold onto their power bases, they wanted a closed-list PR election in a single nation-wide district instead. The United States and the United Nations, running election logistics, agreed to the plan, since it made it easier to hold elections quickly. The result was that the elections became a blatant identity referendum. In turn, this ensured that constitutional negotiations would proceed along sectarian lines and contributed to setting in motion the ethnic security dilemma dynamic that spiraled into civil war.[7] Moreover, during and after the civil war, political order such as there was in the country rested upon sectarian and regional patron–client networks. Replicating the pervasive neopatrimonial rent distribution of the Saddam Hussein era, a small group of post-conflict Iraqi elites ensured their continued political dominance through the narrow, particularist distribution of

[7] Kaufmann 2007.

spoils – including the country's oil wealth as well as foreign arms and money – to their supporters.[8]

Major UN peacebuilding interventions have been staged across the Great Lakes region of Africa – in Burundi, the Democratic Republic of the Congo, Rwanda, and Uganda – with the support of regional and international power-brokers. Devon Curtis's analysis of the Burundian case illustrates that the liberal peacebuilding endeavor there interacted with domestic elite preferences in much the same manner as observed in Cambodia, East Timor, and Afghanistan.[9] The Burundian experience – which shares the characteristic transitional design of the interventions examined here, albeit without international governance – is often promoted as a peacebuilding success story. There, a domestic power-sharing approach to liberal governance, underpinned by carefully designed institutional engineering by the international community, is believed by many to have achieved a good measure of the political stability and effective and legitimate governance sought through peace operations. Yet Curtis demonstrates convincingly how Burundian elites, over time, have reinterpreted liberal governance, reappropriating its symbols and resources to build a political order where coercion and neopatrimonialism remain central to the country's stability. For those Burundian elites, "the practice of peacebuilding as control became dominant."[10] Traditional governance in the country functioned on the basis of clientelism and patronage, with elites seeking and distributing rents in order to ensure political support and to protect and advance their own economic interests.

The international community believed that Burundian elites, by agreeing to the power-sharing mechanisms negotiated in the Arusha peace process, would become socialized to the norms of liberal governance. But power-sharing was, in reality, a mechanism for these elites to pragmatically expand the spoils of neopatrimonial order among themselves, just enough to ensure stable governance. Mirroring how Cambodian elites also accepted power-sharing as a necessary way station on the path to asserting more hegemonic control, Burundian elites embraced the institutional designs advanced by the international community as a way to buy themselves time to adjust to the changing power

[8] Erika Solomon. 2016. "Iraq's Parliament in Turmoil as MPs Battle Over Attempt to Curtail Patronage." *Financial Times*, April 14.
[9] Curtis 2013. [10] Ibid.: 74.

balance in the country. Thus, "Power-sharing governance was a tool of control, not a break from neo-patrimonial logic."[11] The way in which government positions were divided and the state captured through the peace process was more akin to elite horse trading than a reflection of any meaningful compromise over the deeper social and political grievances that affected the population. Susanna Campbell notes that important attempts were made by peacebuilders to build meaningful local accountability into the process and these successes should not be diminished.[12] Nevertheless, as in the cases considered in this book, the overall impact of international intervention was to confer legitimacy on specific elites who had not earned that legitimacy in the eyes of the Burundian people. In so doing, it reinforced their grip on authority and perpetuated the neopatrimonial and hegemonic political order they preferred.[13]

Whither Peacebuilding?

Peacebuilding has gone through a remarkably fast cycle over the past 25 years: coming into its own as a major international undertaking in the immediate post-Cold War period with great optimism about the possibility of what interventions could achieve; moving on at the turn of the century to a big surge in peace operations, increasingly complex and ambitious, across the globe; and turning today to more humility in the scope and scale of interventions, with the retrospective recognition that much of this global endeavor has been filled with hubris. Yet the implicit theory that sociopolitical transformation is desirable and possible in post-conflict states has remained unchanged. The practice of peacebuilding has suffered from a lack of critical thinking about this underlying theory, abetted by two major assumptions. First, the implicit theory underpinning the transformative peacebuilding endeavor is highly normative. It reflects the consensus reached in the second half of the twentieth century on the logic of the appropriateness of the bureaucratic nation-state form rather than resting on any empirical case for the success of that form in achieving effective

[11] Ibid.: 82.
[12] Susanna Campbell, 2015, "Global Governance and Local Peace: Accountability and Performance in International Peacebuilding," Unpublished book manuscript.
[13] Curtis 2013: 85. Also International Crisis Group 2012.

and legitimate governance. Second, the implicit theory of peacebuilding represented in the UN's transitional governance strategy for constructing a stable and lasting peace reflects the uncontested assumption that state- and democracy-building are complementary processes.

The scholarly approach to the topic of peacebuilding has, in many respects, abetted this faulty logic. The literature on peacebuilding has gone a long way toward conceptualizing peacebuilding practice and its various guises, identifying the contextual factors that support the probability of success of peace operations at their close, and developing technocratic lessons for improving interventions. Yet the almost exclusively short-term focus in the peacebuilding literature combined with the logic of appropriateness inherent in the "liberal peace" perspective regarding the Weberian state and electoral democracy has resulted in a narrow focus on the formal institutions transplanted through peacebuilding without any systematic attention being paid to outcomes in the aftermath of intervention.[14] I have sought to develop a logic of consequences by generating a theoretically informed and causally oriented explanation of outcomes to explain why the international community is not really building the peace it thinks it is in post-conflict countries.

The practical dilemma faced by international peacebuilders at the turn of the twenty-first century has been sharply articulated by Roland Paris.[15] On the one hand, peacebuilding operations were under pressure to expand their scope and duration in order to build the necessary state capacity and legitimate governance for sustainable peace to take hold. The evolution of the peacebuilding model from Cambodia to East Timor, where the latter was more all-encompassing and more intrusive into the sovereign affairs of the state, can be seen in this technocratic mindset. More recently, on the other hand, these interventions have also faced pressure to reduce the extent of international intrusion and increase local ownership. This sentiment is best captured in Lakhdar Brahimi's "light footprint" approach for the Afghanistan operation. As Paris observes pithily, neither the heavy nor the light footprint seems to have worked.[16]

[14] Critical theorists have, of course, argued that the liberal objectives underpinning the model are an inappropriate imposition of externally generated ideals in post-conflict countries. See, for example, Chandler 2006; Hughes 2009a; Mac Ginty and Richmond 2013; Pugh 2005.

[15] Paris 2010. [16] Ibid.: 343.

The pendulum has swung back and forth on such questions of the "right" degree, scope, and modes of implementation of UN peacebuilding presence, with critics remarking upon the UN's tendency, like generals in war, to develop strategic plans that fight the last battle. The lack of critical thinking about peacebuilding theory has generated a series of policy prescriptions that address only a truncated subset of the problems with the international community's peacebuilding practice. Incremental adjustments of mandate and organization represent a series of decisions about the optimal *operational* structure for implementing the transitional governance strategy – they do not challenge the implicit *theory* of peacebuilding. The latter has remained constant, with the UN time and again attempting to pursue simultaneous state- and democracy-building in a manner that defines the state and democracy in normative terms and assumes that they are complementary.

Sequencing the Pursuit of Effective and Legitimate Governance

The key to improving peacebuilding rests in rethinking the theory that motivates and orients it, not in tinkering with the size of the footprint or the precise mechanisms of institutional engineering deployed by international peacebuilders. A major root of the disappointing consolidated outcomes of peacebuilding through transitional governance is that the UN and the international community writ large tend to see peacebuilding as a technocratic puzzle that can be solved with the right mandates and institutional design, rather than seeing it for the domestic political game it truly is. A sustainable post-conflict peace that rests on modern political order must be crafted from the inside, rather than delivered from the outside. In turn, this requires viewing the pursuit of modern political order as a sequence in time – and recognizing, therefore, that the process of strengthening the state must be separated from the process of democratization. Otherwise, the elites left most powerful at the end of the conflict period capture the nascent institutions of the state even as they ostensibly abide by the peace settlement. The make-up of the state comes to mirror the political balance and the long-term organic project of statebuilding is in turn hijacked by political maneuvering to stay in power.

The single most important implication of this book is that the international community must fundamentally change the way it perceives the peacebuilding enterprise if it is to achieve its goal of creating effective and legitimate governance in post-conflict countries. Improving peacebuilding is a task worth undertaking in the interests of both human security in post-conflict countries and global stability. Paris has noted that "denunciations of liberal peacebuilding are both unwarranted and imprudent,"[17] a sentiment with which I concur. Transitional governance mechanisms are valuable and probably necessary for initiating peacebuilding processes in post-conflict countries because they provide much-needed international assistance in carrying out the functions of the state as well as the political space and incentives for elites to agree on a new institutional architecture. The question then becomes: how can transitional governance be improved? Since the strengthening of the state and democratization act at cross-purposes to each other when pursued at the same time, different elements of the two projects must be somehow separated and sequenced. What if the international community privileged either the statebuilding or the democratization side of the equation?

Focusing on the Leviathan

Leading peacebuilding scholars have emphasized the need to focus on capacity-building and institutionalization in post-conflict contexts, some even arguing that political liberalization through elections may have to be put off in order to achieve statebuilding goals.[18] This book's assessment adds the following insight: not only is capacity-building hindered by an emphasis on early elections, but it is also stunted by the very process through which transitional governance assumes state administrative functions and designates a semi-sovereign counterpart for day-to-day governance and post-transition planning. The strategy of transitional governance itself constrains the potential depth of capacity-building because international officials are more concerned with carrying out their immediate administrative tasks than transferring long-term skills to their local partners. In addition, because interventions focus on a specific subset of domestic counterparts, the potential scope of capacity-building is also constrained because the organizationally most powerful domestic group is essentially handed the reins of the administrative apparatus. The story of UNTAET's

[17] Ibid.: 338. [18] For example, Caplan 2005; and Paris 1997, 2004.

travails with "Timorization" acutely distills both these patterns, which are also on display in Cambodia and Afghanistan.

Logically, then, deepening the statebuilding dimension of peace operations would entail two things. First, it would require devoting greater resources to skills transfer to local administrative officials over a longer transitional period that is better oriented toward effective international–domestic collaboration in governance. Skills transfer and capacity-building through technical assistance is a notoriously difficult endeavor. Despite a strong consensus on the notion that an effective state is an essential basis for setting post-conflict countries on the path toward sustainable peace, the international community has yet to devise a coherent strategy for reconstructing and strengthening administrative institutions in post-conflict settings.[19] Yet instances of institutional success in fragile and conflict-affected states offer important lessons about capacity-building, which include: identifying specific capacity obstacles to fulfilling an agency's immediate objectives; developing a building-block approach to deploy existing capacities more effectively and expand them more gradually; deliberately cultivating organizational identity and pride; developing monitoring tools and analytical skills for self-evaluation; and building implementation partnerships to tap into complementary capacity.[20]

Second, meaningfully reconstructing the leviathan would entail deferring the political contestation of electoral democracy to first build up the state as a countervailing arena of legitimacy and authority in the nascent polity. This complements the view that a push for early elections in peace operations has the adverse effect of destabilizing the political arena and hence that elections should be postponed until further institution building has been undertaken.[21] Following Samuel Huntington, scholars have focused on the need for greater political institutionalization before elections and argued that democracy can only serve constructive participatory and integrative ends following political stabilization and institutional consolidation. Roland Paris warns, for example, that elections, if held at the wrong time and in the wrong manner, can legitimize the power of elected politicians to subsequently sabotage the transition to democracy and never again face

[19] OECD 2008a; and World Bank 2011.

[20] Barma, Huybens, and Viñuela 2014; and Cliffe and Manning 2008.

[21] See, especially, Chesterman 2004; and Paris 2004.

a democratic challenge.[22] The Cambodia case study sharply illustrates how such a dynamic can play out, while East Timor and Afghanistan also show signs of truncated democratization. To avoid this trap, Paris suggests a strategy of "institutionalization before liberalization" that would specifically postpone elections and concentrate on constructing a framework of effective state and political institutions before promoting political competition.[23]

Yet postponing elections to focus on statebuilding does not necessitate the wholesale rejection of the democratization objective. Instead, statebuilding can itself comprise approaches to trump political fissures. In this view, the international community should consider alternative mechanisms of political participation that could be complementary to enhancing state capacity – because concerns that UN transitional administrations can be dictatorships, even if benevolent ones, are worth heeding.[24] In addition to the suggestions I outline further below, Charles Call and Susan Cook appeal, for example, for moves toward democratization that better integrate legitimate local voice and participatory practices into post-conflict governance institutions, recognize the multiplicity of legitimate governance models, and exercise patience in building representative institutions.[25] In Afghanistan, the use of the traditional consensus-building institution of the *loya jirga* for outlining the transitional administration arrangements and ratifying the constitution was an intelligent choice that went a long way toward balancing competing political groups and fostering a sense of inclusion in an otherwise externally mandated process. Andreas Wimmer and Conrad Schetter suggest that the *loya jirga* format should have been institutionalized as a traditional consensus-building system among bureaucrats, warlords, and tribal chiefs over the medium term, instead of deployed only for the purposes of transitional governance.[26] Susanna Campbell shows that what measure of peacebuilding success was achieved in Burundi can be attributed to the local accountability mechanisms that the international presence put in

[22] Paris 2004: 164. Diamond 1996 called the sabotage and manipulation of democratic procedure and legitimacy by elected strongmen "pseudo-democracy"; Levitsky and Way 2002 characterized the outcome as "competitive authoritarianism"; and Zakaria 2003 termed it "illiberal democracy."
[23] Paris 2004.
[24] Caplan 2005; Chandler 2006; Chesterman 2004; and Chopra 2000.
[25] Call and Cook 2003. [26] Wimmer and Schetter 2003: 530.

place.[27] In East Timor, by contrast, lost opportunities to incorporate subnational political participation and the failure to widen political inclusion at the center while UNTAET still governed had lasting adverse consequences for the statebuilding dimension of the peace operation and the country's longer-term stability.

Letting Democracy Make the State?

The less obvious insight that can be drawn from this book is that it may be possible to achieve greater success in building sustainable peace in post-conflict countries by focusing on democratization and leaving aside the statebuilding dimension in the immediate term. Such a strategy would follow the United States' path to nationhood and democracy, where statebuilding was purposefully retarded and central administrative institutions kept deliberately weak to allow the flourishing of democracy, albeit at the cost of a high level of patronage.[28] In turn, robust democracy and the civil society it nourished led eventually to the Progressive Era of successful state and administrative institution building. A number of scholars have advanced the perspective that enabling democratization first can even play a significant role in the development of state capacity, especially if a basic state infrastructure exists – which is almost invariably the case in the twenty-first century, even in fragile states.[29] In particular, where competitive elections lead to party-building, those parties encourage elected governments to enhance their ability to deliver programmatic and collectively oriented policies and public services.[30] Even in competitive authoritarian regimes there is evidence that experience with elections can result in "liberalizing electoral outcomes," especially when opposition elites mount a strategically coordinated challenge to the incumbent.[31]

Could a sequence of putting democracy before the state work in post-conflict developing countries, as contrarian as it might seem? Alex Bellamy and Paul Williams have argued, from a critical theory perspective that deconstructs the international norms of statehood, that it may be desirable to de-emphasize the state during the course of

[27] Susanna Campbell, 2015, "Global Governance and Local Peace: Accountability and Performance in International Peacebuilding," Unpublished book manuscript.
[28] Shefter 1994; and Skowronek 1982.
[29] Carbone and Memoli 2015; and Mazzuca and Munck 2014.
[30] Reilly 2013; and Slater 2008. [31] Howard and Roessler 2006.

peacebuilding in order to "help open up the space for conflict resolution within civil society."[32] If this tactic had been implemented in Afghanistan, for example, an emphasis on democracy in lieu of central statebuilding could have been pursued in a decentralized, even federal manner. This might have successfully given the voters the voice in governance they still crave by making local strongmen accountable to them for providing security and public services rather than being able to blame an illusory central government. In practice, patches of better governance in Afghanistan have emerged on an ad hoc basis when certain local strongmen undertook this contract with their societies.[33]

For the goal of building a democratic process that encourages accommodation between groups of elites rather than the reach for hegemonic control, Philip Roeder and Donald Rothchild suggest that "power-dividing" solutions are better placed to ensure democratic consolidation in post-conflict countries than the typical power-sharing solutions favored by the international community.[34] Michael Barnett raises the same notion in his suggestions to build a "republican peace."[35] One of the hallmarks of the power-dividing approach – also pursued through institutional design, especially via constitutional constraints – is the elevation of civil liberties instead of a state-centric orientation, along with the support of civil society and bottom-up governance mechanisms. This approach potentially opens opportunities for dynamic, issue-specific majorities to form, thereby moving away from the reification of the social cleavages upon which power-sharing is predicated and from the static power freezes that often result. The caveat is that the utility of the power-dividing approach may be hampered in post-conflict peacebuilding efforts because it is, to some extent, predicated on reasonable degrees of state capacity, rule enforcement, and norm adherence that do not often exist in many developing countries, let alone those that have undergone violent conflict.

Six Principles and a Caveat for Modifying Peacebuilding Practice

In reality, it is unlikely that thinking on or the practice of peacebuilding will shift in a wholesale manner such that it moves toward

[32] Bellamy and Williams 2004: 13. [33] Migdal 1988; and Mukhopadhyay 2014.
[34] Roeder and Rothchild 2005. [35] Barnett 2006.

separating statebuilding and democratization in the attempt to build lasting peace in post-conflict countries. The international community has a strong normative commitment to the rationalized bureaucracy and electoral democracy that define modern political order – and pursuing effective *and* legitimate governance resonates more with international norms than pursuing effective *or* legitimate governance. As a result, peacebuilders face a basic practical conundrum: they need counterparts for the purposes of statebuilding but they must attempt to be neutral in initiating democratization. The UN transitional governance process essentially takes a shortcut on the statebuilding side by relying on specific elites as local governing counterparts and agents of progressive change – and, as a result, privileges those elites in the run-up to electoral competition.

Giuseppe Di Palma observed that social scientists have blind spots that lead them to consider democratic regime transitions "as a kind of black box – interchangeable steps to a foreclosed outcome – rather than open processes of interaction."[36] I now offer six complementary principles – each with some specific, incremental suggestions – for attempting to modify the transitional governance approach to peacebuilding, along with one important caveat. Each principle emerges from the recognition that state- and democracy-building are indeed open processes of interaction between international interventions and domestic elites.

Keep the Power Balance Fluid

The mutating nature of domestic elite incentives over the peacebuilding pathway becomes apparent when we view this pathway as a series of concrete phases. Critics of power-sharing solutions attempted through institutional engineering have observed that while they may seem necessary for the *initiation* of a peace settlement, they adversely affect the *consolidation* of peace and democracy.[37] In other words, power-sharing may be necessary to reach agreement at the time an initial peace settlement is being negotiated but subsequently the dominant political group's impetus to share power is much lessened. The international community undertakes institutional engineering with the intention of making politics a non-zero-sum game. In the unstable,

[36] DiPalma 1990: 10. [37] Rothchild and Roeder 2005: 12; also Licklider 2001.

disequilibrated reality of post-conflict states, however, these choices of institutional architecture can freeze a stalemated and typically quite arbitrary political balance over the longer term. The transitional governance process in each of the cases examined – albeit to varying degrees – facilitated the entrenchment of already powerful groups rather than ensuring the dynamic political contestation over time that is the hallmark of a consolidated democracy. Thus, the power-sharing approach is of questionable utility as a means to building peace and democracy in highly conflictual political environments where power-holding is seen as zero-sum. Any power-sharing concessions that are necessary to reach a settlement should be bounded in time and later renegotiated so as to allow more fluid power dynamics to manifest themselves and be accommodated.[38]

The international community must, quite simply, avoid picking winners during the transitional period and thereby avoid locking in a particular domestic power configuration. Elections, too, can reinforce the strength of the already powerful and lead to anti-democratic outcomes. Considerable care must thus be taken at the outset in designing democratic procedures. The goal should be, perhaps counterintuitively, to enforce uncertainty rather than inevitability about who will take the reins of power at transition and thereby align competing elite incentives toward moderation in institutional design. If elites are uncertain about their prospects, they will be more willing to agree on institutional arrangements that make elite alternation more likely and increase overall political inclusion and participation. For example, Jeremy Weinstein argues that in an excessively centralized and therefore zero-sum political system, Mozambican elites unsure of the results of the next election should have supported electoral decentralization that would have diffused political power away from the elected government and made some degree of power-sharing possible.[39] Similarly, the one-shot game of constitution-writing introduced by the transitional governance process is problematic because elites with short time horizons

[38] Du Toit 2003 discusses the notion of coming to "post-settlement settlements" to deal with the changing incentives over time in democratic transitions. The same would apply to post-conflict settlements and transitions. On the recognition that power-sharing deals may not have the desired consequences for the longer-term project of creating a sustainable peace, see also Jarstad 2008; Rothchild 2002; and Sisk 2013.

[39] Weinstein 2002.

will write rules that entrench themselves in power. The possibility of revising the rules of the game at several defined future intervals could, by contrast, encourage more moderate institutional choices. A genuinely participatory constitution-writing process could be mandated *before* national elections. The benefits would be twofold: preventing powerful groups from dominating decisions about institutional architecture; and encouraging a nascent democratic participatory culture.

Charles Call's fascinating account of security and justice sector reforms in El Salvador offers the insight that major and rapid state transformation is possible in a context in which the "prior state is not victorious" – with the proviso that the window of opportunity for formal institutional reform is short, while informal attitudes are difficult to change so quickly.[40] This is the flipside of the coin to the argument I have advanced here, which holds that the UN transitional governance model's need for a domestic counterpart perversely enables specific elites to get that precious grip on the state. Echoing the insight that the fluid uncertainty of transitions creates moments of extraordinary agency, Call points out that the window of opportunity can be seized in the service of lasting reform instead of captured by status quo forces – but that antecedent context determines how likely this will be. Another possible, albeit difficult, adaptation of the transitional governance model would be to ban elites central to the transitional process and its attendant institutional decisions from taking elected office for some specified period of time post-transition – for example, in the first five or ten years. This approach would turn the cadre of domestic elites who act as counterparts in transitional administration officials into a caretaker government – like Ayad Allawi's Iraqi Interim Government, which was term-limited in this manner. It would, importantly, meet the UN's practical need for collaboration with domestic elites while preventing those particular elites from entrenching themselves in power through the transitional governance process.

Focus on the Non-Electoral Ingredients of Democratization

To similarly prevent state capture by anointed elites, a gradual and more expansive course of peacebuilding that defers elections and focuses on institutionalization seems inescapable. Roland Paris's

[40] Call 2003: 859–860; also Wood 2003.

call for a strategy of "institutionalization before liberalization," for example, is echoed by Francis Fukuyama, who argues that democratization before statebuilding is often a recipe for patronage and corruption.[41] Moreover, both the peacebuilding and democratization literatures hold that the transition to democracy in post-conflict states is inherently more destabilizing than stabilizing, especially as elites seek ways to mobilize popular support in thinly institutionalized contexts.[42] Thus, a gradual and expansive course of democracy-building that defers elections seems most desirable, together with processes of political accommodation and institution building to strengthen political and governance arrangements at national and subnational levels.

In particular, postponing elections does not mean that participation has to be attenuated. Non-electoral forms of national- and local-level input can be brought into policymaking and accountability mechanisms – through, for example, traditional consensus institutions such as the Afghan *loya jirga*, or grand council meeting, or the Timorese *nahe biti bo'ot* system of conflict resolution handled by village elders.[43] But it is almost invariably the case that the various UN agencies and partners associated with multidimensional peace operations view elections as the main end point and goal of the transformative peacebuilding effort, even if they are not explicitly mandated as an exit strategy.[44] Hastily designed and held elections from Bosnia to Afghanistan to the Congo have further polarized political groups and reinforced the authority of political entrepreneurs with non-moderate viewpoints.

Traditional sources of authority, by contrast, while certainly often arbitrary and parochial, typically serve some of the objectives associated with effective and legitimate governance, especially when customary forms of participation and consultation are built in. This is not to propose traditional authority in lieu of democratic legitimacy, nor to suggest that the traditional is intrinsically desirable; it is simply to note that the innovative coexistence of different forms of governance is possible and can be constructive. Indeed, transformative attempts that ignore customary governance practices typically find major obstacles to constructing effective and legitimate governance.[45] Even kinship-based patrimonial networks, in this view, might serve as important

[41] Fukuyama 2005, 2011; and Paris 2004.
[42] Mansfield and Snyder 1995; Paris 2004; and Snyder 2000.
[43] Anderson 2014b. [44] Caplan 2012; Lyons 2002; and Zaum 2012.
[45] Bowles and Chopra 2008; and Boege, Brown, and Clements 2009.

building blocks of effective and legitimate political order – in particular, neopatrimonial networks can serve a crucial function in binding local elites to a center-driven statebuilding process.[46] Attempts to incorporate traditional forms of authority into a peacebuilding strategy must, of course, be rooted in locally contextualized knowledge and engagement. Caution and even skepticism are certainly warranted as to the notion that international actors could properly interpret traditional practices and incorporate them into interventions – but peace operations could and should at least create political and institutional spaces in which traditional practices could assert themselves more organically. This would constitute a peacebuilding approach very different from the technocratic norm managed by international agencies from on high.

In a similar vein, instead of relying simply on a centralized semi-sovereign body to provide local input and validation, peacebuilding interventions can emphasize and foster broader political involvement during the transitional process at both the central and subnational levels. Here, I am echoing Oliver Richmond's call to view peace formation as a bottom-up process emerging from non-elite sites of legitimate authority.[47] In East Timor, the UN failed to capitalize on an ambitious community empowerment project that could have helped it to generate and incorporate political participation at the provincial level, thereby paving the way for FRETILIN to consolidate its power at the center. In Cambodia and Afghanistan, too, the focus of transitional governance was squarely on the capital city and a small strata of urban political elites, with little attention paid to subnational participation even as peacebuilders recognized the importance of state–society and political ties at the local level. In Afghanistan, and probably also in Cambodia after the defection of the Khmer Rouge, this approach was due in part to the security situation – but it also reflected the elite-oriented nature of the theory underpinning these interventions.[48] In all three countries, the elites empowered by the UN as key counterparts were able to rely on and build upon their existing subnational infrastructure – and, in each case, that strategy deepened after the first election. The policy implication is straightforward: more attention must be paid to

[46] Kelsall 2012; Migdal 1988; and Smith 2014.
[47] Richmond 2005, 2014.
[48] Autesserre 2010 delivers a vivid indictment of the capital- and elite-centric strategy of the UN's peace operation in the Democratic Republic of the Congo.

subnational political dynamics and potential power balancers outside the capital.

Political Parties are the Key to Programmatic Policy

The political arena closes down very rapidly during and after transitional governance interventions, as the case narratives in this book have made clear. This recognition points to the broad imperative to introduce the space and mechanisms necessary to encourage legitimate political opposition and healthy political dialogue during transition. Transformative peacebuilding approaches have quite simply lacked the space for opposition. Governments of national unity are convenient counterparts for peacebuilders but breed an absolutist form of power.[49] A major plank of the deeper political institutionalization that is necessary is a nonpartisan process of party-building. Benjamin Reilly observes that "there is an increasing focus in the policy world – which has yet to be adequately digested by scholars – on the need to build broad-based, programmatic political parties in new democracies, and to avoid the narrow, personalized and sectarian parties and party systems that have undermined so many democracies."[50] Developing a nonpartisan program of party-building as part of peacebuilding interventions is thus an important area for both policy experimentation and further scholarship.

In terms of the political economy perspective advanced in this book, party-building is essential toward achieving effective and legitimate governance because it cuts into the vicious circle of weak credibility that enables neopatrimonialism to thrive. Parties serve as institutionalized mechanisms to enhance the credibility of the political elite and thus reorient their incentives toward providing broad-based programmatic policies and public goods rather than distributing narrow patronage spoils.[51] To be sure, partisan political mobilization is not without its dangers in conflict-affected countries. Leaders in all three countries studied here have expressed a fear of political parties as a vehicle for hardening lines between political factions. They offer their countries' experiences – Cambodia's civil war factions, East Timor's antagonistic independence parties, ethnoregional

[49] Thier and Chopra 2002. [50] Reilly 2002: 134.
[51] Joshi and Mason 2011; Keefer and Vlaicu 2008; and Reilly 2013.

factions in Afghanistan – in maintaining that political parties draw lines between social groups that contribute to rigid and escalating conflict between them. More cynically, however, powerful individuals dislike parties because they undermine their own political advantages. Privileged elites will be more dominant where there are no powerful parties; and the absence of programmatic parties appealing to collectivist values makes it easier for them to perpetuate the particularist and instrumental logic that underpins neopatrimonial political order. Political parties also enforce discipline and compliance within their organizations;[52] in turn, therefore, they offer an opportunity to weaken opportunistic and parasitic elites who exploit formal institutions.[53] The key to the party-building imperative is to emphasize the value of programmatic approaches to policy and governance.

Expand and Extend International Post-Conflict Engagement

There is no doubt that the short timeframe of transitional governance interventions, typically two to three years, contributes to some of the perverse outcomes on display in the countries examined here. The logical implication would be to extend the transitional period and international assistance in order to enhance the prospects of both state capacity-building and political institutionalization. The practical limitations facing suggestions to lengthen the transitional process are simple and twofold. First, most external actors are simply unwilling or unable to accept the enormous human and financial responsibilities of extended transitional support. The desire of foreign stakeholders to disengage from the Cambodian civil conflict was instrumental in reaching the Paris Peace Agreement but also meant that there was no will to extend the UNTAC mandate. Second, would-be recipient countries have become increasingly concerned, even resentful, regarding the sovereignty implications of extended international tutelage. The early enthusiasm of Timorese elites for an extended transitional period quickly evaporated in the face of their frustration with UNTAET's approach to shared governance. Nevertheless, the costs associated with premature international exit have become all too clear, not least in the attenuated peacebuilding experiences discussed here. The international community must develop pragmatic mechanisms through which to

[52] Keefer 2011. [53] Mahoney and Thelen 2010: 24.

remain constructively involved in recovering post-conflict states. Some scholars have gone so far as to suggest extended co-governance periods of neotrusteeship or shared sovereignty.[54] David Lake and Christopher Fariss have cautioned, however, that trusteeship-type models fail due to the mismatch between international and domestic incentives, in a perspective complementary to that in this book.[55]

The more promising strategy lies in what Aila Matanock characterizes as "governance delegation agreements," whereby host countries enter into arrangements with external actors to exercise joint authority over specific statebuilding tasks.[56] Mark Baskin, for instance, encourages the substitution of the idea of "engagement" for that of "exit" to prevent would be domestic spoilers from simply waiting out the international intervention.[57] A strategy that emphasizes international engagement could lengthen the shadow of the future, allowing the evolution of combined international–domestic forms of authority in which various agents are responsible for those tasks they can implement effectively. Similarly, Jarat Chopra advocates an approach of peace maintenance, where transitional administration is seen as a "brokerage framework" in which ministries and departments are contracted out for some period of time to those agents who can best provide the service or perform the function, be they international organizations, development agencies, nongovernmental organizations, or private companies.[58]

The notion that transitional administrations could perform better by serving brokerage or coordinating functions is crucial for three additional reasons. First, there is a need to improve domestic capacity-building through governance that is truly joint. As was clear in East Timor, too high a degree of international involvement stifles the building of the effectiveness, legitimacy, and accountability the state needs going forward. Astri Suhrke aptly named this the international community's "too tight embrace" of post-conflict countries.[59] Second, there is a need for better harmonization of international assistance toward the pursuit of collaborative strategic goals. Devon Curtis illustrates vividly how fragmented and contradictory international assistance in the Burundian case increased the leverage of domestic elites;[60] much the same can be seen in the three cases considered in this book. The

[54] Fearon and Laitin 2004; and Krasner 2004.
[55] Lake and Fariss 2014; also Krasner and Risse 2014.
[56] Matanock 2014.
[57] Baskin 2004.
[58] Chopra 1999.
[59] Suhrke 2009.
[60] Curtis 2013: 82.

international development community has devoted a great deal of attention to this issue over the past decade, resulting in frameworks of aid coordination principles.[61] Aid harmonization of this sort has two major inter-related benefits: it allows strategic coordination, preventing donors from working at cross-purposes to each other; it also emphasizes "country ownership" in a manner that should enhance capacity building. Third, a major test of any state-building experiment should be the extent to which it enhances the ability of the governing regime to deliver on the state–society compact and thereby generate at least a process-based form of legitimacy, if not normative legitimacy. If domestic elites know they will be penalized for failing to continue to deliver on that compact, they might even moderate their extractive behavior at least enough to remain in power.

View the State–Society Compact as Multidimensional

In addition to considering longer timeframes to elections, the international community would do well to emphasize alternative, non-electoral mechanisms for building the state–society compact, particularly from the ground up. Séverine Autesserre has noted the persistence and effects of the post-conflict peacebuilding culture and framework orienting international interventions in her study of the extensive UN peace operation in the Democratic Republic of the Congo.[62] Two of the faulty elements of this framework are that international peacebuilders view the national level as the appropriate forum for intervention and tend to believe that holding elections is the suitable and effective route to peacebuilding, instead of finding local mechanisms and forums for statebuilding and peacebuilding endeavors. This is a particularly problematic set of blinkers since a great deal of conflict across the world emerges from micro-level contestation over traditional, kinship-based claims to authority as well as land and other resources.

Moreover, this bias in international intervention is difficult to overcome because, as Autesserre demonstrates, individual habit as well as organizational culture and narrative in international agencies is reinforced by the need to implement practical, workable solutions on the ground that can be linked to log frames and exit strategies.[63] But

[61] OECD 2005, 2008b. [62] Autesserre 2009, 2010. [63] Autesserre 2014.

the local level is a crucial site for reform of international peacebuilding practice.[64] In addition to the conflict resolution systems identified above, potential locally oriented service delivery models include decentralized development programs like Cambodia's Seila community program, aimed at increasing local-level participation; and Afghanistan's National Solidarity Program, a similar community-level block grant initiative. The risk with such programs may be that they fail to build state institutions – but at least they enhance participation and ensure some element of programmatic, non-instrumental service delivery. A complementary tactic could be the contracting out of service delivery to the agents that can best perform the function – be they enclaves within government or a range of external providers, both public and private.[65] The goal is for international donors to focus their partnerships with post-conflict governments on providing public services to the collective – thereby undercutting the value to elites of providing particularistic benefits to targeted groups of supports.

Focus on Institutional Function, Not Form

Finding ways to improve peacebuilding means recognizing that institutionally engineered, "ideal" forms of governance are the enemy of "good enough governance," a concept first articulated by Merilee Grindle that has become increasingly popular in the field of international development.[66] The notion centers on discarding best-practice governance recommendations for good-fit approaches, or contextually grounded and feasible institutional arrangements that achieve a *de minimis* degree of quality sufficient to enable government agencies to fulfill their purpose.[67] Scholars of development and governance have, more generally, asserted the importance of focusing on the development of functional ability to execute core administrative activities instead of focusing on specific institutional forms, arguing, for example, that the latter can create a "capability trap" instead of enhancing capacity.[68] The core insight is the importance of finding heterodox means of working with elite and social incentives to achieve specific

[64] Autesserre 2008 emphasizes the importance of "thinking local, acting local" in the Congo.
[65] Chopra 1999. [66] Grindle 2004, 2007.
[67] Barma, Huybens, and Viñuela 2014; and Levy 2014.
[68] Pritchett, Woolcock, and Andrews 2013.

ends, instead of butting up against those incentives by blindly attempting the orthodox.[69]

The transitional governance model of peacebuilding, with its institutional engineering approach to building modern political order and its static emphasis on institutional form as outcome, becomes co-opted in implementation by post-conflict elites. Yet I have also shown, as the historical institutionalist paradigm would suggest, that some institutional outcomes were not sought by any particular actors, coming about instead as the unintended consequences of distributional battles.[70] Over time, too, these institutions become "multi-purpose tools" that can be used to different ends and continue to have contested functions.[71] The peacebuilding literature, especially the large body of practitioner work on the subject, typically treats institutional choice as bounded, rational, and technical. This study has instead demonstrated that the institutions that emerge from the design process engineered by peacebuilding interventions represent a series of "messy contradictions abounding with inconsistencies and contradictions based on coalitions of convenience."[72]

This institutional mismatch between what domestic political actors want and what outcomes actually obtain represents an important opportunity. A more subtle peacebuilding approach attuned to institutional function would instead focus on reforming and building the facets of the state that serve and resonate with elite incentives. Timorese elites invested a great deal of energy into building the capacity of the Ministry of Social Solidarity in the aftermath of the 2006 political crisis because it was central to the new coalition government's strategy of delivering a peace dividend to the population through social transfer programs.[73] As Cambodia faces the prospect of a unified market within the Association of Southeast Asian Nations, government and party officials have elevated the importance of enhancing education service delivery.[74] The insight here is that surprising governance improvements can be achieved if the puzzle is approached through the lens of the governance challenges and problems that domestic elites must solve, instead of through the typical international intervention approach of

[69] Rodrik 2014. [70] Mahoney and Thelen 2010: 22–23.
[71] Hacker, Pierson, and Thelen 2015: 185.
[72] Ibid.: 192. [73] Anderson 2014b.
[74] Author interviews with donor officials and Cambodian analysts; Phnom Penh, Cambodia, October 2014.

offering to these elites predesigned solutions and institutions that, in reality, challenge their interests and incentives. Function obviously dictated form in these ways in the long-term, organic processes of state formation and democratization in Western Europe and the United States.

Cutting-edge work in the field of the political economy of development pushes this line of thinking one step further. Borrowing concepts from physics and evolutionary biology, Owen Barder asserts that all human systems – political, social, economic, government – are "complex adaptive" systems, which do not display linear properties of change.[75] As a result, attempting to deliberately engineer these systems is folly. Instead, the inherent adaptiveness of political systems should be exploited for its advantages – and the way to do this is through processes that encourage innovation and experimentation. As unwelcome, even threatening, as such recommendations may seem to technocratic international peacebuilders, this book's account of the causal logic that unfolds along the peacebuilding pathway certainly supports a more adaptive, incentive-based, and experimental approach to attempting to build effective and legitimate governance in post-conflict states.

The Caveat: A Neopatrimonial Peace?

These half-dozen suggestions for improving the pursuit of modern political order notwithstanding, it is dangerous to view neopatrimonial political order as a way station to more effective and legitimate governance. It is much more realistic, both intellectually and pragmatically, to view neopatrimonialism as an extremely persistent, even default, equilibrium – as evidenced over time and across the world. What is surprising, in light of this insight, is not that peacebuilding fails but that that any elements of the institutions transplanted by transitional governance prevail at all – and yet they do. The political and institutional spaces in which limited successes are achieved illuminate what incremental movements toward better governance may continue to be

[75] Owen Barder. 2012. "Complexity, Adaptation, and Results." *Center for Global Development* blog, September 7. www.cgdev.org/blog/complexity-adaptation-and-results (accessed on May 7, 2015). See also Ramalingam 2013.

gained. Yet international interventions are not immune from neopatrimonial dynamics – on the contrary, they in part enable and are co-opted by them. The transitional governance strategy provides new sources of patronage, power, and legitimacy to domestic elites, even rewarding those who begin with the strongest patron–client networks, because they are the elites the international community must have on board. The international community's relative failure in fully meeting its goals of rationalized bureaucracy and electoral democracy can be equally viewed as the success of domestic elites in serving their own governing vision and objectives much more concretely.

The hybrid political order logic reminds us that modern political order hardly exists outside the advanced, industrialized world – and that statebuilding in post-conflict developing countries could be better achieved if combined with traditional modes and customary practices of governance and legitimacy, which show considerable adaptiveness and resilience.[76] It is possible to argue that the political economy of patronage is simply to be expected in post-conflict states, that collusive rent-seeking among elites and the distribution of benefits through patron–client networks are simply the price of peace and are preferable to outright conflict.[77] In this line of thinking, moreover, neopatrimonial political order represents a secular improvement in the post-conflict country's journey from war to sustainable peace, with patronage systems representing a form of routinization of politics and governance in a thinly institutionalized environment. Post-conflict elites have co-opted transitional governance to put in place a neopatrimonial peace – and great care must be taken with regard to any further decisions that would disrupt what measure of stability and order that equilibrium affords.

Future Research and Theoretical Implications

Although the foregoing discussion has focused on the practical implications of this study, the six principles advanced for modifying peacebuilding practice, as well as the caveat, each point to potential

[76] Boege, Brown, and Clements 2009; and Smith 2014.

[77] I am indebted to Ed Aspinall for this point. Cheng and Zaum 2012 outline this logic and illustrate how international assistance can become complicit due to the rapid disbursement of aid, a reliance on local elites, an emphasis on stability, and the push for quick elections.

agendas for problem-driven research. This final section reflects on how rethinking peacebuilding in the manner I have suggested also opens up new lines of theoretical inquiry.

Indigenous Statebuilding and Peacebuilding

Given how widespread is the consensus that statebuilding is a crucial element of peacebuilding, there is a significant intellectual lacuna in the lack of attention paid to how the construction of effective states and the achievement of lasting peace are related to each other.[78] The experiences of post-conflict Cambodia, East Timor, and Afghanistan illustrate that different types of elite bargain are necessary at different critical junctures on the pathway to peace. In particular, the nature of the elite settlement required to achieve a peace agreement is very different from that required to sustain peace and build state capacity in the long term. The former requires locking in elite commitments to peace maintenance and stability such that they are credible. The latter, by contrast, requires creating an incentive structure that institutionalizes uncertainty and hence encourages elites to build intertemporal credibility, accountability, and state capacity by delivering programmatic policies and collective public goods.

A crucial avenue for future research thus lies in problematizing the relationship between statebuilding and peacebuilding – with the goal of better understanding the trade-offs and complementarities between the two processes, along with empirical investigation of the conditions under which those trade-offs and complementarities hold.[79] An important element of this research program is to gain a better understanding of how countries that have *not* been the targets of ambitious peacebuilding interventions have, nevertheless, achieved significant gains through their own, autonomously driven and implemented statebuilding programs. There are numerous instances of indigenous efforts by domestic actors to pursue reforms to achieve sustainable peace and improvements in state capacity in the relative absence of coordinated international intervention: a partial list would include, at different points in time, Angola, Eritrea, Indonesia, Laos, Lebanon,

[78] Jones and Chandran 2008 and Paris and Sisk 2009 are notable exceptions that have helped to identify the problem.

[79] Barma, Levy, and Piombo 2015 outline the conceptual motivation for such a program of research, along with one proposed method for undertaking it.

Rwanda, Sri Lanka, Somaliland, and Uganda.[80] Yet surprisingly little comparative research has been undertaken on the similarities and differences between international peace operations and what can be thought of as autonomous or indigenous processes of statebuilding and peacebuilding.[81] It seems likely that the establishment of neopatrimonial political order by post-conflict elites will be a recurring theme. Ricardo Soares de Oliveira, for example, defines "illiberal peacebuilding" experiences in Angola, Rwanda, and Sri Lanka as processes of post-war reconstruction by hegemonic elites who structure the political economy of rent extraction and distribution in their favor.[82] Ironically, the neopatrimonial outcomes in post-conflict countries that have gone through international interventions, such as those described and explained here, may come to reflect, in large part, how post-conflict elites structure political order when left entirely to their own devices.

Peacebuilding, Historical Institutionalism, and Political Science

A number of the principles for modifying peacebuilding discussed above bring to bear accumulated knowledge on the comparative political economy of development on the pressing policy issue of post-conflict peacebuilding. Some of the conclusions of this book also have implications for theoretical debates in political science. Peacebuilding through transitional governance is, for example, part of a broader post-Cold War trend in which the international community has increasingly emphasized liberal interventionism to protect individual human rights. In tandem with the material challenges to international order that resulted from the increasing incidence of internal conflict immediately after the Cold War, thinking around the sovereignty norm has begun to shift away from the inviolability of borders and the presumption of nonintervention in the internal affairs of a state.[83] The UN's

80 A number of revealing single-country case studies indicate that this would be a fruitful research effort. On Angola, see Soares de Oliveira 2011; on Indonesia, see Smith 2014; and, on Uganda, see Weinstein 2005.

81 Weinstein 2005.

82 Soares de Oliveira 2011.

83 Krasner 1999 examines the ways in which sovereignty has always been compromised in the modern international system. International Commission on Intervention and State Sovereignty 2001 articulates the "Responsibility to Protect" doctrine, which is emblematic of the rethinking of the sovereignty norm.

peacebuilding strategy is built on an internal contradiction regarding Westphalian sovereignty: the transitional governance approach is predicated on and designed to replicate and preserve the foundations of Westphalian order by emphasizing the formal trappings of nation-statehood, but it implements these international norms by violating in part the state sovereignty that is the most fundamental Westphalian assumption.[84] As peacebuilding theory and practice evolve, they will necessarily continue to impact international relations scholarship on the sovereignty norm.

One major insight I take from this study of building the institutions of the modern state is the need to construct multiple centers of legitimate authority in post-conflict and developing countries. Legitimacy is, of course, not solely a function of the electoral process. Non-elected branches of government, such as the bureaucracy, judiciary, and military, must also embody legitimacy and authority to function effectively– and these attributes come from systematic attention to institutional capacity-building. A strong state, in turn, can exist "only with a tremendous concentration of social control";[85] otherwise, fragmented social control weakens the state and poorly institutionalized governance reinforces fragmentary social control. We know that the state and society disintegrate together in the course of state failure, so it is only reasonable that they must be reconstituted together for a successful process of state regeneration. A promising avenue of research would be to widen the historical institutionalist lens adopted here to investigate how the nature of the state–society compact evolves over the course of the peacebuilding pathway.

This book has tried to improve our understanding of peacebuilding by bringing to its study insights from the political economy of development literature on how institutions and resources shape elite incentives to deliver political order, economic development, and a collectively oriented state–society compact. In their landmark volume, *Bringing the State Back In*, Peter Evans, Dietrich Rueschemeyer, and Theda Skocpol believed that "comparative and historical examinations of watershed periods in which state apparatuses are constructed or reconstructed may be the most promising approach" to sharpen our understanding of the state while allowing us to grapple with substantive problems.[86]

[84] Zaum 2007. [85] Migdal 1988: 262.
[86] Evans, Rueschemeyer, and Skocpol 1985: 361.

A deep, contextualized analysis of transformative events that is centered on cases adds much that cannot be determined by probabilistic analysis resting on variable-based coding of cases.[87] The causal theoretical framework of this book, which focuses on how post-conflict elites could be expected to respond to transformative events, is generalizable to other subsets of contemporary governance challenges, such as international–domestic forms of collaboration around natural resource governance or public goods provision. In particular, development interventions would be fruitfully viewed in time, with the specific goal of understanding the path-dependent and endogenous change they bring about – and through which their outcomes affect the sociopolitical context in developing countries in deep and lasting ways. The case-centered, conjunctural logic of this study is also amenable to the comparative analysis of development interventions, typically studied with a variable-centered evaluative logic. Moreover, the practice of international development assistance offers a promising issue area in which to make advances on historical institutionalist theory itself. Scholars working in this paradigm have focused mostly at either the comparative or the international level. Although they have examined, as in this book, how international–domestic interaction occurs, political science scholarship would benefit from deeper theorizing about how feedback loops of such interaction across different levels of analysis occur around critical junctures of transformation.

Conclusion

The fact that it is difficult, if not impossible, to refashion post-conflict states in the guise of modern states, effectively governed and democratically legitimate, has become a truism – and yet we still do not fully know why. The historical institutionalist lens applied in this book has contributed to a better understanding of why peacebuilding typically falls short of its aspirations. It has done so by combining an analysis of exogenously imposed transformative peacebuilding interventions, conventional in the literature, along with a unique examination of the more gradual and endogenous processes of institutional change that occur during their implementation and in their wake. Viewing

87 Thelen and Mahoney 2015: 13–14.

international interventions in this temporal manner leads to the important recognition that peacebuilding comprises a series of critical junctures, each with its own distinct set of challenges and incentives. The approach illuminates how international interventions and domestic elites approach the peacebuilding puzzle of how to construct post-conflict political order in two very different ways. The peacebuilding pathway represents a series of connected phases over time in which competing local and international visions of political order are manifested through the contestation of governance institutions. The bad news is that the international community's peacebuilding approach is, at least in part, itself responsible for the eventually disappointing governance outcomes that emerge in post-conflict countries. The good news is that – if we are prepared to rethink the theory that motivates and orients peacebuilding – there is still much that could be done to improve the prospects of interventions that aim to contribute to political order in post-conflict states.

Appendix: Interviews Conducted

Afghanistan

Pamela Constable, Deputy Foreign Editor and former Kabul Bureau Chief, *Washington Post*. March 29, 2005, Berkeley.

Kevin Evans, United Nations Development Program Governance Advisor. June 18, 2002, Kabul.

Ray Jennings, World Bank Consultant. June 22, 2002, Kabul and November 1, 2004, Washington, DC.

Nick Leader, Advisor, Afghan Assistance Coordination Authority. June 28, 2002, Kabul.

Clare Lockhart, Advisor and Assistant to the Director, Afghan Assistance Coordination Authority. June 28, 2002, Kabul.

Nick Manning, Governance and Public Sector Advisor, South Asia Region, World Bank. June 13 and July 3, 2002, Washington, DC.

Raquel Ragrario, United Nations Development Program payroll office. June 17, 2002, Kabul.

Abdul Ahad Sartep, Employment Chief of the Education Ministry, Personnel Department. June 19, 2002, Kabul.

Larry Seale, US Treasury, Budget Advisor to the Minister of Finance. June 18 and June 26, 2002, Kabul.

Alex Thier, Director of the Project on Failed States at Stanford University's Center on Democracy, Development, and the Rule of Law and former legal advisor to Afghanistan's Constitutional and Judicial Reform Commissions. February 16, 2005, Palo Alto.

Anne Tully, Deputy Country Director for Afghanistan, World Bank. June 13, 2002, Kabul.

Juanita Villarosa, United Nations Development Program payroll office. June 17 and June 24, 2002, Kabul.

Sami Walli, Advisor to the Minister of Finance. June 17, June 19, and June 27, 2002, Kabul.

Jim Wasserstrom, Consultant to the United Nations Development Program Law and Order Trust Fund for Afghanistan. June 23, 2002, Kabul.

Fazel Wassit, World Bank Consultant. June 21, 2002, Kabul.

Director and Officials at the Manpower Department, Ministry of Labor and Social Affairs. June 22, 2002, Kabul.

Officials at the Office of Administrative Affairs. June 22, 2002, Kabul.

Officials at the Personnel Department, Ministry of Health. June 20, 2002, Kabul.

Professors in the Economics Faculty, University of Kabul. June 27, 2002, Kabul.

Cambodia

Rebecca Black, Chief of Mission, USAID, US Embassy. October 17, 2014, Phnom Penh.

John Burroughs, AusAID Governance Advisor. May 17, 2005, Phnom Penh.

Stacey Crevello, Country Director, International Relief & Development. October 14, 2014, Phnom Penh.

Kate Elliot, AusAID Representative. May 17, 2005, Phnom Penh.

Eng Netra, Cambodian Development Research Institute. October 21, 2014.

Tsuyoshi Fukao, Education Specialist, World Bank. October 17, 2014, Phnom Penh.

Christophe Grundmann, Director, University Research in Cambodia. October 23, 2014.

Kao Kim Hourn, Secretary of State, Ministry of Foreign Affairs and International Cooperation, and President, University of Cambodia. May 16, 2005, Phnom Penh.

Keat Sukun, Professor, Panyasasra University. May 18, 2005, Phnom Penh.

Kem Sokha, Director, Cambodian Center for Human Rights. May 18, 2005, Phnom Penh.

Paul Keogh, Counsellor, Development Cooperation, Australian Embassy. October 20, 2014.

Kristina Kuhnel, Head of Development Cooperation, SIDA. October 23, 2014.

Lao Mong Hay, Head of Legal Unit, Center for Social Development, former Director, Khmer Institute for Democracy. May 10, 2005, Phnom Penh.

Nareth Ly, Health Operations Officer, World Bank. October 24, 2014.

Eva Mysliwiec, former Director, Cambodian Development Research Institute. May 11, 2005, Phnom Penh.

Jan Noorlander, CARE International. October 20, 2014.

Ok Serai Sopheak, Center for Peace and Development. May 16, 2005, Phnom Penh.

Jackie Pomeroy, Resident Representative, The Asia Foundation. May 11, 2005, Phnom Penh.

Say Bory, Member of Constitutional Council and former expert on Constitution Drafting Committee. May 17, 2005, Phnom Penh.

Son Chhay, Member of Parliament (Sam Rainsy Party). May 12, 2005, Phnom Penh.

Son Soubert, Senator, Constitutional Council and former expert on Constitution Drafting Committee. May 17, 2005, Phnom Penh.

Birgit Strube, Deputy Head of Cooperation, German Embassy. October 16, 2014, Phnom Penh.

Robert Taliercio, Country Economist, The World Bank. Several conversations in October 2005, Phnom Penh.

Un Leang, Department of Higher Education, Ministry of Education, Youth, and Sport. October 16, 2014, Phnom Penh.

East Timor

Mericio Akara, Director, Luta Hamutuk (NGO – governance). February 20, 2013, Dili.

Saku Akmeemana, Advisor, Justice for the Poor Program, World Bank. March 1, 2013, Dili.

Dionisio Babo Soares, Deputy Director, Asia Foundation. April 15, 2005, Dili.

Laura Bailey, World Bank Consultant. April 18, 2005 and April 20, 2005, Dili.

Hans Beck, Senior Country Economist, World Bank, February 26, 2013, Dili.

Maria Braz, Human Resources Unit, Ministry of Planning and Finance. April 26, 2005, Dili.

Nelson Belo, Director, Fundasaun Mahein (NGO – conflict/security). February 21, 2013, Dili.

Pedro Belo Da Silva. Deputy Director (Civil Society), Catholic Relief Services. May 1, 2005, Bali (Indonesia).

Keryn Clark, Program Director, AusAID. February 27, 2013, Dili.

Deborah Cummins, Subnational Governance Advisor, Asia Foundation. February 22, 2013, Dili.

Aderito Hugo D'Acosta, Editor, *Timor Post*. April 19, 2005, Dili.

Pamela Dale, Social Development Specialist, World Bank. February 28, 2013, Dili.

Angelo De Almeida, Head of Internal Revenue, Ministry of Planning and Finance. April 22, 2005, Dili.

Sarah Dewhurst, Program Director, Belun (NGO – conflict/security). March 1, 2013, Dili.

Jill Engen, former UNTAET Subdistrict Administrator. April 26, 2005, Dili.

Hugo Fernandes, Unit Manager, Asia Foundation. February 25, 2013, Dili.

João Cancio Freitas, Director, Dili Institute of Technology. April 20, 2005, Dili.

Ambassador Peter Galbraith, former Director of UNTAET's Department of Political, Constitutional, and Electoral Affairs. February 25, 2005, by telephone.

Louis Gentile, Law and Justice Specialist, Asia Foundation. April 21, 2005, Dili.

Edio Guterres, Program Coordinator and Advisor, Justice for the Poor Program, World Bank, February 21, 2013, Dili.

Vergilio Guterres, Director, Haburas (NGO – environment and land). February 27, 2013, Dili.

David Hook, Governance and Public Sector Specialist, World Bank, February 23, 2013, Dili.

Elisabeth Huybens, Country Manager and Resident Representative, World Bank. April 17, 2005 and April 19, 2005, Dili.

Fidelis Magalhaes, Chief of Staff, Office of the President of Timor-Leste. February 20, 2013, Dili.

Francisco Monteiro, President and CEO, Timor GAP (National Oil Company). February 27, 2013, Dili.

Guteriano Neves, Economist Analyst, Office of the President of Timor-Leste. February 28, 2013, Dili.

Rui Paulo, Health Sector Specialist, World Bank. April 20, 2005, Dili.

Lucio Pinto, Subdistrict Administrator, Viqueque Province. April 30, 2005, Viqueque.

Doug Porter, Advisor, Justice for the Poor Program, World. March 1, 2013, Dili.

Jose Ramos-Horta, President of RDTL. November 7, 2009, Dili.

Anita Reddy, AusAID. April 22, 2005, Dili.

Edward Rees, Political Economy Analyst (independent). March 2, 2013, Dili.

Tamrat Samuel, Department of Political Affairs, United Nations and former Representative of the United Nations Assistance Mission in East Timor. March 4, 2005, New York.

Estanislau Saldanha, Rector, Dili Institute of Technology. February 20, 2013, Dili.

Joao Saldanha, Senior Management Advisor for Economic Policy, Ministry of Finance of Timor-Leste. March 1, 2013, Dili.

Alexandre Sarmento, National Advisor, National Development Agency of Timor-Leste. February 26, 2013, Dili.

Charles Scheiner, Director, La'o Hamutuk (NGO – governance, petroleum/budget management). February 25, 2013, Dili.

Nicole Seibel, Resident Representative, USAID. April 27, 2005, Dili.

Aderito Soares, President, Timorese Jurists Association. April 27, 2005.

Aderito Soares, Commissioner, Anti-Corruption Commission of Timor-Leste. February 26, 2013, Dili.

Karol Soltan, Professor of Government and Politics, University of Maryland and former Deputy Director of UNTAET's Department of Political, Constitutional, and Electoral Affairs. November 1, 2004, by telephone.

Jose Teixeira. Member of FRETILIN Central Committee and former Ministry of Natural Resources. February 21, 2013, Dili.

Manuel Tilman, Member of Parliament (KOTA), Chair of Economic, Finance, and Planning Committee. April 21, 2005, Dili.

Adelgiza Ximenes, Member of Parliament. April 22, 2005, Dili.

Luis Ximenes, Director, Belun (NGO – conflict/security). February 22, 2013, Dili.

Valentim Ximenes, Dean, Faculty of Social and Political Studies, National University of Timor Leste. April 14, 2005, Dili.

Additional

Matt Cordova, Office of Reconstruction and Stabilization, US State Department. October 27, 2004, Washington, DC.

Ambassador James Dobbins, RAND. February 28, 2005, Berkeley.

Michael Doyle, Professor of International and Public Affairs, Columbia University and former Assistant Secretary-General and Advisor to Secretary-General Kofi Annan at the United Nations. March 2, 2005, New York.

Gordon Hein, Vice President, Asia Foundation. August 8, 2007, San Francisco.

Lise Howard, Director of MA Program in Conflict Resolution, Georgetown University. October 28, 2004, Washington, DC.

Ray Jennings, Senior Fellow, United States Institute of Peace. 2005, Washington, DC.

Homi Kharas, Chief Economist, East Asia and Pacific Region, World Bank. October 26, 2004, Washington, DC.

Lizanne McBride, Director, International Rescue Committee. February 16, 2005, Palo Alto.

Kara McDonald, Office of Reconstruction and Stabilization, US State Department. October 27, 2004, Washington, DC.

Barbara Nunberg, Governance and Public Sector Manager, East Asia and Pacific Region, World Bank. Numerous conversations over the course of 2002–2007, Washington, DC and Phnom Penh.

Murray Proctor, Director, Governance Division, AusAID. April 25, 2002, Dili.

Jim Tullock, Resident Representative in Cambodia, World Health Organization and former Minister of Health in the East Timor Transitional Administration. May 17, 2005, Phnom Penh.

Bibliography

Acemoglu, Daron and James Robinson. 2012. *Why Nations Fail: The Origins of Power, Prosperity, and Poverty*. New York: Crown Publishers.

Afghanistan Bonn Agreement. 2001. *Agreement on Provisional Arrangements in Afghanistan Pending the Re-Establishment of Permanent Government Institutions*, December 5.

Anderson, Catherine. 2014a. "Timor-Leste Case Study: Ministry of Health." In *Institutions Taking Root: Building State Capacity in Challenging Contexts*, edited by Naazneen H. Barma, Elisabeth Huybens, and Lorena Viñuela, 303–345. Washington, DC: The World Bank.

Anderson, Catherine. 2014b. "Timor-Leste Case Study: Ministry of Social Solidarity." In *Institutions Taking Root: Building State Capacity in Challenging Contexts*, edited by Naazneen H. Barma, Elisabeth Huybens, and Lorena Viñuela, 261–302. Washington, DC: The World Bank.

Andrews, Matt. 2013. *The Limits of Institutional Reform in Development: Changing Rules for Realistic Solutions*. New York: Cambridge.

Ashley, David W. 1998. "The Failure of Conflict Resolution in Cambodia." In *Cambodia and the International Community: The Quest for Peace, Development, and Democracy*, edited by Frederick Z. Brown and David G. Timberman, 49–78. New York: Asia Society.

Aucoin, Louis, and Michele Brandt. 2010. "East Timor's Constitutional Passage to Independence." In *Framing the State in Times of Transition: Case Studies in Constitution Making*, edited by Laurel E. Miller, 245–274. Washington: United States Institute of Peace.

Autesserre, Séverine. 2008. "The Trouble With Congo: How Local Disputes Fuel Regional Conflict." *Foreign Affairs* 87 (May/June): 94–110.

Autesserre, Séverine. 2009. "Hobbes and the Congo: Frames, Local Violence, and International Intervention." *International Organization* 63: 249–280.

Autesserre, Séverine. 2010. *The Trouble With the Congo: Local Violence and the Failure of International Peacebuilding*. New York: Cambridge University Press.

Autesserre, Séverine. 2014. *Peaceland: Conflict Resolution and the Everyday Politics of International Intervention.* New York: Cambridge University Press.

Babo Soares, Dionisio. 2003. "Branching From the Trunk: East Timorese Perceptions of Nationalism in Transition." PhD dissertation, Australian National University, Canberra.

Ballentine, Karen, and Jake Sherman, eds. 2003. *The Political Economy of Armed Conflict: Beyond Greed and Grievance.* New York and Boulder: International Peace Academy and Lynne Rienner.

Baltazar, Alipio. 2004. "An Overview of the Constitution Drafting Process in East Timor." *East Timor Law Journal* 9.

Barfield, Thomas. 2010. *Afghanistan: A Cultural and Political History.* Princeton: Princeton University Press.

Barma, Naazneen H. 2006. "Brokered Democracy-building: Developing Democracy Through Transitional Governance in Cambodia, East Timor and Afghanistan." *International Journal on Multicultural Societies* 8 (2): 127–161.

Barma, Naazneen H. 2007. "Crafting the State: Transitional Governance and the International Role in Post-Conflict Peacebuilding." PhD dissertation, University of California, Berkeley.

Barma, Naazneen H. 2012a. "Peacebuilding and the Predatory Political Economy of Insecurity: Evidence from Cambodia, East Timor, and Afghanistan." *Conflict, Security & Development* 12 (3): 273–298.

Barma, Naazneen H. 2012b. "Petroleum, Governance, and Fragility: The Micro-Politics of Petroleum in Post-Conflict States." In *Beyond the Resource Curse*, edited by Brenda Shaffer and Taleh Ziyadov, 330–351. Philadelphia: University of Pennsylvania Press.

Barma, Naazneen H. 2014. "Pathways From Petroleum Dependence to Conflict in Rentier States: A Case Study of Timor-Leste." Paper presented at ISSS–ISAC Joint Annual Conference, Austin, Texas, November 2014.

Barma, Naazneen H., Elisabeth Huybens, and Lorena Viñuela, eds. 2014. *Institutions Taking Root: Building State Capacity in Challenging Contexts.* Washington, DC: The World Bank.

Barma, Naazneen H., Naomi Levy, and Jessica Piombo. 2015. "Creating a Sustainable Peace? Disentangling the Processes of Statebuilding and Peacebuilding." Paper presented at the Annual Meeting of the International Studies Association, New Orleans, Louisiana, February.

Barnett, Michael. 2006. "Building a Republican Peace." *International Security* 30 (4): 87–112.

Barnett, Michael, and Martha Finnemore. 1999. "The Politics, Power, and Pathologies of International Organizations." *International Organization* 53 (4): 699–732.

Barnett, Michael, and Martha Finnemore. 2004. *Rules for the World: International Organizations in Global Politics*. Ithaca and London: Cornell University Press.

Barnett, Michael, Hunjoon Kim, Madalene O'Donnell, and Laura Sitea. 2007. "Peacebuilding: What Is in a Name?" *Global Governance* 13: 35–58.

Barnett, Michael, and Christoph Zürcher. 2009. "The Peacebuilder's Contract: How External Statebuilding Reinforces Weak Statehood." In *The Dilemmas of Statebuilding: Confronting the Contradictions of Postwar Peace Operations*, edited by Roland Paris and Timothy D. Sisk, 23–52. New York: Routledge.

Baskin, Mark. 2004. "Between Exit and Engagement: On the Division of Authority in Transitional Administrations." *Global Governance* 10: 119–137.

Bates, Robert H. 2001. *Prosperity & Violence: The Political Economy of Development*. New York: W.W. Norton & Company.

Bates, Robert H. 2008a. *When Things Fell Apart: State Failure in Late Century Africa*. New York: Cambridge University Press.

Bates, Robert H. 2008b. "Probing the Sources of Political Order." In *Order, Conflict, and Violence*, edited by Stathis N. Kalyvas, Ian Shapiro, and Tarek Masoud, 17–42. New York: Cambridge University Press.

Beauvais, Joel C. 2001. "Benevolent Despotism: A Critique of UN State-Building in East Timor." New York *University Journal of International Law and Politics* 33 (4): 1101–1178.

Bellamy, Alex J., and Paul Williams. 2004. "Introduction: Thinking Anew About Peace Operations." *International Peacekeeping* 11 (1): 1–15.

Bellamy, Alex J., Paul Williams, and Stuart Griffin. 2004. *Understanding Peacekeeping*. Cambridge: Polity Press.

Bermeo, Nancy. 1997. "Myths of Moderation: Confrontation and Conflict During Democratic Transitions." *Comparative Politics* 29 (3): 305–322.

Blattman, Christopher, and Edward Miguel. 2010. "Civil War." *Journal of Economic Literature* 48 (1): 3–57.

Blunt, Peter. 2009. "The Political Economy of Accountability in Timor-Leste: Implications for Public Policy." *Public Administration and Development* 29: 89–100.

Bockman, Johanna, and Gil Eyal. 2002. "Eastern Europe as a Laboratory for Economic Knowledge: The Transnational Roots of Neoliberalism." *American Journal of Sociology* 108 (2): 310–352.

Boege, Volker, M. Anne Brown, and Kevin P. Clements. 2009. "Hybrid Political Orders, Not Fragile States." *Peace Review* 21 (1): 13–21.

Boix, Carles. 2015. *Political Order and Inequality: Their Foundations and Their Consequences for Human Welfare*. New York: Cambridge University Press.

Boutros-Ghali, Boutros. 1992. *An Agenda for Peace: Preventive Diplomacy, Peacemaking, and Peace-Keeping*. A/47/277; S/24111. New York: United Nations, June 17.

Boutros-Ghali, Boutros. 1995. *Supplement to "An Agenda for Peace": Position Paper of the Secretary-General on the Occasion of the Fiftieth Anniversary of the United Nations*. A/50/60; S/1995/1. New York: United Nations, January 3.

Bowles, Edith, and Tanja Chopra. 2008. "East Timor: Statebuilding Revisited." In *Building States to Build Peace*, edited by Charles T. Call with Vanessa Wyeth, 271–302. Boulder: Lynne Rienner.

Boyle, Michael J. 2009. "Explaining Strategic Violence After Wars." *Studies in Conflict and Terrorism* 32: 209–236.

Brady, Henry E., and David Collier, eds. 2004. *Rethinking Social Inquiry: Diverse Tools, Shared Standards*. Lanham: Rowman& Littlefield.

Brahimi, Lakhdar. 2000. "Report of the Panel on United Nations Peace Operations (The Brahimi Report)." A/55/305; S/2000/809. New York: United Nations.

Bratton, Michael, and Nicolas Van de Walle. 1994. "Neopatrimonial Regimes and Political Transitions in Africa." *World Politics* 46 (4): 453–489.

Bratton, Michael, and Nicolas Van de Walle. 1997. *Democratic Experiments in Africa: Regime Transitions in Comparative Perspective*. Cambridge: Cambridge University Press.

Brown, Frederick Z., and David G. Timberman. 1998. "Introduction: Peace, Development, and Democracy in Cambodia – Shattered Hopes." In *Cambodia and the International Community: The Quest for Peace, Development, and Democracy*, edited by Frederick Z. Brown and David G. Timberman, 13–31. New York: Asia Society.

Brown, M. Anne. 2009. "Security, Development and the Nation-building Agenda – East Timor." *Conflict, Security & Development* 9 (2): 141–164.

Bueno de Mesquita, Bruce, Alastair Smith, Randolph M. Siverson, and James D. Morrow. 2003. *The Logic of Political Survival*. Cambridge, MA: MIT Press.

Butler, Michael J. 2012. "Ten Years After: (Re) Assessing Neo-Trusteeship and UN State-building in Timor-Leste." *International Studies Perspectives* 13 (1): 85–104.

Call, Charles T. 2003. "Democratisation, War and State-Building: Constructing the Rule of Law in El Salvador." *Journal of Latin American Studies* 35: 827–862.

Call, Charles T. 2008. "Knowing Peace When You See It: Setting Standards for Peace-Building Success." *Civil Wars* 10 (2): 173–194.

Call, Charles T., ed., with Vanessa Wyeth. 2008. *Building States to Build Peace*. Boulder: Lynne Rienner.

Call, Charles T. 2012. *Why Peace Fails: The Causes and Prevention of Civil War Recurrence*. Washington, DC: Georgetown University Press.

Call, Charles T., and Susan E. Cook. 2003. "On Democratization and Peacebuilding." *Global Governance* 9: 233–246.

Campbell, Susanna P., and Peter S. Uvin. 2015. "The Burundi Leadership Training Program." In *Across the Lines of Conflict: Facilitating Cooperation to Build Peace*, edited by Michael Lund and Steve McDonald, 281–312. New York: Columbia University Press.

Caplan, Richard. 2005. *International Governance of War-Torn Territories: Rule and Reconstruction*. Oxford: Oxford University Press.

Caplan, Richard, ed. 2012. *Exit Strategies and State Building*. New York: Oxford University Press.

Capoccia, Giovanni. 2015. "Critical Junctures and Institutional Change." In *Advances in Comparative-Historical Analysis*, edited by James Mahoney and Kathleen Thelen, 147–179. New York: Cambridge University Press.

Carbone, Giovanni, and Vincenzo Memoli. 2015. "Does Democratization Foster State Consolidation? Democratic Rule, Political Order, and Administrative Capacity." *Governance* 28 (1): 5–24.

Center on International Cooperation. 2006. *Annual Review of Global Peace Operations 2006*. Boulder: Lynne Rienner.

Chandler, David. 2006. *Empire in Denial: The Politics of Statebuilding*. London: Pluto Press.

Chandler, David P. 1991. *The Tragedy of Cambodian History: Politics, War, and Revolution since 1945*. New Haven: Yale University Press.

Chandler, David P. 1998. "The Burden of Cambodia's Past." In *Cambodia and the International Community: The Quest for Peace, Development, and Democracy*, edited by Frederick Z. Brown and David G. Timberman, 33–47. New York: Asia Society.

Chandrasekaran, Rajiv. 2006. *Imperial Life in the Emerald City: Inside Iraq's Green Zone*. New York: Knopf.

Chayes, Sarah P. 2006. *The Punishment of Virtue: Inside Afghanistan After the Taliban*. New York: Penguin Press.

Cheng, Christine S., and Dominic Zaum. 2012. "Selling the Peace? Corruption and Post-Conflict Peacebuilding" In *Corruption and Post-Conflict Peacebuilding*, edited by Christine S. Cheng and Dominic Zaum, 1–25. New York: Routledge.

Chesterman, Simon. 2002. "East Timor in Transition: Self-Determination, State-Building and the United Nations." *International Peacekeeping* 9 (1): 45–76.

Chesterman, Simon. 2004. *You, The People: The United Nations, Transitional Administration, and State-Building*. New York: Oxford University Press.

Chesterman, Simon, Michael Ignatieff, and Ramesh Thakur, eds. 2005. *Making States Work: State Failure and the Crisis of Governance*. Tokyo: United Nations University Press.

Chopra, Jarat. 1999. *Peace-Maintenance: The Evolution of International Political Authority*. London and New York: Routledge.

Chopra, Jarat. 2000. "The UN's Kingdom of East Timor." *Survival* 42 (3): 27–39.

Chopra, Jarat. 2002. "Building State Failure in East Timor." *Development and Change* 33 (5): 979–1000.

Cliffe, Sarah, and Nick Manning. 2008. "Practical Approaches to Building State Institutions." In *Building States to Build Peace*, edited by Charles T. Call with Vanessa Wyeth, 163–184. Boulder: Lynne Rienner.

Collier, Paul, and Anke Hoeffler. 1998. "On Economic Causes of Civil War." *Oxford Economic Papers* 50 (4): 563–573.

Collier, Paul, Anke Hoeffler, and Måns Söderbom. 2008. "Post-Conflict Risks." *Journal of Peace Research* 45 (4): 461–478.

Collier, Ruth Berins, and David Collier. 1991. *Shaping the Political Arena: Critical Junctures, the Labor Movement, and Regime Dynamics in Latin America*. Princeton: Princeton University Press.

Costy, Alexander. 2004. "The Dilemma of Humanitarianism in the Post-Taliban Transition." In *Nation-Building Unraveled? Aid, Peace and Justice in Afghanistan*, edited by Antonio Donini, Norah Niland, and Karin Wermester, 143–165. Bloomfield: Kumarian Press.

Cramer, Christopher, and Jonathan Goodhand. 2002. "Try Again, Fail Again, Fail Better? War, the State, and the 'Post-Conflict' Challenge in Afghanistan." *Development and Change* 33 (5): 885–909.

Cristalis, Irene. 2002. *Bitter Dawn: East Timor, A People's Story*. London and New York: Zed Books.

Croissant, Aurel. 2007. "International Interim Governments, Democratization, and Post-Conflict Peace Building: Lessons from Cambodia and East Timor." In *Interim Governments: Institutional Bridges to Peace and Democracy?*, edited by Karen Gutierri and Jessica Piombo, 217–238. Washington, DC: United States Institute of Peace Press.

Curtis, Devon. 2007. "Transitional Governance in Burundi and the Democratic Republic of the Congo." In *Interim Governments: Institutional Bridges to Peace and Democracy?*, edited by Karen Gutierri and Jessica Piombo, 171–194. Washington, DC: United States Institute of Peace Press.

Curtis, Devon. 2013. "The International Peacebuilding Paradox: Power Sharing and Post-Conflict Governance in Burundi." *African Affairs* 112 (446): 72–91.

Curtis, Devon, and Gwinyayi A. Dzinesa. 2012. *Peacebuilding, Power, and Politics in Africa*. Athens: Ohio University Press.

Dale, Pamela, Lena Lepuschuetz, and Nitin Umapathi. 2014. "Peace, Prosperity and Safety Nets in Timor-Leste: Competing Priorities or Complementary Investments?" *Asia & the Pacific Policy Studies* 1 (2): 287–296.

Della Porta, Donatella. 2013. *Clandestine Political Violence*. Cambridge: Cambridge University Press.

Diamond, Larry. 1996. "Is the Third Wave Over?" *Journal of Democracy* 7 (3): 20–37.

Diehl, Paul F. 2014. "Behavioral Studies of Peacekeeping Outcomes." *International Peacekeeping* 21 (4): 484–491.

Diehl, Paul F., and Daniel Druckman. 2010. *Evaluating Peace Operations*. Boulder: Lynne Rienner.

DiPalma, Giuseppe. 1990. *To Craft Democracies: An Essay on Democratic Transitions*. Berkeley: University of California Press.

Donini, Antonio. 2004. "Principles, Politics, and Pragmatism in the International Response to the Afghan Crisis." In *Nation-Building Unraveled? Aid, Peace and Justice in Afghanistan*, edited by Antonio Donini, Norah Niland, and Karin Wermester, 117–142. Bloomfield: Kumarian Press.

Donini, Antonio, Norah Niland, and Karin Wermester, eds. 2004. *Nation-Building Unraveled? Aid, Peace and Justice in Afghanistan*. Bloomfield: Kumarian Press.

Doornbos, Martin. 2002. "State Collapse and Fresh Starts: Some Critical Reflections." *Development and Change* 33 (5): 797–815.

Downs, George, and Stephen J. Stedman. 2002. "Evaluation Issues in Peace Implementation." In *Ending Civil Wars: The Implementation of Peace Agreements*, edited by Stephen J. Stedman, Donald Rothchild, and Elizabeth M. Cousens, 43–69. Boulder: Lynne Rienner

Doyle, Michael W. 1995. *UN Peacekeeping in Cambodia: UNTAC's Civil Mandate*. Occasional Paper Series, International Peace Academy. Boulder: Lynne Rienner.

Doyle, Michael W. 1996. "Peacebuilding in Cambodia." IPA Policy Briefing Series. New York: International Peace Academy.

Doyle, Michael W. 2001. "War Making and Peace Making: The United Nations' Post-Cold War Record." In *Turbulent Peace: The Challenges of Managing International Conflict*, edited by Chester A. Crocker, Fen Osler Hampson, and Pamela Aall, 529–560. Washington, DC: United States Institute of Peace Press.

Doyle, Michael W., and Nicolas Sambanis. 2000. "International Peacebuilding: A Theoretical and Quantitative Analysis." *American Political Science Review* 94 (4): 778–801.

Doyle, Michael W., and Nicolas Sambanis. 2006. *Making War and Building Peace: United Nations Peace Operations*. Princeton and Oxford: Princeton University Press.

Du Toit, Pierre. 2003. "Why Post-Settlement Settlements?" *Journal of Democracy* 14 (3): 104–118.

Dunn, James. 2003 [1983]. *East Timor: A Rough Passage to Independence*. Haberfield, NSW: Longueville Books.

Dupree, Louis. 1973. *Afghanistan*. Princeton: Princeton University Press.

Durch, William J. 2003. "Picking Up the Peaces: The UN's Evolving Post-Conflict Roles." *Washington Quarterly* 26 (4): 195–210.

Eckstein, Harry. 1975. "Case Studies and Theory in Political Science." In *Handbook of Political Science* (Vol. 7), edited by Fred Greenstein and Nelson W. Polsby, 79–138. Reading, MA: Addison–Wesley.

Ertman, Thomas. 1997. *Birth of the Leviathan: Building States and Regimes in Medieval and Early Modern Europe*. Cambridge: Cambridge University Press.

Evans, Peter B. 1995. *Embedded Autonomy: States and Industrial Transformation*. Princeton: Princeton University Press.

Evans, Peter B., and James E. Rauch. 1999. "Bureaucracy and Growth: A Cross-National Analysis of the Effects of 'Weberian' State Structures on Economic Growth." *American Sociological Review* 64 (5): 748–765.

Evans, Peter B., Dietrich Rueschemeyer, and Theda Skocpol, eds. 1985. *Bringing the State Back In*. Cambridge: Cambridge University Press.

Fearon, James D. 2010. "Governance and Civil War Onset." Background paper for the *World Development Report 2011: Conflict, Security, and Development*. Washington, DC: The World Bank.

Fearon, James D., and David Laitin. 2003. "Ethnicity, Insurgency, and Civil War." *American Political Science Review* 97 (2): 75–90.

Fearon, James D., and David D. Laitin. 2004. "Neo-Trusteeship and the Problem of Weak States." *International Security* 28 (4): 5–43.

Fearon, James D., and David D. Laitin. 2008. "Civil War Termination." Paper presented at the annual meetings of the American Political Science Association, Chicago, Illinois, August 30–September 1, 2007.

Fortna, Virginia Page. 2004. *Peace Time: Cease-Fire Agreements and the Durability of Peace*. Princeton: Princeton University Press.

Fortna, Virginia Page. 2008. *Does Peacekeeping Work? Shaping Belligerents' Choices After Civil Wars*. Princeton: Princeton University Press.

Fortna, Virginia Page, and Lise Morjé Howard. 2008. "Pitfalls and Prospects in the Peacekeeping Literature." *Annual Review of Political Science* 11: 283–301.

Freeman, Christopher. 2007. "Introduction: Security, Governance and State-building in Afghanistan." *International Peacekeeping* 14 (1): 1–7.

Fukuyama, Francis. 2004. *State-Building: Governance and World Order in the 21st Century*. Ithaca: Cornell University Press.

Fukuyama, Francis. 2005. "'Stateness' First." *Journal of Democracy* 16 (1): 84–88.

Fukuyama, Francis. 2011. *The Origins of Political Order: From Prehuman Times to the French Revolution*. New York: Farrar, Straus and Giroux.

Fukuyama, Francis. 2014a. *Political Order and Political Decay: From the Industrial Revolution to the Globalization of Democracy*. New York: Farrar, Straus and Giroux.

Fukuyama, Francis. 2014b. "States and Democracy." *Democratization* 21 (7): 1326–1340.

Galbraith, Peter W. 2006. *The End of Iraq: How American Incompetence Created a War Without End*. New York: Simon & Schuster.

Gans-Morse, Jordan, Sebastián Mazzuca, and Simeon Nichter. 2014. "Varieties of Clientelism: Machine Politics During Elections." *American Journal of Political Science* 58 (2): 415–432.

George, Alexander L., and Andrew Bennett. 2005. *Case Studies and Theory Development in the Social Sciences*. Cambridge, MA: MIT Press.

Ghani, Ashraf, and Clare Lockhart. 2008. *Fixing Failed States: A Framework for Rebuilding a Fractured World*. New York: Oxford University Press.

Girod, Desha M. 2015. *Explaining Post-Conflict Reconstruction*. New York: Oxford University Press.

Giustozzi, Antonio. 2009. *Empires of Mud: War and Warlords of Afghanistan*. New York: Columbia University Press.

Giustozzi, Antonio. 2013. "March Toward Democracy? The Development of Political Movements in Afghanistan." *Central Asian Survey* 32 (3): 318–335.

Gleditsch, Nils Petter, Peter Wallensteen, Mikael Eriksson, Margareta Sollenberg, and Håvard Strand. 2002. "Armed Conflict 1946–2001: A New Dataset." *Journal of Peace Research* 39 (5): 615–637.

Goldstone, Anthony. 2004. "UNTAET With Hindsight: The Peculiarities of Politics in an Incomplete State." *Global Governance* 10: 83–98.

Goldstone, Anthony. 2012. "East Timor." In *Exit Strategies and State Building*, edited by Richard Caplan, 177–193. New York: Oxford University Press

Goodhand, Jonathan. 2008. "Corrupting or Consolidating the Peace? The Drugs Economy and Post Conflict Peacebuilding in Afghanistan." *International Peacekeeping* 15 (3): 405–423.

Goodson, Larry. 2003. "Afghanistan's Long Road to Reconstruction." *Journal of Democracy* 14 (1): 82–99.

Goodson, Larry. 2005. "Bullets, Ballots, and Poppies in Afghanistan." *Journal of Democracy* 16 (1): 24–38.

Gottesman, Evan. 2003. *Cambodia After the Khmer Rouge: Inside the Politics of Nation Building*. New Haven, CT: Yale University Press.

Goulding, Marrack. 1993. "The Evolution of United Nations Peacekeeping." *International Affairs* 69 (3): 451–464.

Greenhill, Kelly M., and Solomon Major. 2007. "The Perils of Profiling: Civil War Spoilers and the Collapse of Intrastate Peace Accords." *International Security* 31 (3): 7–40.

Gregorian, Vartan. 1969. *The Emergence of Modern Afghanistan: Politics of Reform and Modernization, 1880–1946*. Stanford, CA: Stanford University Press.

Grindle, Merilee S. 2004. "Good Enough Governance: Poverty Reduction and Reform in Developing Countries." *Governance* 17 (4): 525–548.

Grindle, Merilee S. 2007. "Good Enough Governance Revisited." *Development Policy Review* 25 (5): 553–574.

Gunn, Geoffrey C. 1997. *East Timor and the United Nations: The Case for Intervention*. Lawrenceville, NJ: Red Sea Press, Inc.

Gutierri, Karen, and Jessica Piombo. 2007. *Interim Governments: Institutional Bridges to Peace and Democracy?* Washington, DC: United States Institute of Peace Press.

Hacker, Jacob S., Paul Pierson, and Kathleen Thelen. 2015. "Drift and Conversion: Hidden Faces of Institutional Change." In *Advances in Comparative-Historical Analysis*, edited by James Mahoney and Kathleen Thelen, 180–208. New York: Cambridge University Press.

Haggard, Stephan, and Robert Kaufman. 1997. "The Political Economy of Democratic Transitions." *Comparative Politics* 29 (3): 263–83.

Hamieri, Shahar. 2010. *Regulating Statehood: State Building and the Transformation of Global Order*. London: Palgrave Macmilllan.

Hartzell, Caroline, and Matthew Hoddie. 2007. *Crafting Peace: Power-Sharing Institutions and the Negotiated Settlement of Civil Wars*. University Park, PA: Pennsylvania State University Press.

Hartzell, Caroline, and Matthew Hoddie. 2015. "The Art of the Possible: Power Sharing and Post-Civil War Democracy." *World Politics* 67 (1): 37–71.

Hartzell, Caroline, Matthew Hoddie, and Donald Rothchild. 2001. "Stabilizing the Peace After Civil War: An Investigation of Some Key Variables." *International Organization* 55 (1): 183–208.

Heder, Steve and Judy Ledgerwood, eds. 1996. *Propaganda, Politics and Violence in Cambodia: Democratic Transition under United Nations Peace-Keeping*. Armonk, NY: M. E. Sharpe.

Hellman, Joel S. 1998. "Winners Take All: The Politics of Partial Reform in Postcommunist Transitions." *World Politics* 50 (2): 203–234.

Hendrickson, Dylan. 2001. "Cambodia's Security-Sector Reforms: Limits of a Downsizing Strategy." *Conflict, Security & Development* 1 (1): 67–82.

Herbst, Jeffrey. 2000. *States and Power in Africa: Comparative Lessons in Authority and Control.* Princeton, NJ: Princeton University Press.

Hobbes, Thomas. 1968 [1651]. *Leviathan.* Edited by C. B. MacPherson. New York: Penguin Books.

Hoddie, Matthew, and Caroline Hartzell. 2005. "Power Sharing in Peace Settlements: Initiating the Transition from Civil War." In *Sustainable Peace: Power and Democracy After Civil Wars*, edited by Philip G. Roeder and Donald Rothchild, 83–106. Ithaca, NY: Cornell University Press.

Hoddie, Matthew, and Caroline Hartzell. 2010. *Strengthening Peace in Post-Civil War States: Transforming Spoilers into Stakeholders.* Chicago: University of Chicago Press.

Horowitz, Donald L. 1985. *Ethnic Groups in Conflict.* Berkeley: University of California Press.

Horowitz, Donald L. 2002. "Constitutional Design: Proposals versus Processes." In *The Architecture of Democracy: Constitutional Design, Conflict Management, and Democracy*, edited by Andrew Reynolds, 15–36. Oxford: Oxford University Press.

Howard, Lise Morjé. 2008. *UN Peacekeeping in Civil Wars.* New York: Cambridge University Press.

Howard, Marc Morjé, and Philip G. Roessler. 2006. "Liberalizing Electoral Outcomes in Competitive Authoritarian Regimes." *American Journal of Political Science* 50 (2): 365–381.

Hughes, Caroline. 2003. *The Political Economy of Cambodia's Transition 1991–2001.* Richmond, UK: Curzon Press.

Hughes, Caroline. 2009a. *Dependent Communities: Aid and Politics in Cambodia and East Timor.* Ithaca, NY: Cornell Southeast Asia Program Publications.

Hughes, Caroline. 2009b. "Reconstructing Legitimate Political Authority through Elections?" In *Beyond Democracy in Cambodia: Political Reconstruction in a Post-Conflict Society*, edited by Joakim Öjendal and Mona Lilja, 31–69. Copenhagen: Nordic Institute of Asian Studies Press.

Huntington, Samuel P. 1968. *Political Order in Changing Societies.* New Haven, CT: Yale University Press.

Hutchcroft, Paul D. 1997. "The Politics of Privilege: Assessing the Impact of Rents, Corruption, and Clientelism on Third World Development." *Political Studies* XLV: 639–658.

Ingram, Sue. 2012. "Building the Wong Peace: Reviewing the United Nations Transitional Authority in East Timor (UNTAET) Through a Political Settlement Lens." *Political Science* 64 (1): 3–20.

International Commission on Intervention and State Sovereignty. 2001. *The Responsibility to Protect*. Ottawa, Canada: International Development Research Centre.

International Crisis Group. 2002. "The Afghan Transitional Administration: Prospects and Perils." July 30.

International Crisis Group. 2003. "Afghanistan: The Constitutional Loya Jirga." December 12.

International Crisis Group. 2006. "Afghanistan's New Legislature: Making Democracy Work." May 15.

International Crisis Group. 2011. "Timor-Leste's Veterans: An Unfinished Struggle?" Asia Briefing No. 129, Dili, Jakarta, and Brussels, November 18.

International Crisis Group. 2012. "Burundi: A Deepening Corruption Crisis." Africa Report 185, March 21.

International Monetary Fund. 2009. *Democratic Republic of Timor-Leste: 2011 Article IV Consultation – Staff Report*. IMF Country Report No. 09/219. Washington, DC: International Monetary Fund.

International Monetary Fund. 2013. *Democratic Republic of Timor-Leste: 2013 Article IV Consultation – Staff Report*. IMF Country Report No. 13/338. Washington, DC: International Monetary Fund.

Jackson, Robert H. 1990. *Quasi-States: Sovereignty, International Relations, and the Third World*. Cambridge: Cambridge University Press.

Jackson, Robert H., and Carl G. Rosberg. 1982. "Why Africa's Weak States Persist: The Empirical and the Juridical in Statehood." *World Politics* 35 (1): 1–24.

Jackson, Robert H. and Carl G. Rosberg. 1984. "Personal Rule: Theory and Practice." *Contemporary Politics* 16 (4): 421–442.

Jarstad, Anna K. 2008. "Power Sharing: Former Enemies in Joint Government." In *From War to Democracy: Dilemmas of Peacebuilding*, edited by Anna K. Jarstad and Timothy D. Sisk, 105–133. New York: Cambridge University Press.

Jarstad, Anna K., and Desirée Nilsson. 2008. "From Words to Deeds: The Implementation of Power-Sharing Pacts in Peace Accords." *Conflict Management and Peace Science* 25: 206–223.

Jarstad, Anna K., and Timothy D. Sisk. eds. 2008. *From War to Democracy: Dilemmas of Peacebuilding*. New York: Cambridge University Press.

Johnson, Chris, William Maley, Alexander Thier, and Ali Wardak. 2003. "Afghanistan's Political and Constitutional Development." London: Overseas Development Institute and United Kingdom Department for International Development.

Jones, Bruce. 2004. "Evolving Models of Peacekeeping: Policy Implications and Responses." External Study, United Nations Department of Peacekeeping Operations. New York: United Nations.

Jones, Bruce, and Rahul Chandran. 2008. *From Fragility to Resilience: Concepts and Dilemmas of State Building in Fragile Situations*. Joint study by the Center on International Cooperation at New York University and the International Peace Academy. Paris: OECD DAC Fragile States Group.

Joshi, Madhav, and T. David Mason. 2011. "Peasants, Patrons, and Parties: The Tension between Clientelism and Democracy in Nepal." *International Studies Quarterly* 55 (1): 151–175.

Kalyvas, Stathis N., Ian Shapiro, and Tarek Masoud. 2008. "Introduction: Integrating the Study of Order, Conflict, and Violence." In *Order, Conflict, and Violence*, edited by Stathis N. Kalyvas, Ian Shapiro, and Tarek Masoud, 1–14. New York: Cambridge University Press.

Karl, Terry Lynn. 1990. "Dilemmas of Democratization in Latin America." *Comparative Politics* 23 (1): 1–21.

Katzman, Kenneth. 2007. "Afghanistan: Post-War Governance, Security, and US Policy." *Congressional Research Service Report for Congress*, Washington, DC, January 11.

Katznelson, Ira. 1997. "Structure and Configuration in Comparative Politics." In *Comparative Politics: Rationality, Culture, and Structure*, edited by Marc Irving Lichbach and Alan S. Zuckerman, 81–112. Cambridge: Cambridge University Press.

Kaufmann, Chaim. 2007. "A Security Dilemma." *Harvard International Review*, April 16.

Kaufmann, Daniel, Aart Kraay, and Massimo Mastruzzi. 2010. "The Worldwide Governance Indicators: A Summary of Methodology, Data and Analytical Issues." World Bank Policy Research Working Paper No. 5430. Washington, DC: The World Bank.

Keefer, Philip. 2011. "Collective Action, Political Parties, and Pro-Development Public Policy." *Asian Development Review* 28 (1): 94–118.

Keefer, Philip, and Razvan Vlaicu. 2008. "Democracy, Credibility, and Clientelism." *Journal of Law, Economics, & Organization* 24 (2): 371–406.

Kelsall, Tim. 2012. "Neo-Patrimonialism, Rent-Seeking and Development: Going with the Grain?" *New Political Economy* 17 (5): 677–682.

Kent, Alexandra. 2016. "Conflict Continues: Transitioning Into a Battle for Property in Cambodia Today." *Journal of Southeast Asian Studies* 47 (1): 3–23.

Keohane, Robert O. 2003. "Political Authority After Intervention: Gradations of Sovereignty" In *Humanitarian Intervention: Ethical, Legal, and*

Political Dimensions, edited by J. L. Holzgrefe and Robert O. Keohane, 275–298. Cambridge: Cambridge University Press.

Kiernan, Ben. 1996. *The Pol Pot Regime: Race, Power, and Genocide in Cambodia under the Khmer Rouge, 1975–79*. New Haven, CT: Yale University Press.

Kiernan, Ben. 2003. "The Demography of Genocide in Southeast Asia: The Death Tolls in Cambodia, 1975–1979, and East Timor, 1975–1980." *Critical Asian Studies* 35 (4): 585–597.

Kitschelt, Herbert, and Steven I. Wilkinson, eds. 2007. *Patrons, Clients, and Policies: Patterns of Democratic Accountability and Political Competition*. New York: Cambridge University Press.

Kohli, Atul. 2002. "State, Society, and Development." In *Political Science: The State of the Discipline*, edited by Ira Katznelson and Helen V. Milner, 84–117. New York and Washington, DC: W. W. Norton and American Political Science Association.

Krasner, Stephen D. 1999. *Sovereignty: Organized Hypocrisy*. Princeton, NJ: Princeton University Press.

Krasner, Stephen D. 2004. "Sharing Sovereignty: New Institutions for Collapsed and Failing States." *International Security* 29 (2): 85–120.

Krasner, Stephen D., and Thomas Risse. 2014. "External Actors, State-Building, and Service Provision in Areas of Limited Statehood: Introduction." *Governance* 27 (4): 545–567.

Lake, David A. 2016. *The Statebuilder's Dilemma: On the Limits of Foreign Intervention*. Ithaca: Cornell University Press.

Lake, David A., and Christopher J. Fariss. 2014. "Why International Trusteeship Fails: The Politics of External Authority in Areas of Limited Statehood." *Governance* 27 (4): 569–587.

Le Billon, Philippe. 2000. "The Political Ecology of Transition in Cambodia 1989–1999: War, Peace and Forest Exploitation." *Development and Change* 31: 785–805.

Le Billon, Philippe. 2003. "Buying Peace or Fuelling War: The Role of Corruption in Armed Conflicts." *Journal of International Development* 15: 413–426.

Lemarchand, René. 2012. "Peacebuilding in the Great Lakes Region of Africa." In *Peacebuilding, Power, and Politics in Africa*, edited by Devon Curtis and Gwinyayi A. Dzinesa, 212–231. Athens: Ohio University Press.

Levi, Margaret. 1989. *Of Rule and Revenue*. Berkeley: University of California Press.

Levi, Margaret. 2006. "Why We Need a New Theory of Government." *Perspectives on Politics* 4 (1): 5–20.

Levitsky, Steven, and Lucan A. Way. 2002. "The Rise of Competitive Authoritarianism." *Journal of Democracy* 13 (2): 51–65.

Levy, Brian. 2014. *Working With the Grain: Integrating Governance and Growth in Development Strategies*. New York: Oxford University Press.

Licklider, Roy. 1995. "The Consequences of Negotiated Settlements in Civil Wars, 1945–1993." *American Political Science Review* 89 (3): 681–690.

Licklider, Roy. 2001. "Obstacles to Peace Settlements." In *Turbulent Peace: The Challenges of Managing International Conflict*, edited by Chester A. Crocker, Fen Osler Hampson, and Pamela Aall, 697–718. Washington, DC: United States Institute of Peace Press.

Lijphart, Arend. 1977. *Democracy in Plural Societies: A Comparative Exploration*. New Haven, CT: Yale University Press.

Lijphart, Arend. 2002. "The Wave of Power-Sharing Democracy." In *The Architecture of Democracy: Constitutional Design, Conflict Management, and Democracy*, edited by Andrew Reynolds, 37–54. Oxford: Oxford University Press.

Linz, Juan J., and Alfred Stepan. 1996. *Problems of Democratic Transition and Consolidation: Southern Europe, South America, and Post-Communist Europe*. Baltimore, MD: Johns Hopkins University Press.

Lipset, Seymour Martin. 1959. "Some Social Requisites of Democracy: Economic Development and Political Legitimacy." *American Political Science Review* 53 (1): 69–105.

Locke, John. 1963 [1698]. *Two Treatises of Government*. New York: Cambridge University Press.

Lyons, Terrence. 2002. "The Role of Postsettlement Elections." In *Ending Civil Wars: The Implementation of Peace Agreements*, edited by Stephen J. Stedman, Donald Rothchild, and Elizabeth M. Cousens, 215–235. Boulder, CO: Lynne Rienner.

Mac Ginty, Roger. 2010. "Warlords and the Liberal Peace: Statebuilding in Afghanistan." *Conflict, Security & Development* 10 (4), 577–598.

Mac Ginty, Roger, and Oliver Richmond. 2013. "The Local Turn in Peacebuilding: A Critical Agenda for Peace." *Third World Quarterly* 34 (5): 763–783.

Mahoney, James and Kathleen Thelen, eds. 2010. *Explaining Institutional Change: Ambiguity, Agency, and Power*. New York: Cambridge University Press.

Mahoney, James and Kathleen Thelen, eds. 2015. *Advances in Comparative-Historical Analysis*. New York: Cambridge University Press.

Maley, William. 2013. "Statebuilding in Afghanistan: Challenges and Pathologies." *Central Asian Survey* 32 (3): 255–270.

Mann, Michael. 1986. *The Sources of Social Power*. New York: Cambridge University Press.

Manning, Carrie. 2007. "Interim Governments and the Construction of Political Elites." In *Interim Governments: Institutional Bridges to Peace and Democracy?*, edited by Karen Gutierri and Jessica Piombo, 53–72. Washington, DC: United States Institute of Peace Press.

Mansfield, Edward D., and Jack Snyder. 1995. "Democratization and the Danger of War." *International Security* 20 (1): 5–38.

Marks, Stephen P. 2010. "The Process of Creating a New Constitution in Cambodia." In *Framing the State in Times of Transition: Case Studies in Constitution Making*, edited by Laurel E. Miller, 207–244. Washington, DC: United States Institute of Peace.

Marten, Kimberly. 2012. *Warlords: Strong-Arm Brokers in Weak States*. Ithaca: Cornell University Press.

Martin, Ian. 2001. *Self-Determination in East Timor: The United Nations, The Ballot, and International Intervention*. Occasional Paper Series, International Peace Academy. Boulder, CO: Lynne Rienner.

Martin, Philip. 2013. "Coming Together: Power-Sharing and the Durability of Negotiated Peace Settlements." *Civil Wars* 15 (3): 332–358.

Matanock, Aila M. 2014. "Governance Delegation Agreements: Shared Sovereignty as a Substitute for Limited Statehood." *Governance* 27 (4) 589–612.

Mazzuca, Sebastián L., and Gerardo L. Munck. 2014. "State or Democracy First? Alternative Perspectives on the State–Democracy Nexus." *Democratization* 21 (7): 1221–1243.

McAdam, Doug, Sidney Tarrow, and Charles Tilly. 1997. "Toward an Integrated Perspective on Social Movements and Revolutions." In *Comparative Politics: Rationality, Culture, and Structure*, edited by Marc Irving Lichbach and Alan S. Zuckerman, 142–173. Cambridge: Cambridge University Press.

Meyer, John W., John Boli, G. M. Thomas, and F. O. Ramirez. 1997. "World Society and the Nation-State." *American Journal of Sociology* 103 (1): 144–181.

Meyer, John W., and Brian Rowan. 1977. "Institutionalized Organizations: Formal Structure as Myth and Ceremony." *American Journal of Sociology* 83 (2): 340–363.

Migdal, Joel S. 1988. *Strong Societies and Weak States: State–Society Relations and State Capabilities in the Third World*. Princeton, NJ: Princeton University Press.

Migdal, Joel S. 1997. "Studying the State." In *Comparative Politics: Rationality, Culture, and Structure*, edited by Marc Irving Lichbach and Alan S. Zuckerman, 208–235. Cambridge: Cambridge University Press.

Migdal, Joel S., Atul Kohli, and Vivienne Shue, eds. 1994. *State Power and Social Forces: Domination and Transformation in the Third World*. New York: Cambridge University Press.

Mill, John Stuart. 1843. *A System of Logic*. Publisher unknown.

Mo, Timothy. 2002. *The Redundancy of Courage*. Hong Kong: Paddleless-Press.

Mukhopadhyay, Dipali. 2014. *Warlords, Strongman Governors, and the State in Afghanistan*. New York: Cambridge University Press.

Nagl, John A., Andrew M. Exum, and Ahmed A. Humayun. 2009. "A Pathway to Success in Afghanistan: The National Solidarity Program." CNAS Policy Brief. Washington, DC: Center for a New American Security.

Newman, Edward, and Oliver Richmond, eds. 2006. *Challenges to Peacebuilding: Managing Spoilers During Conflict Resolution*. New York: United Nations University Press.

Nicol, Bill. 1978. *Timor: The Stillborn Nation*. Melbourne: Visa Books.

Nilsson, Desirée, and Mimi Söderberg Kovacs. 2011. "Revisiting an Elusive Concept: A Review of the Debate on Spoilers in Peace Processes." *International Studies Review* 13: 606–626.

Niner, Sarah. 2009. *Xanana: Leader of the Struggle for Independent Timor-Leste*. Melbourne: Australian Scholarly Publishing.

Nixon, Hamish, and Richard Ponzio. 2007. "Building Democracy in Afghanistan: The Statebuilding Agenda and International Engagement." *International Peacekeeping* 14 (1): 26–40.

North, Douglass C., John J. Wallis, and Barry R. Weingast. 2009. *Violence and Social Orders: A Conceptual Framework for Interpreting Recorded Human History*. New York: Cambridge University Press.

Nunberg, Barbara, Naazneen Barma, Mark Abdollahian, Amanda Green, and Deborah Perlman. 2010. "At the Frontier of Practical Political Economy: Operationalizing an Agent-Based Stakeholder Model in the World Bank's East Asia and Pacific Region." *World Bank Policy Research Working Paper Series* No. 5176. Washington, DC: The World Bank.

Nunberg, Barbara and Robert R. Taliercio. 2012. "Sabotaging Civil Service Reform in Aid-Dependent Countries: Are Donors to Blame?" *World Development* 40 (10): 1970–1981.

O'Dwyer, Conor. 2006. *Runaway State-Building: Patronage Politics and Democratic Development*. Baltimore, MD: Johns Hopkins University Press.

OECD. 2005. *The Paris Declaration on Aid Effectiveness*. Paris: Organization for Economic Cooperation and Development.

OECD. 2008a. *Concepts and Dilemmas of State Building in Fragile Situations: From Fragility to Resilience*. Paris: Organization for Economic Cooperation and Development.

OECD. 2008b. *The Accra Agenda for Action*. Paris: Organization for Economic Cooperation and Development.

OECD. 2011. *From Power Struggles to Sustainable Peace: Understanding Political Settlements*. Paris: Organization for Economic Cooperation and Development.

Olson, Mancur. 1993. "Dictatorship, Democracy, and Development." *American Political Science Review* 87 (3): 567–576.

Ottaway, Marina. 2002. "Rebuilding State Institutions in Collapsed States." *Development and Change* 33 (5): 1001–1023.

Pak, Kimchoeun, Vuthy Horng, Netra Eng, Sovanna Ann, Sedara Kim, Jenny Knowles, and David Craig. 2007. *Accountability and Neo-Patrimonialism in Cambodia: A Critical Literature Review*. Working Paper No. 34. Phnom Penh: Cambodia Development Resource Institute.

Paris, Roland. 1997. "Peacebuilding and the Limits of Liberal Internationalism." *International Security* 22 (2): 54–89.

Paris, Roland. 2001. "Wilson's Ghost: The Faulty Assumptions of Postconflict Peacebuilding." In *Turbulent Peace: The Challenges of Managing International Conflict*, edited by Chester A. Crocker, Fen Osler Hampson, and Pamela Aall, 765–784. Washington, DC: United States Institute of Peace Press.

Paris, Roland. 2003. "Peacekeeping and the Constraints of Global Culture." *European Journal of International Relations* 9 (3): 441–473.

Paris, Roland. 2004. *At War's End: Building Peace After Civil Conflict*. New York: Cambridge University Press.

Paris, Roland. 2010. "Saving Liberal Peacebuilding." *Review of International Studies* 36: 337–365.

Paris, Roland, and Timothy D. Sisk, eds. 2009. *The Dilemmas of Statebuilding: Confronting the Contradictions of Postwar Peace Operations*. New York: Routledge.

Parsons, Talcott. 1951. *The Social System*. London: Routledge & Kegan Paul.

Peou, Sorpong. 2002. "Implementing Cambodia's Peace Agreement." In *Ending Civil Wars: The Implementation of Peace Agreements*, edited by Stephen J. Stedman, Donald Rothchild, and Elizabeth M. Cousens, 499–530. Boulder, CO: Lynne Rienner.

Pierson, Paul. 1996. "The Path to European Integration: A Historical Institutionalist Perspective." *Comparative Political Studies* 29 (2): 123–163.

Pierson, Paul. 2004. *Politics in Time: History, Institutions, and Social Analysis*. Princeton, NJ: Princeton University Press.

Pierson, Paul. 2015. "Power and Path Dependence." In *Advances in Comparative-Historical Analysis*, edited by James Mahoney and Kathleen Thelen, 123–146. New York: Cambridge University Press.

Pierson, Paul, and Theda Skocpol. 2002. "Historical Institutionalism in Contemporary Political Science." In *Political Science: The State of the Discipline*, edited by Ira Katznelson and Helen V. Milner, 693–721. New

York and Washington, DC: W. W. Norton and American Political Science Association.

Ponzio, Richard. 2011. *Democratic Peacebuilding: Aiding Afghanistan and other Fragile States*. Oxford: Oxford University Press.

Powell, G. Bingham. 1989. "Constitutional Design and Citizen Electoral Control." *Journal of Theoretical Politics* 1 (2): 107–130.

Pritchett, Lant, and Michael Woolcock. 2002. "Solutions When the Solution is the Problem: Arraying the Disarray in Development." Working Paper No. 10. Washington, DC: Center for Global Development.

Pritchett, Lant, Michael Woolcock, and Matt Andrews. 2013. "Looking Like a State: Techniques of Persistent Failure in State Capability for Implementation." *Journal of Development Studies* 49 (1): 1–18.

Przeworski, Adam, and Henry Teune. 1970. *The Logic of Comparative Social Inquiry*. New York: Wiley.

Pugh, Michael. 2005. "The Political Economy of Peacebuilding: A Critical Theory Perspective." *International Journal of Peace Studies* 10 (2): 23–42.

Ragin, Charles C. 1987. *The Comparative Method: Moving Beyond Qualitative and Quantitative Strategies*. Berkeley and Los Angeles: University of California Press.

Ramalingam, Ben. 2013. *Aid on the Edge of Chaos*. Oxford: Oxford University Press.

Rangelov, Iavor, and Marika Theros, 2012. "Abuse of Power and Conflict Persistence in Afghanistan." *Conflict, Security & Development* 12 (3): 227–248.

Ratner, Steven R. 1995. *The New UN Peacekeeping: Building Peace in Lands of Conflict After the Cold War*. New York: St. Martin's Press and Council on Foreign Relations.

Reilly, Benjamin. 2002. "Elections in Post-Conflict Scenarios: Constraints and Dangers." *International Peacekeeping* 9 (2): 118–139.

Reilly, Benjamin. 2013. "Political Parties and Post-Conflict Peacebuilding." *Civil Wars* 15 (S1): 88–104.

Rees, Edward. 2004. "Under Pressure: Falantil-Forcas de Defesa de Timor Leste – Three Decades of Defence Force Development in Timor Leste 1975–2004." Working Paper No. 139. Geneva: Centre for the Democratic Control of Armed Forces.

Reno, William. 2004. "Reconstructing Peace in Liberia." In *Durable Peace: Challenges for Peacebuilding in Africa*, edited by Taisier M. Ali and Robert O. Matthews, 115–141. Toronto: University of Toronto Press.

Reynolds, Andrew, ed. 2002. *The Architecture of Democracy: Constitutional Design, Conflict Management, and Democracy*. Oxford: Oxford University Press.

Reynolds, Andrew. 2006. "Electoral Systems Today: The Curious Case of Afghanistan." *Journal of Democracy* 17 (2) (April): 104–117.

Reynolds, Andrew, and Andrew Wilder. 2004. *Free, Fair or Flawed: Challenges for Legitimate Elections in Afghanistan*. Kabul: Afghanistan Research and Evaluation Unit.

Richmond, Oliver P. 2005. *The Transformation of Peace*. New York: Palgrave Macmillan.

Richmond, Oliver P. 2006. "The Problem of Peace: Understanding the 'Liberal Peace'." *Conflict, Security & Development* 6 (3): 291–314.

Richmond, Oliver P. 2014. *Failed Statebuilding: Intervention, the State, and the Dynamics of Peace Formation*. New Haven, CT: Yale University Press.

Richmond, Oliver P., and Jason Franks. 2009. *Liberal Peace Transitions: Between Statebuilding and Peacebuilding*. Edinburgh: Edinburgh University Press.

Roberts, David. 2009. "The Superficiality of Statebuilding in Cambodia: Patronage and Clientelism as Enduring Forms of Politics." In *The Dilemmas of Statebuilding: Confronting the Contradictions of Postwar Peace Operations*, edited by Roland Paris and Timothy D. Sisk, 149–169. New York: Routledge.

Roberts, David. 2011. *Liberal Peacebuilding and Global Governance: Beyond the Metropolis*. New York: Routledge.

Robinson, James A. 2001. "When is a State Predatory?" Unpublished manuscript.

Rodrik, Dani. 2014. "When Ideas Trump Interests: Preferences, Worldviews, and Policy Innovations." *Journal of Economic Perspectives* 28 (1): 189–208.

Roeder, Philip G., and Donald Rothchild, eds. 2005. *Sustainable Peace: Power and Democracy After Civil Wars*. Ithaca, NY: Cornell University Press.

Rostow, Walt W. 1962. *The Stages of Economic Growth: A Non-Communist Manifesto*. Cambridge: Cambridge University Press.

Rotberg, Robert I., ed. 2004. *When States Fail: Causes and Consequences*. Princeton, NJ: Princeton University Press.

Rothchild, Donald. 2002. "Settlement Terms and Post-Agreement Stability." In *Ending Civil Wars: The Implementation of Peace Agreements*, edited by Stephen J. Stedman, Donald Rothchild, and Elizabeth M. Cousens, 117–138. Boulder, CO: Lynne Rienner.

Rubin, Barnett R. 2000. "The Political Economy of War and Peace in Afghanistan." *World Development* 28 (10): 1789–1803.

Rubin, Barnett R. 2002. *The Fragmentation of Afghanistan: State Formation and Collapse in the International System*. (2nd ed.) New Haven, CT: Yale University Press.

Rubin, Barnett R. 2004. "Creating a Constitution for Afghanistan." *Journal of Democracy* 15 (3): 5–19.

Rubin, Barnett R. 2006. "Afghanistan's Uncertain Transition From Turmoil to Normalcy." CSR No. 12. New York: Council on Foreign Relations.

Rubin, Barnett R., and Humayun Hamidzada. 2007. "From Bonn to London: Governance Challenges and the Future of Statebuilding in Afghanistan." *International Peacekeeping* 14 (1): 8–25.

Rustow, Dankwart. 1970. "Transitions to Democracy: Toward a Dynamic Model." *Comparative Politics* 2 (3): 337–363.

Saikal, Amin. 2005. "Afghanistan's Weak State and Strong Society." In *Making States Work: State Failure and the Crisis of Governance*, edited by Simon Chesterman, Michael Ignatieff, and Ramesh Thakur, 193–209. Tokyo: United Nations University Press.

Scambary, James. 2009. "Anatomy of a Conflict: The 2006–2007 Communal Violence in East Timor." *Conflict, Security & Development* 9 (2): 265–288.

Scott, James C. 1972. "Patron–Client Politics and Political Change in Southeast Asia." *American Political Science Review* 66(1): 91–113.

Scott, James C. 1998. *Seeing Like a State: How Certain Schemes to Improve the Human Condition Have Failed.* New Haven, CT: Yale University Press.

Shain, Yossi, and Juan J. Linz, eds. 1995. *Between States: Interim Governments and Democratic Transitions.* New York: Cambridge University Press.

Sharan, Timor. 2011. "The Dynamics of Elite Networks and Patron–Client Relations in Post-Bonn Afghanistan." *Europe–Asia Studies Journal* 63 (6): 1109–1127.

Shawcross, William. 1994. *Cambodia's New Deal.* Contemporary Issues Paper #1. Washington, DC: Carnegie Endowment for International Peace.

Shefter, Martin. 1977. "Party and Patronage: Germany, England, and Italy." *Politics and Society* 7: 403–451.

Shefter, Martin. 1994. *Political Parties and the State: The American Historical Experience.* Princeton, NJ: Princeton University Press.

Sisk, Timothy D. 1996. *Power Sharing and International Mediation in Ethnic Conflicts.* Washington, DC: United States Institute of Peace.

Sisk, Timothy D. 2013. "Power-Sharing in Civil War: Puzzles of Peacemaking and Peacebuilding." *Civil Wars* 15 (S1): 7–20.

Skocpol, Theda. 1979. *States and Social Revolutions: A Comparative Analysis of France, Russia, and China.* Cambridge: Cambridge University Press.

Skocpol, Theda. 1985. "Bringing the State Back In: Strategies of Analysis in Current Research." In *Bringing the State Back In*, edited by Peter B.

Evans, Dietrich Rueschemeyer, and Theda Skocpol, 3–37. Cambridge: Cambridge University Press.

Skocpol, Theda. 1988. "Social Revolutions and Mass Military Mobilization." *World Politics* 40 (2): 147–68.

Skowronek, Stephen. 1982. *Building a New American State: The Expansion of National Administrative Capacities, 1877–1920*. New York: Cambridge University Press.

Slater, Dan. 2008. "Can Leviathan Be Democratic? Competitive Elections, Robust Mass Politics and State Infrastructural Power." *Studies in Comparative International Development* 43 (3): 252–272.

Slater, Dan. 2010. *Ordering Power: Contentious Politics and Authoritarian Leviathans in Southeast Asia*. New York: Cambridge University Press.

Slater, Dan, and Erica Simmons. 2010. "Informative Regress: Critical Antecedents in Comparative Politics." *Comparative Political Studies* 43 (7): 886–917.

Smith, Claire Q. 2014. "Illiberal Peace-building in Hybrid Political Orders: Managing Violence During Indonesia's Contested Political Transition." *Third World Quarterly* 35 (8): 1509–1528.

Smith, Michael G., with Moreen Dee. 2003. *Peacekeeping in East Timor: The Path to Independence*. Occasional Paper Series, International Peace Academy. Boulder, CO: Lynne Rienner.

Smith, Steven S., and Thomas F. Remington. 2001. *The Politics of Institutional Choice: The Formation of the Russian State Duma*. Princeton, NJ: Princeton University Press.

Snyder, Jack. 2000. *From Voting to Violence: Democratization and Nationalist Conflict*. New York: W. W. Norton.

Soares de Oliveira, Ricardo. 2011. "Illiberal Peacebuilding in Angola." *Journal of Modern Africa Studies* 49 (2): 287–314.

Solarz, Stephen. 1990. "Cambodia and the International Community." *Foreign Affairs* 69 (2): 99–115.

Soltan, Karol E. 2002. "The United Nations and the Development of Constitutional Order." Paper presented at the Annual Meeting of the International Studies Association, 2002.

Springer, Simon. 2009. "The Neoliberalization of Security and Violence in Cambodia's Transition." In *Human Security in East Asia: Challenges for Collaborative Action*, edited by Sorpong Peou, 125–141. New York: Routledge.

Srinivasan, Sharath. 2012. "The Politics of Negotiating Peace in Sudan." In *Peacebuilding, Power, and Politics in Africa*, edited by Devon Curtis and Gwinyayi A. Dzinesa, 195–211. Athens: Ohio University Press.

Stark, David, and Laszlo Bruszt. 1998. *Postsocialist Pathways: Transforming Politics and Property in East Central Europe*. Cambridge: Cambridge University Press.

Stedman, Stephen J. 1997. "Spoiler Problems in Peace Processes." *International Security* 22 (Fall 1997): 5–53.

Stedman, Stephen J., Donald Rothchild, and Elizabeth M. Cousens, eds. 2002. *Ending Civil Wars: The Implementation of Peace Agreements*. Boulder, CO: Lynne Rienner.

Steinmo, Sven. 2008. "Historical Institutionalism." In *Approaches and Methodologies in the Social Sciences: A Pluralist Perspective*, edited by Donatella della Porta and Michael Keating, 118–138. Cambridge: Cambridge University Press.

Stinchcombe, Arthur L. 1999. "Ending Revolutions and Building New Governments." *Annual Review of Political Science* 2: 49–73.

Stokes, Susan C., Thad Dunning, Marcelo Nazareno, and Valeria Brusco. 2013. *Brokers, Voters, and Clientelism: The Puzzle of Distributive Politics*. New York: Cambridge University Press.

Strangio, Sebastian. 2014. *Hun Sen's Cambodia*. New Haven, CT: Yale University Press.

Suhrke, Astri. 2001. "Peacekeepers as Nationbuilders: Dilemmas of the UN in East Timor." *International Peacekeeping* 8 (4): 1–20.

Suhrke, Astri. 2009. "The Dangers of a Tight Embrace: Externally Assisted Statebuilding in Afghanistan." In *The Dilemmas of Statebuilding: Confronting the Contradictions of Postwar Peace Operations*, edited by Roland Paris and Timothy D. Sisk, 227–251. New York: Routledge.

Suhrke, Astri. 2013. "Statebuilding in Afghanistan: A Contradictory Engagement." *Central Asian Survey* 32 (3): 271–286.

Tansey, Oisín. 2009. *Regime-Building: Democratization and International Administration*. Oxford: Oxford University Press.

Tansey, Oisín. 2014. "Evaluating the Legacies of State-Building: Success, Failure, and the Role of Responsibility." *International Studies Quarterly* 58 (1): 174–186.

Tarrow, Sidney. 1998. *Power in Movement: Social Movements and Contentious Politics*. Cambridge: Cambridge University Press.

Taylor, John. 1999. *East Timor: The Price of Freedom*. London: Zed Books.

Thakur, Ramesh. 2001. "Cambodia, East Timor and the Brahimi Report." *International Peacekeeping* 8 (3): 115–124.

Thakur, Ramesh, and Albrecht Schnabel, eds. 2001. *United Nations Peacekeeping Operations: Ad Hoc Mission, Permanent Engagement*. Tokyo: United Nations University Press.

Thelen, Kathleen. 1999. "Historical Institutionalism in Comparative Politics." *Annual Review of Political Science* 2: 369–404.

Thelen, Kathleen, and James Mahoney. 2015. "Comparative-historical Analysis in Contemporary Political Science." In *Advances in*

Comparative-Historical Analysis, edited by James Mahoney and Kathleen Thelen, 3–36. New York: Cambridge University Press.

Themnér, Lotta, and Peter Wallensteen. 2014. "Armed Conflict, 1946–2013." *Journal of Peace Research* 51 (4): 541–554.

Thier, J. Alexander. 2004. "The Politics of Peace-building: Year One: From Bonn to Kabul." In *Nation-Building Unraveled? Aid, Peace and Justice in Afghanistan*, edited by Antonio Donini, Norah Niland, and Karin Wermester, 39–60. Bloomfield, CT: Kumarian Press.

Thier, J. Alexander. 2010. "Big Tent, Small Tent: The Making of Constitution in Afghanistan." In *Framing the State in Times of Transition: Case Studies in Constitution Making*, edited by Laurel E. Miller, 535–562. Washington, DC: United States Institute of Peace.

Thier, J. Alexander, and Jarat Chopra. 2002. "The Road Ahead: Political and Institutional Reconstruction in Afghanistan." *Third World Quarterly* 23 (5): 893–907.

Tilly, Charles. 1985. "War Making and State Making as Organized Crime." In *Bringing the State Back In*, edited by Peter B. Evans, Dietrich Rueschemeyer, and Theda Skocpol, 169–191. Cambridge: Cambridge University Press.

Tilly, Charles. 1990. *Coercion, Capital, and European States, AD 990–1992*. Cambridge: Blackwell Publishers.

Toft, Monica Duffy. 2010. *Securing the Peace: The Durable Settlement of Civil Wars*. Princeton, NJ: Princeton University Press.

Turner, Mark. 2013. "Why is it So Difficult to Reform Some Asian Bureaucracies? Building Theory from Cambodian Evidence." *Public Administration and Development* 33: 275–285.

Un, Kheang. 2005. "Patronage Politics and Hybrid Democracy: Political Change in Cambodia, 1993–2003." *Asian Perspective* 29 (2): 203–230.

United Nations. 2004. *A More Secure World: Our Shared Responsibility – Report of the Secretary-General's High-level Panel on Threats, Challenges and Change*. New York: United Nations.

United Nations Security Council. 2006. "Report of the Secretary-General on Timor-Leste pursuant to Security Council Resolution 1690 (2006)." New York: United Nations.

United States Library of Congress. 2009. *East Timor: Political Dynamics, Development, and International Involvement*. Written by Rhoda Margesson and Bruce Vaughn, Congressional Research Service. CRS Report RL33994. Washington, DC: Office of Congressional Information and Publishing, June 17.

Van de Walle, Nicolas. 2007. "Meet the New Boss, Same as the Old Boss? The Evolution of Political Clientelism in Africa." In *Patrons, Clients, and Policies: Patterns of Democratic Accountability and Political Competition*, edited by Herbert Kitschelt and Steven I. Wilkinson, 50–67. New York: Cambridge University Press.

Vernon, Raymond. 1971. *Sovereignty at Bay: The Multinational Spread of U.S. Enterprises*. New York: Basic Books.

Waldner, David. 1999. *State Building and Late Development*. Ithaca, NY: Cornell University Press.

Walter, Barbara F. 1999. "Designing Transitions from Civil War: Demobilization, Democratization, and Commitments to Peace." *International Security* 24 (1): 127–155.

Walter, Barbara F. 2002. *Committing to Peace: The Successful Settlement of Civil Wars*. Princeton, NJ: Princeton University Press.

Walter, Barbara F. 2009. "Bargaining Failures and Civil Wars." *Annual Review of Political Science* 12: 243–261.

Weber, Max. 1978 [1922]. *Economy and Society*. Edited by Guenther Roth and Claus Wittich. Berkeley, CA: University of California Press.

Weinstein, Jeremy. 2002. "Mozambique: A Fading UN Success Story." *Journal of Democracy* 13 (1): 141–156.

Weinstein, Jeremy. 2005. "Autonomous Recovery and International Intervention in Comparative Perspective." Working Paper Number 57. Washington, DC: Center for Global Development.

Weir, Margaret. 1992. *Politics and Jobs: The Boundaries of Employment Policy in the United States*. Princeton, NJ: Princeton University Press.

Westendorf, Jasmine-Kim. 2015. *Why Peace Processes Fail: Negotiating Insecurity After Civil War*. Boulder, CO: Lynne Rienner.

Whalan, Jeni. 2013. *How Peace Operations Work: Power, Legitimacy, and Effectiveness*. Oxford: Oxford University Press.

Wilde, Andreas, and Katja Mielke. 2013. "Order, Stability, and Change in Afghanistan: From Top-down to Bottom-up State-making." *Central Asian Survey* 32 (3): 353–370.

Wimmer, Andreas, and Conrad Schetter. 2003. "Putting State Formation First: Some Recommendations for Reconstruction and Peace-Making in Afghanistan." *Journal of International Development* 15: 525–539.

Wood, Elisabeth Jean. 2003. *Forging Democracy from Below: Insurgent Transitions in South Africa and El Salvador*. Cambridge: Cambridge University Press.

World Bank. 2004. *Subnational Administration in Afghanistan: Assessment and Recommendations for Action*. Report No. 28435-AF. Washington, DC: The World Bank.

World Bank. 2011. *World Development Report 2011: Conflict, Security, and Development*. Washington, DC: The World Bank.

Zakaria, Fareed. 2003. *The Future of Freedom: Illiberal Democracy at Home and Abroad*. New York: W. W. Norton.

Zartman, William. 1985. *Ripe for Resolution: Conflict and Intervention in Africa*. Oxford: Oxford University Press.

Zartman, William, ed. 1995. *Collapsed States: The Disintegration and Restoration of Legitimate Authority*. Boulder: Lynne Rienner.

Zaum, Dominick. 2007. *The Sovereignty Paradox: The Norms and Politics of International Statebuilding*. Oxford: Oxford University Press.

Zaum, Dominik. 2012. "Exit and International Administrations." In *Exit Strategies and State Building*, edited by Richard Caplan, 137–158. New York: Oxford University Press.

Zürcher, Christoph, Carrie Manning, Kristie D. Evenson, Rachel Hayman, Sarah Riese, and Nora Roehner. 2013. *Costly Democracy: Peacebuilding and Democratization After War*. Stanford, CA: Stanford University Press.

Index

CPSIA information can be obtained
at www.ICGtesting.com
Printed in the USA
LVHW04*2100120618
580473LV00011B/217/P

9 781107 169319